RAN HOUR

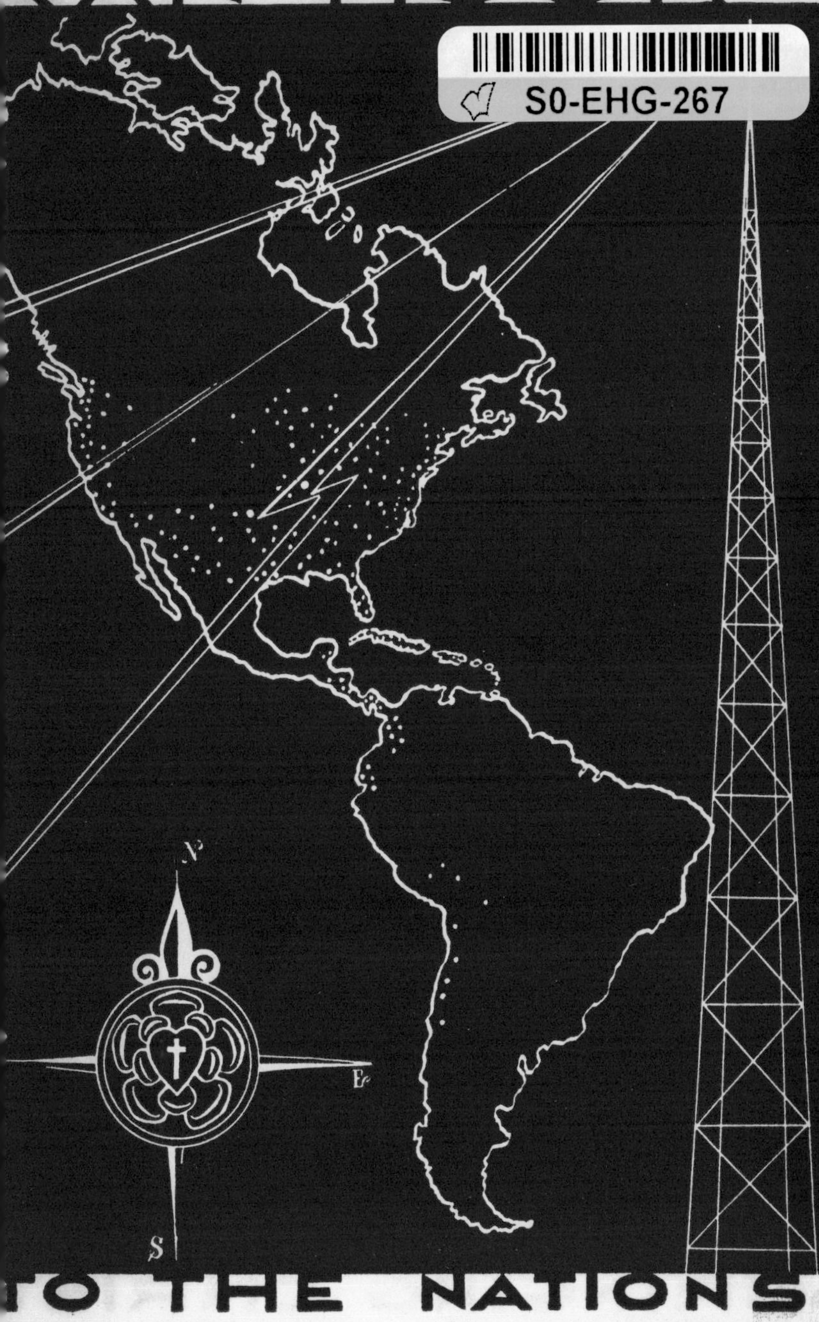

FROM CONTINENT TO CONTINENT

TO THE NATIONS

Courage in Christ

RADIO MESSAGES BROADCAST IN

THE EIGHTH LUTHERAN HOUR

By

WALTER A. MAIER, PH. D.

Professor of the Old Testament
Concordia Theological Seminary
Saint Louis, Missouri

"Repentance and remission
of sin should be preached in
His name among all nations."
Saint Luke 24:27

St. Louis, Mo.
CONCORDIA PUBLISHING HOUSE
1941

FOREWORD

WRITTEN during a turbulent world crisis, these messages mirror the moving issues of our day, particularly those which affect the Christian and his Church. War is discussed in greater detail than in previous volumes. Avoiding the errors of pacifism and the menace of militarism, these references to current hostilities seek to restate and apply the Biblical utterances concerning international conflicts. With Luther, I have emphasized the disastrous consequences following wide-spread warfare. I have denounced the tyranny and despotism of Naziism, Fascism, and Communism; but I have tried not to blind myself to the serious dangers confronting our own national life: the breakdown of the home, godless education, rampant crime, corruption of justice, class struggle, radical, anti-Scriptural theories of government and administration, the disloyalty to Christ in modernist circles, and particularly the religious indifference that keeps more than half our population away from the Church.

These conditions, however, were discussed only incidentally, as the background for the one message to which every Lutheran Hour address has been dedicated: the free, completed, assured Gospel of Jesus Christ, the divine Redeemer. Every time I stepped before the microphone, I was prayerfully conscious that multitudes would doubtless be tuned in who were unacquainted with the clear promises of the atonement through the Savior, and I felt it a sacred duty to show the way of salvation in each message, to explain how for every problem the penitent, trusting soul can find courage in Christ.

It has never been popular to preach the Law in its severity and the Gospel in its divine comfort; yet through the undeserved grace of God the eighth Lutheran Hour brought a greater response than ever before. About 200,000 individual letters and postal cards were received at the headquarters and in my office — as high as 13,000 in a single week, more than 5,000 in one day! These communications came from practically all the religious groups in our country and from varied social strata. Correspondence from State governors, members of Congress, mayors of cities, college presidents, authors, shows the ever-widening influence of our mission. Most gratifying was the extensive tribute from the labor group. Particularly welcome was information like this, "We are passing the word in our factories at Toledo that your broadcast is the one radio message that is genuinely interested in the working classes."

Criticism of the Lutheran Hour was, of course, not missing, although the number of dissenting letters, including the anonymous communications, was smaller than one tenth of 1 per cent of the total.

The radio mail also reveals increasing support from Christians who love the Scripture but are distracted either by the modernist tendencies of their pastors or the overemphasis laid on various and contradictory theories of unfulfilled prophecies. The growing tendency in many Fundamentalist circles to find the present conflict forecast in detail by the Scriptures, and the frequent incorrect identification of Biblical personages and localities, have sometimes shifted interest from the atoning Christ to speculations in millenarian conjectures.

Several vital lessons can be learned from the remarkable God-granted results of this radio mission. First of all, our experiences astonishingly illustrate God's power. In 1935, when we returned to the air, we had only two stations: WXYZ in Detroit and WLW in Cincinnati. No human ability or ingenuity could increase the number of stations to 300 within six short years. Whenever people search for twentieth-century evidence of answered prayer, let them behold the Lutheran Hour and say, "How marvelously God has sent His promised help!"

In the second place, our broadcasting shows that sermons centering in the crucified Savior still have the promise of divine blessing. No matter how completely international scenes may be shifted, the personal soul-questions remain; and nothing men have ever devised can bring the comfort to be found by faith in the Savior's cleansing blood, atoning grace, and life-giving death. Let pastors and laymen who wonder whether the old Gospel has lost its appeal look to our broadcast and understand from this nation-wide demonstration that the one message which has the assurance of blessing is the good news of a Savior slain for the sins of an evil world!

This Mission of the Air proves the value of radio as a Gospel-proclaiming agency. For the first time during a period of national conscription the message of salvation has been brought into military, naval, and air-training camps by means of the radio. Almost every national cantonment was within the range of our radio, and replies from selectees were numerous. Sailors on ships and submarines were also listed among our correspondents. Once again listeners in remote and inaccessible regions were served. Hundreds of hospitals, sanatoria, homes for the incurables, orphanages, asylums, institutions of public and private charity, regularly received our message. We were particularly gratified that many cooperative wardens each week made our broadcasts available to the prisoners under their care.

Outstanding during the eighth Lutheran Hour has been the remarkable extension of our foreign broadcasting. On April 30 a total of 64 foreign broadcasting stations were in use or had been pledged to join our system as soon as suitable arrangements could be made: in Bolivia, 3; Chile, 5; China, 1; Colombia, 6; Costa Rica, 2; Cuba, 11; Ecuador, 4; Mexico, 10; Nicaragua, 2; Panama, 5; Paraguay, 1; Philippine Islands, 1; Puerto Rico, 6; Santo Domingo, 4; Uruguay, 3; Hawaii, 1.

From this tabulation it will be noted that we have outlets in Mexico. The government regulations banning religious programs from the air have been officially interpreted, at least in some districts, as permitting the broadcast of our evangel. We pray for a steady addition in Mexican facilities. Border stations in Texas have proved helpful in bringing Christ to the other side of the Rio Grande.

We are blessed in having the generous cooperation of many Latin-American station-owners. In South America our field continually widens. Short-wave stations on this hemisphere like HCJB at Quito, Ecuador, one of the first to carry our message, give the Gospel remarkable coverage. Stations KZRM in Manila, KGMB in Honolulu, XMHA in Shanghai, KFQD in Anchorage, Alaska, spread the message through Eastern Asia and adjacent territories.

As unprecedented as our foreign work has been, the task of exploring the entire field has hardly begun. Tremendous possibilities of expansion await us, and with divine guidance and the help of those who realize the radio's importance in fulfilling the Savior's command, "Go ye into all the world and preach the Gospel to every creature," we hope eventually to have an all-year, world-wide broadcasting system, which in dozens of languages will bring the comfort and courage to be found in the crucified Savior even to the most remote regions.

Some may question, however, whether foreign-language broadcasting pays. Although our work is still new, we have already received marked evidence of divine blessing. Our missionary in Mexico City, the Rev. C. A. Lazos, writes: "As a result of the broadcasts from Quito, Ecuador, General —— and his entire family are now taking catechetical instructions with me." The Director of Missions for the Spanish-speaking people, the Rev. W. H. Bewie, informs us that so many Mexican people wrote the Laredo, Tex., radio office to express their appreciation for the Lutheran Hour that as a direct result of our program a new mission is to be started there. Our missionary executive secretary, the Rev. O. H. Schmidt, who personally visited the Philippine Islands, has spoken enthusiastically to encourage our foreign endeavors. A young man from Manila writes to inquire concerning the possibility of his being baptized. Negotiations are under way with Generalissimo Chiang Kai-Shek in the hope that we may broadcast Chinese messages over stations in the unoccupied territory of these undaunted people. One mail from a Dominican Republic station brought 182 touching letters of gratitude for the Savior's Gospel. Even before our radio system is fully organized in South America, we see the unmistakable imprint of the Spirit's power.

It should, however, not be our first purpose to ask for calculable results. The blessing comes only from God. Ours is the duty and privilege to preach the Gospel with all the power we can. How we ought to rejoice that by the means of the radio we have been permitted to reach masses in countries in which our Church has never had a missionary! Think of it, our message of the crucified Savior is being heard for the first time from stations in Cuba, Costa Rica, the Dominican Republic, Nicaragua, Honduras, Guatemala, Panama, Venezuela, Bolivia, Chile, Ecuador, the Philippine Islands! Through transmitters in these and other countries our Gospel is also being brought to unnumbered villages and towns in Indo-China, Malaya, India, Australia, New Zealand, Hawaii, Alaska, otherwise untouched by our missionary messengers.

Difficulties, of course, arise in certain localities owing to local religious prejudice. Every Sunday afternoon one of our stations in Nicaragua broadcasts the Spanish Lutheran Hour from the city plaza. The response was so wide that the Catholic churches attacked the broadcast in their newspapers and after Mass officially requested their people not to tune to our program. Despite such antagonism the number of listeners in Nicaragua has steadily increased.

When the war is over and the new social order begins, we must be ready to enter more fields, notably in Europe and Africa. Remarkable short-wave facilities have already been promised us, by which we can reach many more millions in various sections of the world. Pray, work, give, so that the everlasting

Gospel may be brought to all the nations as the radio may serve to introduce our missionaries and make their task easier!

Next to divine blessing, richly showered upon us, we owe the success of the Lutheran Hour to the whole-hearted support from listeners in all stations of life and in every Christian denomination. Almost $100,000 was contributed directly by the members of the audience; the rest of the amount required to meet broadcasting expenses, approximately $90,000, was received indirectly through congregational contributions, pledges, and solicitations. These gifts of Christian love ranged from a few pennies offered by children or by those who eagerly shared their meager funds, to $700, the largest single contribution, sent by a Wisconsin nurse in addition to other substantial assistance. The average mail donation was less than one dollar, and the Lutheran Hour, without special support from any financial leaders, is thus a definitely popular program, endorsed by increasing masses of the common people.

A large part of our support comes from listeners outside our Church. They have recognized in the principles which this broadcast emphasizes a restatement of Biblical Christianity and have therefore been eager to aid the spread of our message. They have not only sent their love offerings regularly, but have also actively publicized the radio mission, distributing Lutheran Hour announcements, inviting the unchurched, either by telephone or personal visit, to tune in each Sunday afternoon. Gratifying results have been recorded through such testimony.

Powerful in their effect and blessing have been the prayers directed to the Throne of Mercy in behalf of this Mission of the Air. Not hundreds, but literally thousands have written us that their petitions regularly wing their way to God; and we know that their pleading has enjoyed the reality of answer. More than ever before this Bringing-Christ-to-the-Nations endeavor needs fervent, effectual intercession of Christians throughout the world. As our broadcasting system grows, the forces of darkness will strengthen their opposition. Our counter-resistance must be fortified through Christian intercession!

We owe much to the patient, week-by-week help of our pastors and teachers. By their regular parish and newspaper announcements of the broadcast, their repeated endorsement of this endeavor, they have done much to strengthen our cause. To them, as also to the pastors outside our communion who have worked untiringly for the Lutheran Hour, we say, "Thank you, and God bless you!"

A radio undertaking as large as ours can be maintained, under God, only by organized supervision. Wide recognition should therefore be given the Lutheran Laymen's League for sponsoring this mission. How noteworthy that from its very beginning this mighty broadcast has been a laymen's movement!

For their friendship, encouragement, and counsel I am personally indebted to all the officers of this organization, particularly to Mr. T. G. Eggers, executive secretary; Pastor Herman Gockel, assistant executive secretary; Mr. Martin Daib, field secretary; and Mr. Oscar Brauer, chairman of the radio committee.

At the height of the broadcasting season thirty-five full-time workers were required to answer our correspondence. In addition, a group of volunteers, members of the Lutheran Woman's League, Evening Division, regularly gave their assistance without compensation.

For six seasons Mr. Reinhold Janetzke has announced the Lutheran Hour, serving without any salary. His help has been invaluable. The hymns on the program ("A Mighty Fortress Is Our God" at the opening and "Beautiful Savior" at the close of each broadcast, with additional selections before and after the message) were sung by the Lutheran Hour Chorus of Concordia Seminary, directed by Mr. Ronald Ross. The Markus Male Chorus, under the direction of Mr. Alvin Burmeister, also furnished the musical framework for a half dozen programs.

Not only were the facilities of Station KFUO, the Gospel Voice, always at our disposal, but the technical counsel of the chief operator, Mr. Carl Meyer, was unstintingly given. Groups of volunteer students of Concordia Seminary cheerfully assumed the task of answering the Spanish mail and assisting in other practical ways.

Advantageous publicity was secured for our broadcasts through bill-board advertising. Local organizations connected with the Outdoor Advertisers of America brought the Lutheran Hour to public attention. Once again we record our indebtedness to Mr. Edward C. Donnelly, Jr., of Boston, through whom 232 of our bill-boards were displayed in New England. More than ever before we enjoyed the cooperation of the press. Outstanding was the Saint Louis *Globe-Democrat* with its frequent notices and a double-page rotogravure spread showing the world-wide character of the Lutheran Hour. The Memphis, Tennessee, *Press Scimitar* and *Commercial-Appeal,* the Jackson, Tennessee, *Sun,* the Sioux Falls, South Dakota, *Daily Argus-Leader,* the Fort Wayne, Indiana, *Journal-Gazette,* the Toledo, Ohio, *Blade,* the Cleveland, Ohio, *Press,* have all shown a sympathetic and appreciative understanding of the pivotal importance which the Christian Church assumes in crisis days like these.

I am deeply grateful again for the privilege of issuing these radio messages in book form. It is encouraging to know that the close of the radio season does not end the usefulness of these sermons, but that in printed permanence they will again be sent throughout the country and even to remote places. Likewise gratifying is the publication of these radio messages in embossed letters for the blind. Most of this transcribing has been done personally by Mrs. Bertha Schroeder and Mr. A. Frederick Graepp or under their direction. These volumes, together with other Christian literature for the sightless, are kept in the Lutheran Library for the Blind at Concordia Seminary and will be sent, upon request and without charge, anywhere in the United States.

Concordia Publishing House, Dr. Edmund Seuel, manager, has given the generous cooperation for which that great Christian enterprise is widely known. Dr. F. Rupprecht, editor for Concordia, personally made the manuscript ready for the printer. Though as in previous years he has modestly requested that his name be omitted, his suggestions have been so helpful that it would be unfair to accede to his request any longer.

I have also enjoyed the loyalty of a self-sacrificing staff that has been ready to help me at all hours and has cheerfully stood by me under the many difficult situations which the stress of an undertaking as vast as ours necessarily produces. Mr. E. Rudolph Bertermann, Ph. D., typed the final copy for each weekly message with the assistance of Miss Lucille Biehl and lent invaluable service. Miss Harriet E. Schwenk gave painstaking help in the manuscript preparation. Professor Wm. Arndt, D. D., Ph. D., has again carefully read both the copy and the proof and offered so much other good counsel each week that he has earned my sustained gratitude. Pastor Richard Jesse, Mount Calvary Church, St. Louis, a member of the Literature Board of our Church, also read the proof. Once more my wife gave generously of her time to offer much practical help in producing this book. My deep personal thanks to these and all others who have in any way cooperated in the happy, blessed work of bringing Christ to the nations!

We have called the collection of this season's radio addresses COURAGE IN CHRIST because only in the eternal Savior, Son of God and Son of man, can this afflicted age discover guidance for this life and the assurance for heaven. May these pages, under the Spirit's benediction, be used mightily in leading peace-robbed, fear-filled men and women to approach the Savior's cross with all their sins, sorrows, doubts, and through faith find this courage in Christ!   WALTER A. MAIER

Concordia Seminary
Saint Louis, Missouri
April 30, 1941

TO

HERMAN A. HANSER, M. D. †

AND

THEODORE H. HANSER, M. D.

THE BELOVED PHYSICIANS

COLOSSIANS 4:14

CONTENTS

THE CALL AT THE CROSSROADS —
REPENT AND BELIEVE!

"Repent ye and believe the Gospel!" — Saint Mark 1:15

God, the Father of All Mercy in Christ Jesus:

We can offer nothing for which we dare ask Thy pardoning love, since we who bear the holy name of Thy Son, our only Savior, have often been indifferent toward His redeeming grace. As a nation we have proved ourselves ungrateful; in our individual lives ugly, degrading sin has repeatedly gained control. O Father, if Thou wert to deal with us according to our iniquities, we could expect only Thy consuming wrath. So we come before Thee with deep-souled repentance, yet with the conquering faith which looks only to Jesus and the cleansing power of His blood. For His sake forgive us! By Thy Comforter strengthen us for the better life! Through Thy love direct our joys and sorrows! In blessing this Mission of the Air, which we again begin in Thy name, Father, Son, and Spirit, help us secure new outlets for Thy broadcast Gospel, additional millions of worshipers throughout the world, many more precious souls won eternally for Christ! We ask this in His blessed name. Amen.

AMERICA, guard your peace! Preserve your liberties! Protect the unequaled blessings with which the Almighty has enriched our land! — Never before, in the seven previous years we have broadcast the Gospel of Jesus Christ, has this pointed appeal been as necessary as in this crisis hour, when our country stands at the crossroads before two pathways, one promising national happiness and the other leading to national disaster. Our American form of government, with its freedom of conscience, worship, and expression, has been attacked on an almost world-wide scale. Despite presidential campaign promises, millions feel that we are being drawn irresistibly into the slaughter of another World War, promoted from within by those who profit through bloodshed and from without by those who seek power through aggression. For the first time in days of peace the nation's youth is conscripted; for the first time, except during years of conflict, we must undertake a gigantic defense program.

Add to these international difficulties our internal problems, the fact that at least 8,000,000 American workers are still unemployed, that government grants and private charity are the sole support of 18,000,000; that many more must exist on a low, discouraging level! Picture the restless, chafing masses in the United States and Canada, weary of waiting and hoping! Survey especially the multitudes whose hearts are heavy with their own personal problems, weighted down by sorrows, sickness, family conflicts, loneliness, bereavement — all the grief many of you know through bitter experience — and you will agree that critical days have dawned upon vast numbers inside our boundaries.

What, then, we ask, is the message needed for these perilous moments? Is it the proposal of new laws? I hope not, for no country has had as many legal statutes, yet as much lawbreaking, as the United States. Within this generation more regulations have been repealed than the whole Babylonian empire observed in the conduct of its affairs. Are we to take refuge in the philosophy of abundance or its opposite, the planned scarcity? Neither of these programs, nor the commendable social improvements the last years have witnessed, can cure inner ills or soothe aching hearts. Are the politicians right when they insist that the nation requires above all their partisan programs? Recalling the dishonesty, graft, drunkenness, profanity, that too often mark politics, we ought to declare openly that this nation needs far more than a Democratic or Republican victory. Should I preach during this Eighth Lutheran Hour what certain clerics insistently proclaim from their pulpits, the constant coaxing into Europe's struggle, which dangles higher prices before the farmers, increased wages before factory-workers, swollen profits before munitions manufacturers, all of which, like a dose of opium, offers temporary stimulation, only to leave its victims worse than before? God forbid! This modern glorification of war, with its shrieking, bombing, wounding, slaughtering, is a hideous folly. War of this kind and proportion can only pave the way for further bloodshed.

As in every crisis, the Church of Jesus Christ today has had only one message. Here it is, the text of our Lord's first recorded Galilean sermon, the message of Peter on the first Pentecost, the challenge in the first of Martin Luther's ninety-five immortal theses, the theme for the first appeal in our present series of Bringing-Christ-to-the-Nations broadcasts, this mighty mission of the air with more than 200 stations — here it is — the one message that can assuredly help America's millions, give you peace and joy, no matter what your personal problems or your soul's perplexities may be:

THE CALL AT THE CROSSROADS —
REPENT AND BELIEVE!

— the words of Jesus Himself, in Saint Mark, chapter one, verse fifteen, *"Repent ye and believe the Gospel!"*

I

REPENT!

This appeal has never been popular. Jesus Christ, the Son of God, preached repentance, and He was crucified. John the Baptist demanded repentance, and he was beheaded. Peter pleaded with his countrymen for repentance, and he was tortured to death. Martin Luther started his Reformation by requiring true repentance, and cruel church machinery sought to crush or bribe him into silence. Today, while such violence has been checked, every preacher of repentance meets opposition. Last week, after I had told a mass-meeting in Cleveland's public hall that before we look down in superior self-righteousness on the European peoples, we ought to acknowledge our own deep-rooted sins, the morning newspaper in that city attacked me editorially, calling my statement "unsound," "unjustifiable," and "unfounded." Because half our population, like the editor of the *Cleveland Plain Dealer,* sees no reason for summoning this nation to repentance, I want to go decidedly farther than last Sunday and declare publicly that a day of financial, moral, and spiritual reckoning lies ahead for America unless our fellow-countrymen penitently return to God. No land can brazenly flaunt the requirements of righteousness, justice, and truth as we have without suffering the consequences of its own folly.

An eternal, unchangeable principle of sacred Scripture states, *"The nation and kingdom that will not serve"* God *"shall perish."* Let our audience across the continent answer this one question: Is America serving God? Honesty demands the confession that the rebellion against the Almighty in our country is greater than ever before, with atheism in some of our political trends, atheism in public education, atheism in a wide-spread life philosophy, which boasts that we can get along without God.

We hold absolutely no brief for European Communism, Fascism, Naziism. How can we when the founders of our Church more than a hundred years ago fled from the Old World's tyranny to find refuge in these United States with its God-granted freedom? How can we have anything but deep-rooted disdain for every restriction of human liberty and the right to worship when we have been entrusted with Martin Luther's heritage? But we love our blessed homeland too much to minimize its serious weaknesses or remain silent when we see smug complacency in high places overlook, excuse, sometimes glorify, the beginning of the same sins which we condemn in Sovietism and totalitarianism across the seas.

The first of all commandments demands, *"Thou shalt love the Lord, thy God, with all thy heart and with all thy soul and with all thy strength."* I ask you, Is America really more devoted to God than the Fascist peoples? At least 70,000,000 of our own people, we are told statistically, are outside America's churches, proportionately at least twice as many as in any European country save Russia. We deplore — and rightly so — the atheism brazenly championed by Communists; but when at Princeton University, founded by pioneer Christians, Dr. Albert Einstein recently declared that he has cast overboard forever the doctrine of a personal God, American papers found his denial newsworthy and acclaimed that scientific atheist a great, distinguished citizen. His features are carved into the imposing portals of a millionaire's church in New York City, while at West Point, with a far greater regard for loyalty, the name of Benedict Arnold, American general who betrayed the Colonies' cause to the British during the Revolution, has been barred. Religious federations publish pamphlets to show that German churches are losing their hold on the people — and may God rebuke any forces in that country which restrain Christ's messages! — but according to the figures published by the United States Government practically all large Protestant denominations lost in membership during the ten-year period previous to the last church census, principally, I believe, because they failed to preach the Gospel and offered "current events" topics as substitutes for sermons on sin and grace. Only one prominent Protestant Church, my own, was able to record an encouraging gain. We decry conditions in France, with its large consumption of alcohol and its dwindling families, but the last years have seen more alcoholism in the United States than at any time since the turn of the century; and while we do little to check its debauch, the Vichy government has taken strenuous measures to restrain overindulgence. Concerning the ravages of birth control — and Marshal Petain said that too few children was a definite cause of France's collapse — let it be recalled that for a recent year the Massachusetts birth-rate was lower than the French. We shake our heads — and God's holy Word justifies our protest — at the racial prejudice which has swept throughout continental Europe and left the Jew a hunted, cowering creature; but if more dangerous days dawn, do not be surprised if the flames of anti-Semitism flare up throughout this country. Besides, must we not feel a deep-rooted sense of shame at our treatment of the American Indian? Negroes in this country also complain that they have been exploited and then pushed aside by white people. In this swollen pride we have complimented ourselves on our all-around moral superiority; yet there are proportionately seven times as many crimes here as in Great Britain and twenty American murders for every British murder. We have more broken families, more teen-age criminals, more corruption in the courts, than any civilized nation — with the possible exception of Soviet Russia.

We ought to face the fact squarely to understand that beyond party platforms, good governmental policies, and the most far-sighted plans of statesmanship we need the penitent spirit by which we bow contritely before the Almighty to acknowledge His grace in sparing us what Europe suffers. Whoever is elected President might well set aside a day for national repentance and thus maintain the early American custom by which in every hour of peril Christians have assembled in their churches, there on bended knees to implore God's forgiveness and His sustaining grace. Repentance saved Nineveh from immediate destruction; repentance brought Israel deliverance from repeated oppressions; repentance would have spared even Sodom and Gomorrah with all their hideous perversions; and by God's promise repentance will bless America if the masses acknowledge their sins, show heartfelt sorrow over their ingratitude, and give evidence of their sincerity by a change of conduct.

However, repentance is first of all personal, individual; and more than national welfare is involved in our Lord's ageless plea *"Repent ye!"* Your own peace of mind and conscience, your own eternal salvation, is at stake. Therefore in the name of Christ I plead with every one of you, *"Repent!"* Return to God! Come contritely before the Almighty to confess the evil in your own heart, the sin on your lips, the wickedness on your own hands!

In the stubbornness of your pride it may be hard to humble yourself and speak the publican's prayer *"God be merciful to me, a sinner!"* You may be so highly esteemed by others, as by yourself, that repentance in your opinion is well in place for the drunkards, prostitutes, murderers, the common rabble in general, but not for you. If that is your attitude, then may a double measure of God's convicting Spirit rest upon my words as I try to impress upon you the truth that no error is more fatal than the denial of sin. God is so all-knowing that He can penetrate into the hidden recesses of your soul to see there the smoldering fires of passion, the dark, hate-filled thoughts, the greedy, overreaching desires, the steady concessions to impurity and untruth — no matter how upright and virtuous you may seem to others. God knows every secret affair in your life, every private sin, every unclean and destructive act committed when you thought that none could see you except your partner in wrong. Do not make the eternally fatal mistake of denying the transgression of God's Law that His justice has marked up against you, for then, the Bible says, you are a self-deceived liar, condemned by this sweeping, exceptionless verdict *"All have sinned!"* Do not join modern scoffers who claim that, after all, wrong-doing is trivial; for if you take that position, the Word brands you as a fool, and it protests, *"The wages of sin is death,"* everlasting separation from heaven, banishment from God. Do not look contemptuously at the wrong in others' lives, for then the Scriptures classify you a hypocrite and tell you first to *"cast out the beam out of thine own eye."* Do not think that you are an exception and can escape sin's punishment; for if you have this vain hope, Holy Writ says that you *"love death"* and stresses God's verdict *"Be sure your sin will find you out!"*

For your soul's sake and the eternity which every one must spend either in heaven or in hell; for peace of mind and God's guidance in your life; for a straight approach to your heavenly Father; for blessing on yourself, your home, your country, I beseech you: Thrust aside all unbelief, overbearing pride and rejection of God! Heed Christ's appeal *"Repent!"* Come before the holy God to say: "O my Father, I have sinned against Thee. I confess my wrongs. I am deeply sorry for them. Be merciful to me! Forgive these transgressions and remove them from me! Help me to walk more closely in Thy Word!" With the sincerity of that repentance you will be prepared to receive Heaven's glorious pardon and strengthening. You will be ready to take the next step for which even the celestial mansions reecho with rejoicing, since it is the promise of Christ Himself that *"joy shall be in heaven over one sinner that repenteth."*

II
BELIEVE THE GOSPEL!

Besides repentance the Lord Jesus asks faith. In three of the most vital words ever spoken on this earth He pleads, *"Believe the Gospel!"* With all the tumult and shouting of the presidential election, the shrieking and bombing of Europe's conflict, this appeal *"Believe the Gospel!"* may be submerged under heated discussions centering about questions of the day. Yet, as William Gladstone, England's great prime minister, once declared, "Talk about questions of the day; there is but one question, and that is the Gospel!"

Now, what is this Gospel, the only hope for this hope-starved age? If unbelief has not hesitated to lay blasphemous hands on Christ and denied that He is the *"very God,"* the eternal *"Son of the Highest"* and the virgin-born Son of Mary, we must expect that His Gospel has been viciously assaulted. Hundreds of Protestant pulpits feature counterfeit gospels, man-made gospels, especially the "social gospel," first to improve labor, living, housing conditions, often to the utter neglect of the soul's perishing condition. But the Gospel that our Lord means, to which we dedicate this broadcast, is the Gospel of Jesus Christ, the world's Savior and your Redeemer, the Gospel of His blood, His agony, His never-to-be-measured suffering, the Gospel of His thorny crown and His gory cross, the Gospel of His pierced hands, His lacerated feet, His wounded side, the Gospel of His sin-atoning death for our life-giving pardon. It is — listen closely, you, the thousands in this audience who up till this moment have never been able to give a clear answer to the question "What is the Gospel?" — it is Heaven's own good news that *"God so loved the world that He gave His only-begotten Son, that whosoever believeth in Him should not perish but have everlasting life."*

It is the best news a man can ever hear, preach, or believe, the promise *"God was in Christ, reconciling the world unto Himself,"* the pledge that through this Gospel we, despite our transgressions, are declared sin-free, assured of our prepared place in our Father's house!

If this Gospel is true — and it must be because it comes from the holy God Himself, because it has proved its power in the lives of countless myriads — you can see that my appeal from this small, Christ-dedicated broadcasting chamber in Saint Louis to you across the country must be, *"Believe the Gospel!"* Learn to know who Jesus is, what He has done for the whole world, but particularly for you! Accept His atonement as the divine, heavenly truth! Build your trust unswervingly on Him as the holy, sin-removing Lamb of God, who cleanses you from the stain of all iniquity! When Jesus says, *"Believe!"* He wants more than a family faith, lip service, head worship, more than outward agreement. He wants your repentant, sin-convicted, but trusting, grace-filled heart. He asks for confident faith, a sure reliance on His power to save to the uttermost.

It is for this blessing on your life that I pray when, beholding you in spirit, I plead, *"Believe the Gospel!"* the good news of this forgiveness for every sin and for every sinner. When Queen Marie Antoinette passed through Strasbourg on her way to Paris, police regulations prohibited all deformed persons, cripples, invalids, from showing themselves on her route. The poet Goethe, unbeliever though he was, wrote a poem to commemorate the contrast with Christ, who especially welcomed the sickly and the poor and the downtrodden. In that Savior's name I tell you, whoever and whatever you may be, Christ's arms are never spread wider in the warmth of their welcome than when He beholds some afflicted, overburdened soul, for whom the rest of the world has little sympathy, and says to him, *"Come unto Me, all ye that labor and are heavy laden, and I will give you rest!"* If the wickedness in your life seems so mountainous that it would shade Jesus, remember: His grace towers above the highest sin, and in this moment Jesus is calling softly and tenderly, "Ye who are weary, come home!"

"Believe the Gospel!" because, being God's truth and the divine guarantee of pardon, peace, and heavenly blessing, it is the sure, unchangeable promise. In his last hour friends asked Philip de Mornay, a distinguished statesman under France's Henry IV and an exemplary Christian, whether he still clung to his hope of future glory, and he answered, "I am as fixed in my confidence of an assured hope for future bliss from the incontestable evidence of the Spirit of God as I ever was from any mathematical truth from all the demonstrations of Euclid." God give you the same unswerving confidence which, without doubt or question, believes Jesus when He says, *"I am the Way, the Truth, and the Life!"*

"Believe the Gospel!" for by that faith we are reborn into a newness of life. The old things of sin have passed away, and we have become new creatures in Christ, with better thoughts and purer desires. Knowing what our transgressions cost the Lord Jesus, we simply cannot continue brazenly in sin. Criminal records tell of a burglar who once entered a Christian home and found in the sitting-room a marble bust of the thorn-crowned Christ. His finger marks on the statue and its changed position showed that, as he set about his burglary, he had turned the features of the agonized Savior to the wall so that he could no longer see His haunting, conscience-prodding face. By the opposite truth, as long as we know that Jesus con-

stantly beholds us, our lives will be strengthened for the highest and noblest achievements.

"Believe the Gospel!" because with that faith even crushing sorrows assume a new meaning. Once you are Christ's in the sincerity of heart-deep trust, you know that every affliction or loss that may come, every sickness that may lay you low for months or even years, every tragedy in your home, comes by God's permission to draw you more closely to Jesus, to protect your blood-bought soul for eternity.

"Believe the Gospel!" for when you accept the Savior you have glorious opportunities for Christian service, for helping your family, fellow-men, country. Jesus chooses His Christian soldiers, not by a goldfish-bowl lottery to see who must prepare himself for military service — as necessary as this is; He gives all His redeemed the privilege of showing men the way to life and salvation. Therefore, to combat antichristian forces, to help bring men to repentance and faith, we need voluntary service, particularly of Christian youth, a spiritual defense program for the churches of Christ. More than ever before the prime objective of Christ's forces in America must be to preach the Gospel. In that spirit this radio mission, through its foreign stations and short-wave facilities reaching half-way round the globe, is trying to meet the Savior's command, as recorded by Luke, *"that repentance and remission of sins should be preached in His name among all nations."* If you need a church in your community that will preach this message and show forth the fulness of the Savior's grace, we will thank God for the privilege of helping you. If you want personal assurance that your sins can be forgiven in Christ, write to us! If you are eager to do your part in helping us spread the good news, let us send you instructions. If you crave joy and peace and happiness, learn the lesson of

repentance and faith! Martin Luther tells us that after he came to Christ and learned the meaning of repentance, no word was sweeter.

"Believe the Gospel!" For in the greatest of mercies Christ's pardon is granted us — this is the climax of our faith, the victory cry of the Reformation — by complete grace. We are to come to the Savior just as we are, burdened by our weakness, heavily weighted by our unworthiness, committing our redemption wholly to Him. Morales, a poor but noted Spanish painter, when summoned to meet his king at court, bought and borrowed elaborate finery and royal apparel; yet his sovereign was displeased at his unnatural appearance, and the audience failed. When later the artist was invited again to the palace, he came just as he was, poor, old, hungry, and he touched Philip's heart so completely that the monarch provided a lifelong endowment for him. When Jesus appeals, *"Come unto Me!"* let us draw near, not in our pride, not with our good intentions, with our borrowed or supposed virtues, but let us come — O God, lead every one to heed these words! — just as we are, with our sins, our weaknesses, our soul-hunger, our helplessness, to Jesus, just as He is, in His endless, depthless, numberless mercies. Then will we be blessed eternally by His promise, *"Him that cometh to Me I will in no wise cast out."* God grant us that assurance for Jesus' sake! Amen!

MORE IMPORTANT THAN THE ELECTION: YOUR DECISION CONCERNING CHRIST

"How long halt ye between two opinions? If the Lord be God, follow Him!" — 1 Kings 18:21

God of All Wisdom and Power:

*A*s the nation prepares for a critical election, do Thou, O Father, lead us to put our own country's welfare above personal gain and partisan prejudices! Through Thy Spirit help us make a choice which under Thy blessing will assure peace at home and abroad, progress in our work, prosperity in our industries, continued enjoyment of free worship! Especially do we entreat Thy mercy by the merits of Jesus Christ, Thy Son, our only Savior; direct us at all times to choose Thee above everything else in life. Show us that at the cross, stained by the life-blood of our blessed Redeemer, we must declare ourselves either for Christ or against Him! Guide our hearts to come penitently, yet confidently, to Jesus, acclaiming Him our sin-atoning Deliverer, our life-giving Lord and God! Warm our hearts with Thy presence, and as we experience Thy power and goodness, let thankfulness banish indifference and faith record daily increase! Bless us for Jesus' sake! Amen.

ON the day after tomorrow the people of the United States will cast their ballots in a momentous choice. The man selected to guide our affairs for the next four years must face problems at least as critical as the conflicts which confronted Washington and Lincoln. In this emergency we should have a 100-per-cent vote, particularly by the Christian citizenry. If church-members neglect to cast their ballots, whom but themselves can they blame if later our country suffers the sudden collapse of representative government that has marked almost all the rest of the world? Many keep their distance from the polls because they are disgusted with corruption, boss rule, gangster tactics, stuffed ballot-boxes, purchased votes. But that antipathy must be overcome! Ours is not only the civic

[14]

duty to help as best we can in choosing the right candidate; we have also Scriptural direction to seek the peace and prosperity of this nation. While I would be the last to advocate the churches' entrance into politics, the call must be sounded for a more determined willingness on the part of Christians to meet their civic obligations, even to assume public office. On Tuesday, then, a day of destiny for America, let us not only vote, but also cast each ballot with serious forethought and personal prayer — the sincere petition that as we place this beloved nation above man or party, the almighty God may forgive us our sins and, despite our thanklessness, keep us in heavenly favor.

As important as the coming presidential election is, however, we dare not forget that every one of us must make a choice of incomparably greater consequence. Legal requirements will prevent at least 70,000,000 under twenty-one and many otherwise unqualified from casting their ballot; but no one, young or old, imprisoned or free, white or black, registered or not, can escape the alternative of this issue that involves their souls, their eternity, their entrance into heaven. Long after both presidential candidates have been laid to their rest and the campaign issues of defense, commerce, agriculture, industry, foreign relations, have given way to new perplexities, this decision will still confront men's souls: the choice which places us either for Christ or against Him, with God or without Him, in support of the Bible or in opposition to its blessings, on the side of righteousness, justice, and truth or in alliance with godlessness, injustice, and falsehood. As I speak particularly to those still uncertain concerning Christ or who think that they can be both for and against their Savior, I ask you: Forget political attacks and counter-attacks! Give God the next few moments to consider a choice

MORE IMPORTANT THAN THE ELECTION:
YOUR DECISION CONCERNING CHRIST

a course suggested by Elijah's ancient plea in First Kings, chapter eighteen, verse twenty-one: *"How long halt ye between two opinions? If the Lord be God, follow Him!"*

I

THE FOLLY OF INDECISION

The prophet spoke these words during dark, perilous days. The Lord of heaven and earth had chosen Israel to be His people and led them out of Egyptian bondage, through the desert's sand and blister, into the Promised Land. The Lord of hosts had defended them against all their enemies. Yet the Israelites lapped in the ease and luxury of their prosperity, had forgotten God and were kotowing in ugly, sensual worship to the Baals, the make-believe gods, of their heathen neighbors. Prophets and priests led this unfaithfulness, and the common people only too gladly followed their treachery. The few faithful were persecuted and imprisoned. When true religion was cast aside, a reign of horrifying lust began. Then it was that God's punishment, which always overtakes national unbelief, closed the heavens so that not a drop of rain descended. Month followed month through a devastating drought, which seared grain-fields, withered orchards, and covered the countryside with thick blankets of dust. One year, two years, three years, and half of a fourth year the leaden skies frowned on a parched brown land as streams dried, cattle perished, and death took heavy human toll. Even in the depths of such suffering, however, the stubborn people did not return to God. The masses thought they could worship both Jehovah and the Canaanite idols. They were unwilling to acclaim God their only Lord; and in one of the most electrifying of Old Testament scenes Elijah prepares to prove that Jehovah alone is Lord and that Israel's allegiance therefore must be given exclusively to

Him. At his request the king gathers at Mount Carmel among others the 450 prophets of Baal, court favorites. There, on the parched slopes of that mountain, formerly the garden spot of Palestine, we see them, row after row of these idolatrous priests; apart from them, to show the complete cleavage between faith and unbelief, stands solitary Elijah; and between them the curious throng, to whom the prophet now speaks these momentous, cutting words, *"How long halt"* (really *"limp"*) *"ye between two opinions?"*

Our own age resembles Israel in those dangerous days. As the priests of Baal secured wide control, so many of the churches' high places are occupied by men who blandly deny Scriptural truth, particularly Christ's atonement. Entire religious groups, some of them with divinity schools built by contributions from Christians, have sold out to modernist unbelief. Who are the most widely quoted and intensely publicized clerical leaders in America today? Are not many of these men with head-line fame entrenched in their rejection of Christ as both God and Savior? They invite into their pulpits outspoken atheists, who, watch in hand, stand before large congregations to give God five minutes in which to strike them dead. They take Bible-stories away from the Sunday-school children and substitute books which picture our ancestors as half ape and half human. As in Elijah's age, when unbelief went hand in hand with brazen sin, so these days, in which much of the old American reverence for God has disappeared, have witnessed a new low in purity and decency. Look at our American family life for a moment — few guides to national honor are better — and you will see more broken homes than ever before. Two of every nine present-day marriages, experts assure us, will end in divorce. Youthful crime is on the increase. The probation officer of our Saint

Louis Juvenile Court writes me that our city, typical, I presume, of similar American communities, had 152 delinquent boys and girls in January of 1940; by a steady and almost uninterrupted growth, September brought 389 delinquent cases, an all-time high. Must we wonder at this when our children play crime games, read crime stories, find entertainment in crime comics, listen to crime broadcasts, and see crime motion-pictures? In addition, who can tabulate all the marital cheating, the nagging and quarreling that often go with the sullen refusal to give Christ His part in the home?

In the face of these and other bold uprisings against God, some people still wonder why our age has suffered loss, hardship, sorrow, not for three and one half years but for eleven. With this rejection of divine mercy, some keep inquiring why the horizon of America's tomorrow is heavy with black clouds, when they ought to know that no nation is too large and wealthy to be overtaken by the outreaching hand of divine justice. Back in 1929 billion-dollar losses were in the day's order; then, as in 1932, when one bank crashed after the other, it was often predicted that these depression years would bring masses in the nation to Christ and that we might soon expect a mighty revival. Eleven years later we ask, Where is the return? Where is the revival? The United States has a larger number of non-Christians than ever before, more than half the nation refusing to acknowledge Christ.

People are still halting, limping, between two opinions, as they did in Elijah's time. Only a few are brazen enough openly to ridicule the Lord Jesus, publicly to denounce His Word. Ninety-nine of every hundred Americans outside Christ's Church will admit that there is something beautiful, unselfish, exalted, about Jesus, but how many will renounce the service of sin and accept Him as their

Savior and their God? Practically all normal men and women agree that the Bible is one of the best books ever written, but at the same time many love their lusts, money, vanity, too completely to follow the Bible's directions. We can understand why a man who has produced *risqué* stage plays has so little sympathy with the Church and its code of decency that he writes a sarcastic, self-contradictory magazine article entitled "Why I Don't Go to Church"; but it is much more difficult to see why some of you are halting between two opinions concerning the Church when even reason points out the earthly blessings that have come from its work.

Stop to think of this startling contrast: Here is the Lord Jesus Himself, God's own Son, who loved every one of you, even the unbeliever, with such a depthless devotion that He came down from heaven and its glories to this sorrow-sown earth to remove your sins, make you right with God, and save you for the greatest joy that even the Almighty can offer. Here in Christ is the peace of mind which many of you crave. Here with Jesus is the power by which you can start life anew and push temptation aside. Here in this blessed Redeemer is the strength to meet adversity, to brave the worst that life may inflict; here are a hundred other blessings which thousands in this audience know to be as real as truth itself. And, on the other hand, what does unbelief offer you? What attractions can you find in unforgiven sin? Drop everything and pay attention to this warning: Without Christ you are under God's wrath. As securely as you may think you can live your godless life, the day of reckoning awaits you. Not peace, but an aroused and restless conscience will be yours; not victory but surrender to destructive forces; not joy but sullen misery; not eternal life but never-ending death; not heaven but hell! Yet despite this tremendous difference between faith in Christ and unbelief, you hesitate, question, doubt; you want to postpone your decision. You are halting, limping uncertainly to and fro, just as those ancient Israelites!

Not all, however, who waver between two opinions are found outside the Church. As the prophet spoke directly to those who had once been members of the Old Testament Church, so I have an earnest word for all backsliders, Christians only in name. They want to worship God on Sunday, but Monday they forget Him. They like to be called "Christian" in church but betray their Savior out in the world. They sing hymns and parrot prayers with the rest of the congregation, but the service is hardly over when they profane God's holy name and by sacrilegious actions show themselves hypocrites. Church officials who piously perform their congregational duties and then mercilessly cheat their fellow-men; members of Christian young people's groups who proclaim Christ publicly and then hurry to serve their secret sins or to deny their Savior openly at disgraceful places of sensual amusement; women who pose as exemplary wives and mothers, but whose children are dirty and untrained, their husbands neglected, their kitchens filthy; even ministers and priests who deliver God's Word from their pulpits but who privately boast that they do not believe all they preach — and not long ago I heard a candidate for the presidency on the Socialist ticket pour out contempt on young clergymen who confidentially admit that they really are radicals but that they preach the opposite to keep their positions and their salaries — all these are halting between two opinions. The condemnation of such two-faced church-members invokes the double wrath of God, since Christ Himself warns, *"Unto whomsoever much is given, of him shall be much required."* To them especially Jesus serves this notice,

"No man can serve two masters," and again, *"He that is not with Me is against Me,"* and, *"Whosoever shall deny Me before men, him will I also deny before My Father which is in heaven."* In only one way can we serve God acceptably — when we follow this golden and repeated direction of Scripture: *"Thou shalt love the Lord, thy God, with all thy heart and with all thy soul and with all thy strength!"* An old naval captain told a young sailor, "On board my ship there are only two choices, duty or mutiny"; and the Captain of our salvation reminds us that finally, as much as we may keep our double-hearted, double-minded, double-handed treachery concealed from men, we cannot deceive God. For every one of us there is a final choice between faith and unbelief, pardon or punishment, heaven or hell, Christ or chaos!

How long, then, will you — the undecided, the lip-worshipers, the backsliders, the worldlings of winning smiles but black hearts — halt between serving Jesus or serving your own lust and greed? Some of you are sixty, seventy, eighty, and more years old; yet despite this long span you are guilty of life's most destructive mistake: you have not accepted the Savior. How much more time do you want? How many more funerals must you attend before realizing that soon you will be carried to the grave and face eternity's terror without Jesus? Some of you are in your prime, yet the supreme glory of Christ's grace has never entered your souls. How long will you halt between obeying the world's enticement and the voice of conscience that appeals for repentance? How many more broadcasts must you hear before falling at the Savior's feet and pleading penitently for His mercy? How much more pain and loss must you endure after God's rebuke has repeatedly hurled you to the ground? Some in this far-flung audience are blessed with youth's bloom and strength. How long do you want to continue rejecting Christ and find false comfort in the delusion that later, after having tasted all of life's alluring pleasures, the time will come to decide for Him? That hour may never arrive, with sudden death taking its quickly increasing toll and the forces of hell working overtime against your soul. This may be — what a terrifying thought! — the last plea for repentance, the final invitation to Christ's mercy, you will ever hear!

II
DECISION — AND ITS BLESSING

Elijah not only denounced; he also voiced this logical, forceful demand, *"If the Lord be God, follow Him!"* Before that day closed, the prophet, in a most compelling Old Testament miracle, proved that Jehovah was God. He asked those devotees of Baal to build an altar on Mount Carmel, place a bullock on it for sacrifice, and then have their idol show his alleged power by sending fire to consume the offering. From morning, through the noon, until late afternoon, the heathen priests screamed, *"O Baal, hear us!"* leaped on the altar, slashed themselves with knives. But no answer came. Their Baal was a fraud — a manufactured lie. Then, shortly before sunset, Elijah acted. He repaired Jehovah's altar, broken down through neglect; and to make the miracle the more challenging, he had twelve large barrels of water poured on his sacrifice to drench the altar's wood. For a moment he bowed before his God in prayer, and he had hardly finished when the heavens were opened and a flame shot down to consume the sacrifice, even the stones and the water within the trench.

We, too, have seen fire fall from heaven as the Almighty proves Himself the God of justice and holiness. The flames of this generation's second World War have revealed His consuming wrath, when men, boasting there would be no more war, forgot that sin and denial of the

Lord can bring conflict as a punishment. Don't think that we in the United States have escaped because we are so much better than the rest of mankind! Our country, too, must face a day of reckoning unless we penitently return to God, just as you and I must pay for every unforgiven sin.

Our heavenly Father proves Himself God even more marvelously by His immeasurable, indescribable grace in Christ. In His Savior-love Jesus did what no man or world of men, no saint or legion of supersaints, no angel or army of heavenly hosts, ever could do. He cleansed our souls of sin's dark stains; He redeemed us from the curse of our transgressions; He pardoned us from the charge of our iniquities; He took away the evil in our lives, without any limitation, any uncertainty, any payment on our part, when on the cross our sins became His sins, our guilt His guilt, our death His death, but His resurrection our life and pledge of heaven.

If the fire of God's love that came down from heaven, not to destroy sin but to purify the sinner, thus proves that Jesus Christ is the eternal Son of the heavenly Father, yes, God Himself, it is our sacred duty to use this Gospel-hookup in crying out much as Elijah did, "If Christ be God, then follow Christ!" Because Jesus suffered and died for you, He has a claim on your soul. You *"are bought with a price,"* His holy, precious blood. A direct personal appeal therefore comes to every one of you. We are not asking faith in some vague, uncertain, mystic opinion, but by God's own truth we do promise that, if you come to Calvary, kneel down before the Crucified, and with a contrite heart cry out: "O Jesus, my Savior, I do believe! I bring all my transgressions to Thee, Thou sin-removing Lamb of God. I trust Thee, Lord Jesus, and from this moment on, with the help of Thy Spirit, my hope is built on nothing less than Thy shed blood and righteousness," if you make this sacred covenant to follow Christ, blessings unnumbered and unending are yours. Henry Clay, warned that a certain just and necessary policy which he supported would ruin his chances for the Presidency, answered, "I would rather be right than President," and while on the eve of this election we hope that every man who aspires to be Chief Executive in this country will honestly make the same assertion, may God — above this — give every one of us the strength to declare, "I would rather be right with Christ than have everything that wealth, power, wisdom, combined, can bestow."

When you say, "Savior, I follow on, Guided by Thee," the fire of the first Pentecost will touch your heart to give you these unsearchable riches in Christ. Write them down one after the other! With Jesus your sins are removed, every one of them, including especially those hideous evils which haunt you with the thought that perhaps your wrongdoing will be discovered and you will be exposed to disgrace. With Christ, no matter what the past has been, you can begin anew with a clean, unblemished start. With the Savior the tyranny of fears is broken, the burden of incessant worries lightened. With that royal Redeemer the weakness by which you fall victim to your pet sins will give way to resolute strength in resisting and conquering temptation. With God's Son, though you meet repeated reverses — and sometimes the most devoted Christians are the most sorely afflicted — though loss of money, good name, health, family happiness, assails you, you can smile through your tears, lift your head high. Beholding the cross, you know that all these trials come from your Father's love, since He wants to refine, purify, strengthen, and preserve you for Himself by keeping pride and haughty self-trust far from your soul. With Christ in a world crushed by suicidal war, you can have joy in your heart and peace in your soul. And for the nation at large, with Jesus in a mighty religious awakening across the American continent that would return the churches to the purpose of their charter, the preaching of the Gospel and the bringing of disinterested masses to Christ, we could have the greatest national blessing of peace and prosperity America has ever known.

Cling to Christ as your God and Savior! Let nothing compete with Him in your heart! Let Him be higher than your human ambitions! Let Him be above your church, especially if that church denies His divine, atoning love; above your parents, particularly if they live in sin and rebellion against God; above your dreams for married happiness, my young Christian friends, notably if you think of pledging yourself in that most intimate of all relations to some one who does not know the Lord Jesus or cannot worship in truth with you!

When William Lloyd Garrison began his struggle against the enslavement of the American Negro, he wrote in the first issue of his publication, *The Liberator:* "I am in earnest. . . . I will not excuse. I will not retreat a single inch." May every one of you in your battle against the slavery of sin be strengthened to pledge: "I am on the side of the Lord Jesus. I am in earnest. I will not retreat a single inch, now and forever!" Then, when the whole race has been run and the last grain of the hour-glass has fallen into eternity, your Savior, who chose you, will say, *"Well done, thou good and faithful servant!"*

With this loyalty unto death, my fellow-countrymen, no matter how you vote next Tuesday, God give you the grace every day to tell an unbelieving world, as you repeat Joshua's ancient pledge, *"Choose you this day whom ye will serve; . . . but as for me and my house, we will serve the Lord."* Our heavenly Father grant all of you from coast to coast this highest of all blessings, for Jesus' sake! Amen!

THE PLEDGE OF PERMANENT PEACE

> *"The mountains shall depart and the hills be removed; but My kindness shall not depart from thee, neither shall the covenant of My peace be removed, saith the Lord that hath mercy on thee."* — Isaiah 54:10

O Christ, Our Heavenly Prince of Peace:

If the heavy hand of divine punishment has long enough rebuked this sinful world, lead the warring nations to an armistice and an honorable peace in which aggression will be checked, hatred restrained, and international cooperation promoted! Shed the Spirit's light into our hearts with the inner calm which comes through faith in Thy sin-removing love! At the cross, where we behold Thee dying in our stead, may we know that as our Substitute Thou, blessed Savior, hast done everything required to assure us of peace with our heavenly Father, our conscience, and our fellow-men! Give wisdom, patience, and courage to all servants of Thy Word who have dedicated their lives to proclaiming the good news of the eternal, world-wide treaty sealed with Thy blood at Calvary! Preserve this country from impenitence! Protect Thy Church within our boundaries against evil counsel! Remove the scales from the eyes of blinded men and help them realize that in Thy truth they have Heaven's pledge for the peace that "passeth all understanding," the joyful assurance that in Thee we shall be the sons of God eternally! Grant us this blessing, Lord Jesus, for Thou hast told us, "Ask and it shall be given you"! Amen.

A S the nation prepares to observe the armistice which ended the first World War, many Christian hearts throughout America are earnestly praying: "O God, give us another truce! Stop this terrifying struggle! Rebuke every aggressor and each agency that promotes conflict for personal profit! O God, bring war-racked men and women up from cellars and underground shelters into the fresh air and sunshine! Give this peace-robbed generation a second armistice and with it the blessing of real peace!"

We must have more than an armistice, however, if international harmony is to prevail. Among the blood-marked lessons taught by the last war this truth stands out boldly: Peace cannot be established by force! No fewer than 8,500,000 brave men laid down their lives on the battle-fields of that first world struggle, which, fought "to end all wars," really helped create the causes for the present upheaval. That conflict two and a half decades ago was to preserve democracy; yet outside our own shores popular government has disappeared. Instead, Communism, Fascism, and Naziism have been systematically advanced. Before we urge this nation to send its youth into Europe's hostilities, let us study the verdict of the past quarter century: We cannot create peace by recourse to armed might. If war does come and this country is drawn into Europe's struggle, that involvement can help undermine our own liberties, add grievously to our financial burden, support the alarming slump in morals, and promote the systematic opposition to God's Word that follows in the wake of all modern warfare. May God strengthen the President of the United States, reelected to direct the country's course during four critical years, in fulfilling his repeated, emphatic promises to help keep this nation removed from that horrifying bloodshed!

If experience has shown that we cannot establish peace by engaging in war, we ought to be similarly convinced that we cannot expect to maintain its blessings by diplomacy and treaties. If one international agreement after the other, each officially signed amid impressive ceremony, has been contemptuously cast aside, what further right have we to expect sincerity among diplomats or honesty in covenant obligations?

Nor can we banish war through organized political efforts. Do you remember how many high hopes for international understanding were placed on the League of

Nations? Hundreds of millions of dollars were eagerly devoted to its work. At one time as many as sixty countries subscribed to its lofty ideals and promised that they would settle all disputes by arbitration. Today the League of Nations is ruined, its $7,000,000 building in Geneva, Switzerland, all but deserted, its staff of 600 workers (not to mention gardeners, watchmen, or less important employees) almost entirely dismissed. Its collapse is a ghastly spectacle of men's failure to work together cooperatively and harmoniously in a world that could offer plenty for every one.

Despite our boasted culture this generation has seen more frequent and devastating strife than any of its predecessors — war not only on the battle-field but also between labor and industry, war among the races, classes, and even religions. How blessed, then, in the midst of spreading conflict and rumors of increasing bloodshed to have

THE PLEDGE OF PERMANENT PEACE!

How reassuring to read the promise of the errorless Word (Isaiah, chapter fifty-four, verse ten), *"The mountains shall depart and the hills be removed; but My kindness shall not depart from thee, neither shall the covenant of My peace be removed, saith the Lord that hath mercy on thee"*!

I

IT OFFERS COMPLETE PEACE THROUGH CHRIST

It is no ordinary peace pact, one of the thousands history has witnessed, that Isaiah here exalts. He describes *"the covenant of"* God's *"peace,"* the treaty between the Lord of heaven and all generations of men.

To understand the rich fulness of this divine grace, we must frankly, unhesitatingly, personally, realize that men in their sin are enemies of God in His holiness. The

Almighty is so perfect, pure, and completely separated from every evil that no man can stand before Him. Every one of us in our wickedness is condemned by His Word, by our consciences, by our own lustful desires and carnal actions. Many want to debate this fact, deny it, or, in the most modern fashion, ridicule it; but an age like ours, which has witnessed human depravity at its low depths, should be the last to question the fact that of themselves all men, by birth and by actual, committed sin, are God's enemies, excluded from heaven, doomed to pay the penalty of their transgressions. You will not applaud that statement. Some of you will shake your heads or completely reject it. Yet the incontestable fact remains: the world today is embattled against its God, and every unforgiven, unconverted sinner fighting his Maker and Master is doomed to defeat in unending death.

The all-important issue for every one of us, then, is this: How can I find peace with God? Don't waste time in the false hope that He will forget your transgressions, close His eyes on your sins, smile at your errors, regard your missteps as too small for notice! Every fracture of God's Law, no matter how insignificant it may seem, is a repeated declaration of war against the Almighty. Rather turn to Isaiah's golden promise and learn that God offers a covenant of peace, history's one all-inclusive treaty made, not in some mirrored, gilded hall but atop an ugly hill, near Jerusalem; a promise not stamped with international seals and initialed by heavily uniformed plenipotentiaries but sealed by the Lord Jesus Christ's holy, precious blood; a peace covenant, not temporary, between nation and nation, but eternal, between God and man. Its articles dictate no crushing terms. Whereas human agreements make the vanquished pay, here the Victor pays a price before which the mortal mind must stagger. Think of this, you parents who love your children with deep devotion: God gave His own beloved Son to become the Mediator between heaven and earth, to take all our sins and guilt upon Himself, so that through His suffering we are free. We pay no indemnity to God for our transgressions; at Calvary Christ paid everything. We need only believe this assurance, *"Being justified by faith, we have peace with God through our Lord Jesus Christ."* Beholding the cross, with the Savior as our Atonement, we can say, "*'He is our Peace!'* He has brought us back to our Father through *'the blood of the everlasting covenant.'* The war is over. We know that God loves us, that He will protect us and preserve us into all eternity."

This *"peace with God"* gives Heaven's own answer to the question "How can I find peace for myself, the inner calm to quiet an accusing conscience? How can I shake off fear's depressing weight and worries to live a happy, contented existence?" Is not this the problem that thousands in our audience have tried to solve in their own lives? The losses through nervous breakdown, mental derangement, suicide, the results of living peace-robbed, dread-ruled lives, are greater than the casualties this country has suffered by its wars. Ask any competent doctor to describe the damage wrought on the human body and mind by the tyranny of fear! Visit the mental hospitals to see for yourself its tragic toll as it sears, twists, or destroys brain power, and you will agree that the most formidable enemy confronting 130,000,000 plus Americans is the shattering force of lashed consciences, tormented souls, and panic-ridden hearts.

Some of you, we know, boast that you fear neither God nor man, that you can stifle every inner protest to silence and live as recklessly as you wish. But the sins you nurture can suddenly turn their relentless fury against you.

Let an emergency break into your life, and you, too, will chatter in terrified agony while your conscience etches the naked evil of your lusts on your terror-stricken mind. You question this? Why is it that men who have climbed the top rungs on the ladder of fame and achievement have often taken the coward's exit from life? Is it not simply that they find no way to overcome the encircling horror of their fears? Why does it happen that, when sudden death seems at hand, men who during their preoccupied lives have little time for God, scant interest in Christ, often lose their calm and frantically seek His help? Must we not find the explanation in the fact that they are afraid to face eternity, afraid to come before the Almighty with their sins' guilt? Not long ago I had to fly from New York to Pittsburgh. On the seat beside me was a successful young scientist, who in the course of our conversation admitted that he had never found much reason to attend church. His closest approach to religion was the rather vague intention to send his little daughter to Sunday-school. After our short conversation he moved to the single seat across the aisle, perhaps to read privately a certain salaciously illustrated magazine that unfortunately claims many readers among the so-called upper classes. Suddenly we were asked to adjust the safety belts, for we were running into an electrical storm. Soon the furious wind shook the plane as though the huge transport were but a plaything for the elements, while lightning lit up the heavens and thunder reechoed across the whole firmament. That self-confident young man who had just admitted scant interest in spiritual things now turned white, dropped his magazine, came over to sit beside me, and asked distractedly: "Do you think the lightning will strike us? You were right; we can be nearer to God than we believe."

Every one of you can be nearer to God than he imagines

in this day's quick change and sudden sorrow. Even if our heavenly Father's unexplained mercy spares you fatal accident or crippling illness, at some time — and there are no exceptions to this rule — your sin will remind you of God's inescapable judgment. Because your souls are involved, I sincerely wish that you who regard faith in Jesus Christ as a chafing restriction could read a portion of the heavy mail this radio mission receives — letters stained with tears of remorse and failure, confessions worded by anguished minds and written by shaking hands, intense pleadings for a positive answer to the question "Where can I find peace for my soul?" Here you would see that the breaking of God's Law which once seemed so enticing and alluring has lost its glamor and turned to bitter reproach. These pleas for peace should warn you against the folly of surrendering to lust for short, quick moments and then living years in restless regret; the fatal mistake of spending a few dollars in the service of sin and then finding that even a life's savings cannot buy forgetfulness, as the one who shared your secret sins constantly points an accusing finger at you.

Peace of mind cannot be found where people often look for it — in money. Some one told Cornelius Vanderbilt, railroad magnate, "How happy you must be with all your millions!" "Happy?" he countered. "Why, I have not had an hour's happiness in my life." Baron Rothschild, once regarded as the world's wealthiest man, when asked, "Are you happy?" similarly answered, "Happy, when just as you are going to dinner, you have a letter placed in your hand saying, 'If you don't lend me £500, I will blow your brains out'? Happy, when you have to sleep with pistols under your pillow?"

Nor can inner strength be found in learning and human science. If political experts, with contacts all over the country, cannot foretell the results of an election, how can we reasonably expect to find any earthly guide for the unmarked future? Modern education, rejecting Jesus Christ, often seeks to unsettle the mind and produce a sense of doubt. A professor at a Mid-Western university begins one of his courses by telling his students, "If I can succeed in making you question everything you have believed, the purpose of this course will have been attained." That cynical, question-mark uncertainty is often responsible for many college suicides.

Again, your peace of heart and mind is not to be found in fortune-telling, even though the newspapers inform us that high Government officials as well as multitudes throughout the country resort to astrology, like all superstitions a contemptible fraud. You cannot drown sorrows in drink; for what a terrifying aftermath follows drunkenness and its debauch!

All else must fail; yet when your soul craves rest, you can find peace — and may God's Spirit help you believe this truth! — in the Lord Jesus! If past sins accuse you, with the Savior you can face them calmly, even the unmentionable, black transgressions you hardly dare admit, yet which, as your letters show, you must confess. For you know that the endless love of Jesus has atoned for every sin and canceled every charge against you. If you doubt this blood-bought pardon and dark, brooding misgivings beset your mind, read your Bible more trustingly, look to Jesus more confidently, pray more earnestly, and His peace will triumph in your soul. If hell itself torments you, you can exult, "I am Christ's, and who shall separate me from the love of God?" When you kneel in faith at the cross, a divine calm will enter your soul as worries fade before the radiance of the Savior's mercy.

As Christ's, we know that, since God loved us with such divine compassion that He *"spared not His own Son but delivered Him up for us all,"* He will direct our entire lives by the power and wisdom of His love. Therefore we are sure that whatever befalls us is for our best, for the strengthening of our inner life and the closer approach to our heavenly Father. Blessed by this confidence, we can join Saint Paul in declaring, *"I have learned in whatsoever state I am therewith to be content."* If our money is taken, we need not forfeit peace, for Christ can restore far more than we have ever had if He so wills; and if not, whatever God ordains is good. If we lose our health, we can still be cheerful with a cleansed, Christ-directed heart; for Jesus, the divine Physician, is able to help and cure, provided healing be in accord with His gracious purpose. If any hard, up-hill road looms before us, Christ's grace will sustain us, as the Savior, fulfilling His promise, *"Lo, I am with you alway, even unto the end of the world,"* walks at our side to say: *"My peace I give unto you. . . . Let not your heart be troubled."* Whatever our burden may be — loneliness, misunderstanding, broken friendship, bereavement — through Christ our *"sorrow shall be turned to joy,"* our afflictions to advantages, earthly losses to heavenly gains and repeated fears to peace, *"perfect peace."*

Though this may seem too glorious to be real, it is Heaven's truth. Give Christ your heart, and it will be filled with a divine calm. How could Christian martyrs, racked by the most horrifying forms of torture pagan fiends might invent, meet death with a hymn of praise on their lips, while their heathen persecutors shrieked in terror when their end came? How could earnest Christians like the founders of my Church gladly leave everything, sacrifice their property, break family ties, and come to a strange country in the search for peace and the freedom to worship God without governmental interference, while others with money, position, and power often lose their minds at even slight reverses? How are some of you, bedridden for twenty, thirty, forty years, radiant with happiness that many others in this audience have never known despite the ease and the health which are theirs! Is not the reason for this wide difference to be found in the glorious truth — prove it in your own lives, my doubting friends! — that Christ's peace, passing human understanding, can make us rich in poverty, spiritually strong though physically weak, exultant even in death?

That peace is too precious to hoard for ourselves. Blessed by God's covenant, we can be peacemakers in this war-fomented age. Put Christ into the home, where, of all places, the family should find a quiet refuge but where, as many of you know, human passions, anger, and selfishness, often exile happiness; and once the Savior rules in parents' and children's hearts and He is daily worshiped in the family circle, His blessing will abide there. Your own experiences bear the most striking testimony to Christ's transforming love as it sanctifies your own households. Enthrone the Savior's faith in the hearts of employers and working-men, and you will reduce the number of labor clashes that are a reproach to the nation. This is illustrated by the many business firms and industries which have applied our Lord's Golden Rule. Let Christ's love dominate our race relations, and such conflicts will be minimized, as the true brotherhood shows which exists between Christians who are white, black, red, or yellow. Let this holy faith work throughout lands of superstition, ignorance, vice, and these citadels of evil must fall. When Charles Darwin first visited the tip of South America, he was dismayed by the bestial conditions of its people. He declared, "The Fuegians are in a more miserable state than I ever expected to see any human being." Thirty years later he returned to Tierra del Fuego and found a transformation to virtue and a civilization that made him write: "I certainly should have predicted that not all the missionaries in the world could have done what has been done. It is wonderful, and it shames me, as I have always prophesied a failure." Let nations bow before Christ, and we shall have the nearest approach to world-wide peace that can ever be ours. When war between Chile and Argentina seemed inevitable, the people of these two South American nations settled their differences quietly and then on their common boundary erected that imposing statue Christ of the Andes, with this inscription: "Sooner shall these mountains crumble into dust than the Argentinians and the Chileans break the peace which at the feet of Christ, the Redeemer, they have sworn to maintain."

Life's cutting tragedy, of course, is this, that sin prevails instead of faith. Therefore, despite roseate campaign speeches which foretold a warless world, we shall always have international conflicts. According to Christ Himself wars and rumors of wars will mark the earth's last days — a prophecy that certainly should make us prepare for His imminent return. Christians, avoiding the error of pacifism, which has usurped a constantly larger place in many American churches, must be ready to defend their country against aggression and invasion. They must do more! They must spread the Savior's message. Every convert to Jesus is an agent for peace. In a world of terrifying strife the preaching of Christ's Gospel and its proclamation *"On earth peace, good will toward men"* is the only effective check we can ever have on the full fury of future war, a struggle which will be incomparably more destructive even than the horrors of the present conflict.

II

IT OFFERS ABIDING PEACE THROUGH CHRIST

Peace with God, peace with our fellow-men, peace with our conscience — these are the glorious blessings of our covenant sealed in the Savior's blood. Yet for tomorrow's uncertainty the riches of God's grace in Jesus are even greater. Our text promises, *"The mountains shall depart and the hills be removed; but My kindness shall not depart from thee, neither shall the covenant of My peace be removed."* Believe that every word of this pledge is heavenly truth, without exaggeration! Step out of your homes, you, my fellow-redeemed near God's hills, Mount Washington in Maine, Mount Baker in Washington, the Appalachians or Alleghenies in the East, the mighty Rockies or the lofty Sierras in the West! You on the plains, picture to yourselves the towering Himalayas! Now believe that, even if these heights could be removed, Christ's peace can never be broken. International documents may become mere scraps of paper; men's promises made under oath before God can be forgotten; marriage vows, as many personally know, are easily violated. Some of you have even betrayed your Savior. The fervent pledge you once made before the Lord Jesus Christ has been withdrawn by your unbelief and your godless life. Everything else in life can change and decay. Men can traitorously turn their backs on their nation, their friends, their home, their Church; but God never spurns any penitent, believing sinner who approaches the mercy-seat in Jesus' name. Today this blood-bought grace is again extended to you as the only permanent blessing in this passing world. Whoever you may be, whatever sins you may have committed, however deeply you may have fallen from grace, remember that this pledge of eternal peace, offered you now through sincere, individual trust in Jesus Christ, can never be broken by all the armies of earth, combined with the legions of hell.

Men with warped minds and twisted morals have sought to destroy this covenant by ridiculing the Savior, persecuting His followers and sanctimoniously attacking His truth. But where are the enemies of Christ? Roman emperors who consigned hosts of martyrs to agonizing death; heathen potentates who slaughtered missionaries and boasted that Jesus would never conquer their realm; antichristian writers, philosophers, and scientists, Voltaire, Renan, Darwin, Hume, Gibbon, Ingersoll, Darrow — where are they? Silenced in defeat by death! Yet the treaty of God's peace with the world, established at Calvary, has not been broken by atheists' million-dollar war funds, persecutors' cruel power, nor anti-Biblical research of misguided minds.

Nor will that peace be destroyed in the future. Christianity will be assailed in the years before us far more viciously than in the past, both from within the Church and without. The difficulties which our beloved nation faces — increasing indebtedness, unemployment, poverty, the specter of war — combine to remind us that radical, antichristian forces may increase during the disturbed days ahead and that the Church may meet serious opposition. Even if our prayers are answered and God in His mercy averts these dangers, there are individual perplexities under which many of you even now stagger. Where, my own countrymen, my fellow-redeemed in Canada, Mexico, and the islands, where in the whole wide world of pain, disease, war, hunger, hatred, can we find an unchanging, immovable, unbroken hope for every sinner and for every sufferer? Where, if not in the blessed Lord Jesus, *"the same yesterday and today and forever"*? Oh, for that Christ-centered faith by which, at time's end, when the mountains have melted away before the final Judgment, we can — O God, may it be every one of us! — stand before the throne of the Lamb to sing in triumph: "We *are* eternally redeemed, O Christ! The covenant of Thy blood-sealed peace has not been broken! We are Thine forever!" God mercifully grant us our Savior's pardon and peace, for His name's sake! Amen.

ON YOUR KNEES, AMERICA!

"If My people, which are called by My name, shall humble themselves and pray and seek My face and turn from their wicked ways, then will I hear from heaven and will forgive their sin and will heal their land." — 2 Chronicles 7:14.

Our God, who hast Promised to Hear Our Prayers:

Mercifully grant that as we behold the cross on which Thy Son, Jesus Christ, shed His atoning, purifying blood, we may receive the courageous trust which takes Thee at Thy word and finds strength in daily prayer! Keep us ever in communion with Thee! Make us strong to petition Thee confidently; humble, to ask according to Thy will; sympathetic, to intercede for our fellow-men; resolute, to plead even though Thine answer may be delayed; faithful, always to pray in our Savior's name! In Him alone we find forgiveness, peace and — God grant this to every one! — the pledged assurance of heaven, face to face with Thee, the Father, the Holy Spirit, and the glorious Redeemer! Until then strengthen us to meet our trials and through firm reliance on Thy grace to overcome temptation! We need Thy sustaining presence constantly, for evil days have come upon us and too easily can we be influenced to deny the truth! As we commend ourselves anew to Thee, O Triune God, hear us, for we trust in Jesus' unfailing promise! Amen.

CONFLICTING cries reecho across our country in these problem-weighted days. "Protect yourself, America!" This plea demands increased armaments, more powerful airplanes, swifter cruisers, heavier cannon, bigger bombs, as the most stupendous defense program in our national history gets under way. With all our hearts we hope that these Titanic efforts will remove the danger of foreign invasion; but we need more protection than even this gigantic rearming project. It took hundreds of thousands of men hundreds of years to build the Chinese Wall, the largest defense structure known to man; but even that barrier —

it would stretch half-way across the United States — could not save China from devastation. The French boasted that the Maginot Line was impregnable, yet it fell without having its strength tested. In 1914 the Germans assembled the greatest war machine known to military science, yet their well-equipped armies surrendered, and their navy was scuttled.

Others cry, "Remove your hidden enemies, America!" Martin Dies, chairman of the committee investigating un-American activities, has just issued a challenging volume in which he shows the Fifth-Column activities of Nazi, Fascist, and particularly of Communist forces. He claims that important youth groups, labor unions, Negro organizations, are Stalin's agents. Two thousand "outright Communists," he maintains, hold Government positions at Washington, with many radicals in the higher salary brackets, some even close to the White House. Again we agree that secret agents of Communists and totalitarians, as treacherous foes of our God and country, should be removed; for as broad as America is, it is not large enough to harbor any one who seeks to undermine our democracy in addition to destroying the Christian religion. Yet if every Fifth Columnist were exiled, other heavy problems would still burden us.

Again, this cry is heard, "Watch your financial structure, America!" Debates on currency and inflation, charges that wealth is being concentrated in fewer hands, fears produced by mounting national indebtedness, fill the air as money experts warn of impending danger. We realize, too, that the nation is living beyond its means, that all the gold safely stored in the Fort Knox vaults may not be sufficient to save us from monetary collapse; but if other nations have regained economic stability after the chaos of wild inflation, we can, too.

Yet, as Christians, we have another cry, incomparably more vital in these question-marked years — not a new plea nor a slogan from our economists, intellectual leaders, Government officials, but an ancient appeal from God Himself. Here it is, the summons which can help bring peace and promise to every one of us and to our whole country, the Lord's demand:

ON YOUR KNEES, AMERICA!

A defenseless nation with prayer is better protected than a heavily armed nation without prayer. America on its knees can accomplish more than America with its head high in proud self-confidence. Far greater power than that afforded by the world's largest store of gold will accrue to the United States through Christian intercession. This is not human theory; it is rather God's truth, recorded in His words to King Solomon, Second Chronicles, chapter seven, verse fourteen: *"If My people, which are called by My name, shall humble themselves and pray and seek My face and turn from their wicked ways, then will I hear from heaven and will forgive their sin and will heal their land."*

I

PRAYER PROMISES NATIONAL BLESSING

This glorious promise of healing for our country's ills is based on the condition that we approach the one true God. The Almighty says, *"Seek My face!"* Too many have the loose idea that any plea, no matter to whom it is addressed, is an effective prayer. So they call upon the "Mighty Spirit," the "Supreme Architect," the "Great Unknown," the "Creative Force," either without actually knowing to whom they are speaking or, what is worse, deliberately directing their petitions to substitutes for the only Lord of heaven and earth. Because there is but one God, not a dozen gods, and only He can answer prayer; because He is revealed unmistakably in the Bible as the Father, His Son, the Lord Jesus Christ, and the purifying Spirit, your petitions must be addressed to that blessed Trinity. If you are praying in any other way, stop now! The true God, beside whom all other objects of men's worship are crude idols, declares, *"Seek* My *face!" "Thou shalt have no other gods before Me."* If you are worshiping saints or angels, hear God say, *"Seek* My *face!" "Put not your trust in men!"* If you utter vague, uncertain supplications without knowing that personal Triune God of power, love, and glory; if you moan through the darkness of your sorrows, *"Oh, that I knew where I might find Him!"* stop now! Your search is ended. For here God the Creator, God the Redeemer, God the Purifier solemnly proclaims: *"Seek* My *face!" "Call upon* Me *in the day of trouble!"* We could erect prayer temples by the thousands; they might be architectural gems, adorned with all the beauty that money and talent can produce. Millions could throng these sanctuaries, but no matter how long, how loud, or even how sincerely, they might pray — the Confucianist bowing down before five hundred ancestral gods prays sincerely — if their words were not addressed to the only God, all this pleading would be empty words, vain vocal exertion. Therefore, when the cry reechoes, "On your knees, America!" it is a summons not simply to prayer, but to the worship of almighty God, the Father of our Lord Jesus Christ; and one of the basic needs in this country today is that millions learn who the one true Lord really is.

Only God's people can pray acceptably. In the text our heavenly Father says: To have your prayers answered you must be one of *"My people, which are called by My name."* Now, to be God's, we must be free from sin, for no man burdened with the wrong inherited by every one of us at birth and acquired by every one during life can approach Him before whom even the sinless angels shield their faces. When the Israelites of old thought that surely they, as the chosen people, with their Temple at Jerusalem, could come before Jehovah, sin-stained though they were, He gave this terrifying rebuke, *"When ye spread forth your hands, I will hide Mine eyes from you; yea, when you make many prayers, I will not hear; your hands are full of blood."* Though we remain on our knees until they are calloused, keep our hands perpetually locked in prayer, and scream until we lose our voices, if we are not right with God, if our sins are not completely removed, we are still children of wrath, and He will not hear our entreaties.

No human agent or intermediary can bring your prayers before the heavenly throne. No church in itself, no minister or priest, possesses the power to make your prayers acceptable. No saint of old, no self-sacrificing mother, no godly husband or wife, can take your place in praying. In the Middle Ages forgiveness of sins was sold at specified rates, and today, with similar folly, people are urged to approach the Almighty by their character, their good intentions, and their good resolutions. You must have your sin forgiven before you can draw near to God.

Here it is that Jesus, the Savior of mankind, comes into our prayer-life with His unfathomable, undeserved mercy. He broke down the barriers that separate us from God by taking away our sins, every one of them, transferring the guilt that rested on us to Himself, paying completely the penalty we should have suffered. All this Jesus did for us when at Calvary He hung on the cross between heaven and earth; and because as our Substitute

He served the sentence that sin pronounced on every one of us; because the anguish and death of God's own Son was the required ransom price He paid to free us, the promise of His holy Gospel is the good news that *"there is therefore now no condemnation to them which are in Christ Jesus."* We have been washed pure, clean, spotless, in the blood of the Lamb. Through Christ we have no more unforgiven sin; and since faith in His reconciling, restoring love makes us the sons of God, nothing can keep us from approaching Him as trusting children petition their loving father. Talk about the great changes in history, the wonders of nature, the marvels of science! There is not in all the centuries, the phenomena of laboratory research, the glories of earth, sea, and sky, a more startling miracle than the change exerted by faith in the Cross of Jesus Christ, which takes sin-stained men and women from the highway to hell, makes them sin-free and sets them on the open road to God and His heaven.

Prayers, to be answered, must come from Christ-dedicated hearts. The Lord Jesus says, *"Whatsoever ye shall ask the Father in My name, He will give it you."* The name of Jesus Christ, our God and Savior, and with it the trust in His fathomless, unfailing mercies — that is the key which opens the door to eternal riches! The name of Jesus Christ, our one Mediator and only Ransom, and with it the unshaken reliance on His power to save to the uttermost — that is the banner under which a praying Church can advance from victory to victory!

Yet that holy name, above all other names, is systematically avoided today, when, more than ever, men should acclaim our Lord. Many, including some nominal Christians, do not like to mention Jesus Christ for fear they may displease those who reject Him. In this spirit certain churches have deleted "Jesus" from their prayers. In many lodges to which, inconsistently, some of you Christian men belong, all reference to Christ has been banned from the ritual. In politics, prayers are spoken which drop His holy name so they will be wide enough to embrace those who deny the Savior's deity and atonement. During the recent presidential campaign one speaker closed his address with a petition for our country taken word for word from *The Book of Common Prayer,* except — and I hope sincerely it was an oversight — that the concluding words of the prayer, "all which we ask through Jesus Christ, our Lord," were completely omitted.

May God give you the loyalty to Christ shown by Samuel F. B. Morse, internationally acclaimed inventor of the electric telegraph, a scientist heaped with honors such as few men have ever received. He testified that in the darkest hours, when everything seemed hopeless, prayer to Jesus brought him light and the assurance of his salvation. He wrote: "To Him, indeed, belongs all the glory. I have evidence enough that without Christ I could do nothing. All my strength is there, and I fervently desire to ascribe to Him all the praise. If I am to have influence, I desire to have it for Christ, to use it for His cause; if wealth, for Christ; if more knowledge, for Christ. I speak sincerely when I say I fear prosperity lest I should be proud and forget whence it comes." May the Holy Spirit similarly grant you the grace to approach your God and say: "Father, I bring these petitions to Thee not in my own name, for who am I, with evil in my heart, on my hands, that I should dare to come before Thee! Rather do I kneel in the name of Thy Son, my own Savior. Hear me for His sake. By His promise bless me and fill me with His love."

If this cry, "On your knees, America!" is to help bring the divine answer to your problems, millions in this country

must pray with contrite sincerity. The text reminds us
that God requires His people to *"humble themselves . . .
and turn from their wicked ways. Then,"* He promises,
"will I hear from heaven." Common reason, not to mention the Bible warning, ought to make this fact clear: we
cannot expect the national benefits which Thanksgiving
week again recalls, to bless our land automatically and indefinitely if the rebellion against the Almighty and the
bold breaking of His Ten Commandments continues un-
checked. We cannot always be the most richly blessed
and at the same time the most crime-ridden nation on earth.
The call, therefore, is for a repentant, prayerful spirit
throughout the land: Back to God, back to the Bible, back
to Christ in humility and contrition!

This cry "On your knees, America!" becomes the more
necessary when we survey the counter-offensive against
Christian prayer waged on every side with an insistence
hitherto unknown. Millions in this country are being
stampeded into a self-reliance which has no room for intercession, an overconfidence which regards trust in God as
effeminate. American Christian homes, basic units in
social and religious improvement, frequently set family
worship aside. American churches have often questioned
the full power of prayer and robbed it of its promise.
American educational theories reject the petitions of children on the ground that dependence on God weakens self-
trust. As a consequence we are paying a prohibitive price
for this neglect, but not nearly as fearful a price as we
may have to pay in the future unless humility, repentance,
and trust in God find a far greater place within our
boundaries. If American Christians neglect the privilege
of prayer, hard and trying times may lie ahead — far worse
than the bread-line, closed-bank, crashed-stock-market days
of the past decade — Heaven's visitation, by which this

country and its churches may be purified and restored to
a deeper recognition of God.

Let us not, however, overlook the strengthening fact
that penitent prayer in Christ's name helped this nation in
the past. George Washington on his knees at Valley
Forge, his face wet with tears, his voice solemnly raised
to God; Abraham Lincoln who, during the crucial years
of the Civil War, started the custom of an annual Thanksgiving Day — these men and millions of humble Christians
joined with them in prayers mightily answered knew God's
ancient promise, which also assures the American people
today that, if they *"humble themselves and pray and seek
My face and turn from their wicked ways, then will I hear
from heaven and will forgive their sin and will heal their
land."* Put confident prayer into the hearts of the nation's
youth, instead of the un-American drivel with which some
of your sons and daughters are being filled today, and we
shall have real patriotism. Nathan Hale, a young man of
twenty-one, was sentenced to die for his country. During
his last moments, instead of surrendering to fear, he turned
his face heavenward and was in such complete communion
with his heavenly Father that he did not even hear the harsh
commands of the British hangman. Strengthened by
prayer, he cried out from the gallows: "If I had ten
thousand lives, I would lay them down for my injured,
bleeding country. I regret that I have but one life to lose
for my country." Bring this humble, penitent, Christian
prayer into our nation's homes; win millions of America's
unchurched for Christ and make them mighty intercessors
for the nation; let each of the quarter million churches in
our forty-eight States intercede for the President, the Congress, and those in authority; teach all of us the power
of Christ-exalting prayer — and, with this obedience to the
cry "On your knees, America!" we can, under God, bring
America to its highest heights!

II

PRAYER PROMISES INDIVIDUAL BLESSING

I thank our heavenly Father for the privilege of telling you by His authority that this promise of answered prayer, forgiven sin, the healed sorrows, can be wholly yours as soon as you say, "Christ, Thou art mine, and by the power of Thy precious blood I am Thine forever." No matter how multiplied your difficulties and how crushing the problems of your money, health, peace, home relations, and general happiness, God tells you, *"I hear from heaven."* Take Him at His word today! Not long ago I read that a business concern employed a famous lawyer at a fee of $100,000 to draw up an unbreakable contract. Some time after the iron-clad document was executed, however, the same concern found reason to change its policies and re-engaged the same attorney, at another $100,000 fee, to break that unbreakable contract; and he did. A recognized insurance director claims: "There is scarcely a law governing business which cannot be broken with more or less impunity — with complete impunity, if the breaker has any brains at all." But there is a law that God Himself can never repeal, His promise *"I hear from heaven,"* if you approach Him in Christ-grounded faith.

Pray confidently, believing that no problem you face is too great for the Almighty, with whom *"nothing shall be impossible."* Henry Ward Beecher tells of a poor Indian Christian woman on Long Island, who faced a Thanksgiving without food. A day or two before the holiday, while standing on a hill overlooking the beach, she saw a large flock of wild geese and prayed, "Oh, that the Lord would give me one of those for Thanksgiving!" She had hardly uttered the words, when a hawk flew into the flock and killed one of the geese, which fell to the ground not far away. Thus did God provide a Thanksgiving feast for an impoverished Indian. God can help you in the same way if you are Christ's. He *"shall supply all your need according to His riches in glory by Christ Jesus,"* if you trust Him fully.

Recall the prayer of Hudson Taylor, consecrated missionary to China! Once the sailing-ship in which he traveled was becalmed close to a cannibal island. To the horror of those aboard, the ship drifted slowly shoreward, and nothing could stop its course toward the savages on the beach, who eagerly prepared for a great feast of human flesh. In that emergency the captain asked Hudson Taylor to beseech God for help. "I will pray," the missionary replied, "provided you set your sails to catch the breeze." At first the captain refused, but Taylor warned, "I will not pray unless you prepare the sails." That request carried out, the heroic man of God knelt in confident pleading. Before long the captain returned to say joyfully, "You had better stop praying now, for we have more wind than we can manage." With the ship a hundred yards from the shore, God had answered by sending a strong wind to save the passengers and the crew.

I can almost hear some of you object, however, "I have prayed, but God has not answered me." Perhaps you have not persevered enough, for our heavenly Father knows far better than we do the best time for answering. Most of us pray far too little, and to teach us the blessing of protracted pleading, God may let us wait. Sometimes Jesus was so busy that He could not eat; but He never was so preoccupied that He could not pray. Regularly He devoted hours to communion with His heavenly Father, and sometimes He spent the whole night in prayer. Yet we — may God forgive us! — are often too engrossed with our petty worries and trivial joys to find time for the Savior who gave His lifetime for us. Pray continually and courageously!

Reviewing the history of his transatlantic cable, Cyrus Field writes: "It has been nearly thirteen years of ceaseless toil. Often my heart has been ready to sink. Many times, when wandering in the forests of Newfoundland in the pelting rain or on the decks of ships on dark, stormy nights, alone, far from home, I have almost accused myself of madness and folly. . . . Yet one hope has led me on; and I have prayed that I might not taste of death till this work was accomplished. That prayer is answered." If his pleading was granted after thirteen years, why do you protest when it seems that God does not hear you after thirteen days or thirteen minutes?

Again, some of you will object, "I have prayed incessantly. I have pleaded humbly and in Jesus' name; and yet God has done just the opposite of what I requested." Some of you clutch a baby's shoe or fondle a little pink garment to recall that you once implored the Almighty with persistent pleas to save an infant life; but the child died. Some of you think of the long nights of prayerful waking and watching with a beloved one, during which you literally wore yourself out; yet God took your dear one home. Some of you have continually prayed for health and happiness, but your bodies are broken beyond repair, your joy of life crushed into a thousand irreparable fragments and you demand, "How can you say that God hears prayer?"

Human reason offers no answer, but faith does. Because you are Christ's, every time it seems such prayers are not heard and God, far from being the Lord of love, has dealt cruelly with you, He has in reality given far more than you have asked. Above our poor powers of understanding, Jesus, who loved us unto the bitter, bleeding end at Calvary, loves us even when it seems He hurts us. That child, snatched away all too young in your opinion, is far better off in the heavenly life than it would be were it to live longer on earth; and because you are the Lord's, you, too, will say in the joyful reunion of eternity, *"He hath done all things well."* The Christian husband or wife, called home against your wishes, was taken by God's mercy and not His cruelty, as hard as it is to understand this. And in the fuller knowledge of the hereafter you will realize His blessed truth *"What I do thou knowest not now; but thou shalt know hereafter."* Would you not prefer heaven through Jesus, after broken health and heaped miseries, to hell without Christ, after the fleeting pleasures of this life?

I know of a man who graduated from a theological seminary and was privileged to serve his Savior three years as a missionary. Then his afflictions began. In the tropics he lost the sight of one eye. A few years later, without a moment's warning, the other eye failed to function. His little girl was smitten by infantile paralysis. His wife, on whom he leaned because of his blindness, was called Home after severe suffering. Three years later his second child died. In the midst of these difficulties his shepherd dog, trained by the Seeing Eye Foundation, was killed in an accident; but as blow followed blow, did this twentieth-century Job rise up to curse God? No! Triumphant over these successive afflictions he declares faith and the power of prayer have taught him that God's Word never fails. He has found the joy and peace which make him tell you in Saint Paul's assurance, *"My God shall supply all your need according to His riches in glory by Christ Jesus."*

Will not you, my fellow-redeemed, turn to our God in prayer and answer the appeal directed personally to every one of you: "On your knees, America! On your knees in penitent, humble prayer! On your knees in sincere and heartfelt prayer! On your knees in trusting, confident prayer! On your knees in the name of Jesus Christ"? God grant that you will for the Savior's sake! Amen.

HELP FOR THE HOME — IN CHRIST

> *"When Jesus was come into Peter's house, He saw his wife's mother laid and sick of a fever. And He touched her hand, and the fever left her: and she arose and ministered unto them."* — Saint Matthew 8:14, 15

Ever-blessed Savior:

By the enlightening power of thy Holy Spirit use our broadcasts mightily to show scoffers the fatal error of unbelief, sinners the perils on every pathway leading away from God! Bring this message into many families throughout the nation and even beyond its borders! Let them know that during these very moments Thou art before their homes, knocking at their doors, eager to be welcomed! Protect our dwelling-places against danger by fire and flood, war and pestilence, famine and destruction; but if Thy divine and all-knowing goodness has decreed that we must face loss, sickness, opposition, give us the faith which recognizes in these reverses the guidance of Thy goodness! Particularly do we beseech Thee to guard our Christian homes against worldliness, unbelief, and denial of Thy grace. Grant us whatever earthly blessings Thy wisdom may see fit to entrust to us! Lead many families to accept Thee as their Savior from sin, their Friend in every need, their Counselor in every problem! Endow our households with Thy loving peace. In poverty, sickness, suffering, misunderstanding, let the light of Thy truth serve as a beacon and brighten our pathway with a foregleam of the heavenly homeland! Hear us by the promise of Thy cross and blood, Thy death and resurrection! Amen.

WHEN the home collapses, the nation is doomed. If throughout our country adultery is smiled on as smart; if young people by instruction of teachers and example of elders are led to believe that men and women are animals who need not obey the laws of purity, that youth should not wait for marriage; if the high and the mighty practice easy divorce; if a growing percentage of marriages is wilfully kept childless; no matter how rich and powerful that country may be, it is headed for disaster.

The United States is no exception to this rule repeatedly proved throughout history. The American revolt against marital morals points unmistakably to Western civilization's decay. France, taught by bitter defeat that the family breakdown was an important cause of its national collapse, has started a government campaign against divorce and artificial birth control. How long before our people, witnessing the ominous increase in broken homes and the startling decrease in family size, will realize that dangerous days have dawned on us? Newspapers throughout the land print the immoral rot of a columnist who deliberately asks Congressional action to help make divorce easy, quick, cheap, and to remove what he calls the "superstition that marriage is sacred." A woman whose lifetime has been devoted to popularizing birth-control methods, thus irreparably injuring the morals of American youth, is honored by medals and applause for a race-suicide program far more serious than any Trojan-horse treachery. A Johns Hopkins University professor asks that every mother of eight children be prevented from having another baby, although the mutilation he proposes would have denied many in this audience as well as some world figures their existence. Harvard University employs a titled English lecturer who has advocated that college students should enter temporary marriages terminable after graduation. He asserts that no man or woman should marry without previous sex experience. When the number of American girls working in taverns exceeds the enrolment of girls studying at our colleges; when publishers who specialize in erotic literature can make the United States the center of printed filth; when Communist leaders promote a pagan free-love program and our own State Legislators constantly compete in loosening divorce laws — devotion to our country, love for our families, reverence for God, demand wide-spread, continued opposition by the nation's Christian forces.

How, then, can American homes be safeguarded against such dangers? Or, looking away from these national issues and focusing our attention on our own homes with their problems, trials, sorrows, how can we find guidance and hope for our families? God grant that in every question of home-life we turn to Jesus, the Son of God and the Savior of the world. If everything else fails; if human promises are broken and our happiness is banished by sin, there is always

HELP FOR THE HOME — IN CHRIST

Our text, one of many similar accounts, illustrates His blessing on the family when it records (Saint Matthew, chapter eight, verses fourteen and fifteen): *"When Jesus was come into Peter's house, He saw his wife's mother laid and sick of a fever. And He touched her hand, and the fever left her: and she arose and ministered unto them."*

I
OUR HOMES NEED HELP

We see from this incident that Peter, later to be the great apostle of Jesus Christ, was married. He found nothing unworthy, unholy, in wedded life. Indeed, it is the clear teaching of God Himself that under normal conditions *"it is not good that the man should be alone."* Today, however, diseased minds ridicule matrimony in dirty stories; the radio, the screen, and the stage too often snicker at its violation; many young people avoid family life because of the restriction on their personal liberties or the drudgery they think it imposes; and, this is the worst, under the guise of religion, even in the holy name of Christ, the claim is raised that to remain single leads to a higher, holier life. How clearly God's Word protests, *"Marriage is honorable in all"!* We ought to understand the perversions which usually follow the ridicule of wedlock and realize that, though disfigured by sin and selfishness, marriage is one of God's most blessed earthly gifts.

When the text speaks of Peter's wife's mother, it offers no indication of the rancor and hatred which the Christless world frequently associates with the mother-in-law. It seems from Saint Mark's account that, far from seeking to avoid his wife's mother, as many do today, Peter took her into the home which he shared with his brother Andrew. Thousands in this audience likewise cannot thank God sufficiently for the blessing that Christian marriage has brought them in their mother-in-law, a second mother in faith, who, with Naomi's devotion to Ruth, has earned the undying love of her sons and daughters by marriage. How gladly many of you would welcome your mother-in-law into your home and care for her as long as she lives! If you have any other feelings, ask God to forgive you! Pray that reconciliation may take the place of estrangement!

Probably it was no ordinary illness that had laid this woman low, for Saint Luke, the beloved physician, calls the fever *"great."* One thing is certain, however, we ought to see clearly from this record, as from scores of similar Scriptural accounts, that the households of God's children will not escape dark hours and heavy afflictions. If it were possible to survey the 30,000,000 homes in America today, we would find hundreds of thousands in which sickness has caused misery, particularly heavy when a mother or father has been a crippled, bedridden invalid for twenty, thirty, forty years, when a child is misshapen and subnormal, when sufferers waste away in apparently incurable disease or, worse, exist in the living death of insanity.

Some have escaped serious sickness, only to endure

other shattering grief. Government figures tell us that
about 2,000,000 American families lost their homes by
mortgage foreclosures the last ten years. Members of this
radio congregation write that they were millionaires in
1929, yet today have hardly the bare necessities. Bad in-
vestments, the treachery of friends, open dishonesty, theft,
may have robbed you of your life's savings and the
resources for declining years. As you face the future with
no money, no income, no possibility even of Government
aid, you ask, "Where can we find help for our family?
Where the support for our children?"

Still others have been the victims of additional afflictions. Here are the husband and wife from whom the
Lord, in His unsearchable wisdom, has withheld the blessing of parenthood. They know that unwanted children
are born into the world every day; and although they have
prayed for years that God would bless them with at least
one child, this gift has been denied. Despite all medical
aid their empty homes will never reecho with the laughter
of their own children. Or here are large numbers of
Christians who repeatedly have asked God if it be His will,
to give them a life's companion and the joy of married
love; yet that happiness may never come to them. Picture
also the households afflicted by that inevitable loss, bereavement. Since I spoke to you a short week ago, some
of your families have been visited by *"the last enemy,"* the
grim reaper, who can cut down life in its prime, youth in
its vigor, even old age all too soon. You would gladly
accept sickness, reverses, poverty, if only the graves in
your cemetery plots would give up their dead and your
loved ones could be restored. And as many of you,
widowed and orphaned, face life alone, the cry that rises
repeatedly from your heart asks, "Where is there help for
this lonely, forsaken home of mine?"

Indescribably hard as all this is, there are homes with needs a hundred times more crucial and agonizing. I mean those families in which sin has ruthlessly blasted away peace. Since I have been broadcasting Christ's Gospel, more than two thirds of a million people have written in, and the problem most frequently voiced by these letters asks for help in the misery that sin imposes on the home. Thus there are those unhappy unions in which husband and wife have unsuccessfully tried to harmonize faith in Christ with the denial of Christ. On your wedding-day many of you thought that by example and prayer you could bring a godless husband to Christ; yet today, despite your love and entreaties, he is farther from repentance and faith than ever. You cannot worship the Savior together here on earth; how terrifying, then, the realization that you will be separated in eternity! Investigation of conditions in unhappy homes often compels me to raise a warning voice even against marriages between Protestants and Roman Catholics; and I say gladly the authorities of the latter group agree with us in issuing this warning. For such unions Protestants are asked to sign a statement involving the denial of their faith. No delusion is greater than the false self-assurance that love can conquer religious differences, even unbelief. If some will regard this as narrow and protest as many of my correspondents did before their unhappy experiences, "We are going to be the exceptions to your rule," let me assure you in friendly concern over your happiness and your soul's salvation that in a mixed marriage you are fighting against overwhelming handicaps which far too often cause unspeakable misery.

Another cutting tragedy is found in the strife-torn household, shattered by selfishness and jealousy. No love, no caresses where, of all places on earth, endearment and affection should reign! No willingness to sacrifice or even cooperate! Instead, separate lives for husband and wife, abuse, curses, profanity, in place of affection and encouragement! Mental cruelty, or actual physical harm, as hot-tempered men and women make their homes, which should be foregleams of heaven, the approach to hell! If you want proof for that clear Biblical doctrine which modern churches too often ridicule, the complete sinfulness of man, look into the American home in the slums or on the gold coast, in dark basements or in gilded penthouses, and you will find men at their worst. The conduct of human beings can become more vile than the actions of beasts when thankless, self-willed children disobey, despise, and finally desert their parents or when a drunken, slobbering, cursing, passion-inflamed father, staggering home from a saloon that has robbed him of his week's salary, tries to lay violent hands on his family.

The tragedy of one domestic sin is still greater — the damnable unfaithfulness which makes a man or woman break sacred marriage vows — the concealed adulteries which, some of you think, can be forgotten or hushed out of existence but which your own consciences will keep alive. These sins not only bring misery into the family, they go much farther; they put you under divine punishment, if not fully in this world, then, as true as God is almighty and all-powerful, in the next. The secret vice that may seem insignificant is such a heinous sin in God's sight that it can bar you from heaven, separate you in the hereafter from your loved ones. The lusts of the flesh which the world applauds are so terrifying that they often receive double punishment: loathsome, nauseating disease during this life and eternal death in hell. As God's Word thunders this denunciation, *"He that soweth to his flesh shall of the flesh reap corruption,"* may you be moved in real repentance to plead: "Oh, give us help for our impure souls, for our broken homes, for our strife-torn families!"

A few of you may have been spared all family sorrows. No one has ever died in your home; serious sickness and want have kept their distance from your doors; you have enjoyed serene family life, generally speaking, with no heavy public sins to mar your happiness. But if you now sit back in self-satisfied smugness and think that you do not need Christ for your family, consider how suddenly disaster may strike! How many of the people whose broken bodies were laid into the mass-graves at bombed Coventry and Birmingham last year thought that their homes would now be destroyed and their souls blasted into eternity? What assurance have you that next November the health, prosperity, happiness, you now cherish may not have departed forever? No matter how firmly built, how well financed your house may be, you, too, need assurance for this uncertain future. You, too, should humble yourselves before the Almighty to plead, "O God, give us help for our homes!"

II

CHRIST CAN HELP OUR HOMES

That prayer is answered definitely by Christ's mercy. As He, our blessed Redeemer, is the only Hope for a world lost in sin, the only Salvation for men's perishing souls, the only Solution to all human difficulties, so we declare publicly from coast to coast, Jesus offers the only lasting, permanent, unfailing blessing for families. See how quickly He shows His saving strength in Peter's home! It is but a small house in despised Galilee, and many a Pharisee or Levite would have refused to cross its threshold. But not Jesus! He is never ashamed to approach those who need His presence; often He is closest to the poor and the afflicted. He steps into that fisherman's cottage as light and love are radiated by His very presence. He touches the sick woman, and because He is God Almighty, the healing Savior, her fever vanishes. There, in the quiet of that humble dwelling, without display and advertising, Jesus proves Himself the divine Helper for the home.

Praise His holy name, Jesus' touch has lost none of its comforting, sustaining force! If you come into believing contact with Jesus through faith, He will do what nothing else can ever accomplish: take away your sins, cleanse you from their stain, free you from their guilt, save you from their punishment. Blessing, peace, and joy that you could never earn He grants you fully and freely when you trust His atoning death on the cross and His life-giving resurrection. But more, we not only have forgiveness in the Savior, but by His Spirit we are also reborn into a higher, better life. Through Christ we can literally become new creatures, with hatred changed to love, fleshly desires checked, selfishness subdued. Pay close attention to this promise! No matter how many books on domestic problems you may have studied, how many college courses on home management and financing you have taken; no matter how many experts have lectured to you on marital relations, sex questions, child-training, parental psychology; with all the assistance these sources may offer, real, upbuilding strength to meet our responsibilities in the family circle comes from the Holy Spirit when you are born again through Christ by Baptism, by faith in His mercies.

These blessings which come with Jesus' presence in the home have been shown too continuously and universally for any question or denial. In the South Sea Islands cannibals used to murder their own children; but after missionaries brought these black-souled pagans to the

Savior, the older among the converts who had killed their offspring wept repentantly over these brutal sins, yet found deep-souled joy when they saw children welcomed, protected, and instructed in the teachings of Christ, who had laid His holy hands on boys and girls of Palestine to say, *"Suffer the little children to come unto Me and forbid them not, for of such is the kingdom of God!"* It was the fiendish custom in dark Africa that aged parents, too weak to pull the plow or carry water jars, were dragged to the jungle, where wild beasts devoured them; but when Christ's missionaries pushed their way into these citadels of heathen darkness, the faith in the Savior changed everything. Instead of exposing their old parents, African Christians gladly honored and supported them until their last breath. In Greece even distinguished leaders whose names are chiseled into monumental granite or the marble of our public buildings, practiced indescribable perversions, while personal purity was laughed to scorn; but Christ's message swept into Athens, Corinth, and other Greek centers; as men and women acclaimed Jesus, they began to hate the unnatural vices that their countrymen applauded. In Rome, swollen with pride, luxury, power, as the mistress of the world, wives were frequently exchanged. Some women were divorced every year. An unknown and unheralded missionary, Paul of Tarsus, came to that city, and on Rome's seven hills he preached the message of the cross on Calvary's hill. With the divine declaration that *"marriage is honorable in all,"* *"Husbands, love your wives, even as Christ also loved the Church and gave Himself for it,"* the rotting props of paganism began to fall.

Today Jesus similarly offers help for your home that no other agency can provide. One of the great British preachers during the last century, Thomas Chalmers, at first neglected Gospel-preaching and did what many churches are trying to do today: he sought to reform his hearers by emphasizing good and denouncing evil. He had to admit, however, that he never reformed any one. Then he began to preach Christ with the promise of His pardon, and the results followed. He declares that "it was not until the free offer of forgiveness of sin through the aton- ing blood of Christ was urged upon men that I ever heard of any transformation." I want to add my testi- mony to the same truth and declare across the length and breadth of this nation, up into Canada and down into Mexico, to islands in the Pacific and the Atlantic, that not until you realize you are lost without Christ but eternally saved with Him, can there be any positive hope of blessing in your home-life, any assurance of victory over the sins which now pull you down to defeat.

In other words, if you want things right in your home, first of all get right with God through Christ. If you want the power to lead a clean life, to break bad habits; if you want a constant, faithful love for your husband or your wife and the ability to overcome the coaxing temp- tation to violate your marriage vow; if you want the strength to defeat drunkenness, come to the Lord Jesus Christ now! Trust Him fully, put everything into His hands, give God His way with your sin-stained life, and He will prove His promise *"Behold I make all things new."* His grace will grant you a clean heart and a right spirit. Hundreds of your letters show that with Christ you can forgive an unfaithful husband, in the Lord Jesus you welcome the little baby whose coming seems ill timed, through Christ you can subdue your passions and love purity. There will always be sin in your home, moments of weakness in your life; but when the Savior forgives and you start anew, you can begin with constantly stronger resolution and success.

Jesus offers more than forgiveness and strength. He whose arms are always outstretched to the weary and world-worn can also give divine comfort for every home sorrow. From the very hour your family is entrusted to Christ and you say, "Come, Lord Jesus, be our Guest," you are under the protection of the Most High. I do not promise that you will be spared all sorrow, that pain will never cross your threshold; but in Jesus' name and by His pledge I can tell you that because you live in Christ, *"there shall no evil befall thee, neither shall any plague come nigh thy dwelling."* It may appear that calamity overwhelms you, yet by God's wisdom and power the deepest family disaster may result in the highest blessing. Even death itself, with the cold loneliness and grief it always leaves, comes to the Christian home, not from God's consuming anger, but from His gracious love. If you are Christ's, not one sorrow will overtake you for which the heavenly homeland will not offer thousandfold joy in its reunion with parents, children, brothers, and sisters who, *"faithful unto death,"* preceded or followed you to eternity.

III

WE OUGHT TO SERVE CHRIST IN OUR HOMES

The text indicates that Peter's mother-in-law was completely cured; for hardly had Christ's healing hand rested on her when, eager to show her thanks, *"she arose and ministered unto them."* It is my earnest, prayer-supported plea that you, too, set everything else aside, no matter how important other issues may seem, and realize that Jesus has healed you from a disease immeasurably more destructive than the fever in Peter's home — the fatal sickness infecting your soul, sin's curse, for which there is no human cure, which brings decay to the body and eternal death to the soul.

Come to the divine Physician now! Kneel humbly before Him to say: "O Lord Jesus, I am weak and sinful, Thou canst help me. Touch me with Thy healing hand, so that through faith I may receive pardon, peace, and eternal life!" As your believing heart speaks this prayer, the curing grace of Christ will begin its blessed work within you. Don't delay, argue, debate, postpone, your coming to Jesus! We are told that Aaron Burr, who played a tragic role in American history, once almost acknowledged his Savior. While studying at Princeton, he was seized with the desire to become a Christian. He discussed his intention with the college president, who gave him the misdirected advice to weigh the matter carefully and return after more serious reflection. But Aaron Burr did not come back and, as far as is known, never confessed Christ. Don't let any one ever keep you from your Savior in that way! Approach Him now!

When you are His, serve Him in your family! Follow the Apostle's injunction, *"Learn first to show piety at home!"* Before you start work even for a church organization, see that Jesus is welcomed in your family circles! Make your houses what many Christian homes were during the first centuries — churches of Christ! You fathers of America who ought to be God's representatives to the group that bears your name, listen attentively! If you are living in the godlessness and sin that gives a destructive example to your own children, urging them to grow up without Christ or against Him, accept the Savior now in repentance and faith! If you think that you are too busy to attend services with the family or enroll your children in Sunday-school, drop some of your activities! Make time for Christ! If you sincerely want to, you certainly can set aside ten or fifteen minutes a day in which, together with your wife and children, you can come before the mercy throne and reverently study God's Word.

You mothers of America, who are daily helping to build your homes either for good or evil, don't let anything, as important, fashionable, entertaining, or helpful it may seem, keep Christ from your home and children! Realize that no woman, however great her political, social, intellectual achievements may be, has any greater privilege than that she bring healthy, happy children into the world, dedicate them to their Savior in Baptism, teach them their first prayers, sing them to sleep with a sacred lullaby, and give them the example of a God-fearing mother!

You children of America, remember what you have cost your parents in money, in work, even in sorrow over your mistakes! No one has ever risen to real success by neglecting or despising his father or mother. If you are estranged from your parents, do not argue as to who is at fault but reread the example of the prodigal! Write home! Return home, follow Jesus as He teaches you to love, honor, and obey your parents!

With Christ our homes can be havens of peace even in a war-crazed world, joy-filled dwellings, despite afflictions, households with pardon and blessing, though we sin daily. Therefore we offer you our services in bringing this help for you. Do domestic problems perplex you? If you have no spiritual counselors, write us! Are you eager to learn more of your Savior and be blessed by the personal promises of His grace? Do you want some one to help you establish family prayer and Scripture reading in your home? Do you want to learn the blessings of Baptism and its cleansing? Are you interested in knowing the details of that vast Christian school system supported by my Church, where children, in addition to receiving secular instruction, every day learn Scripture-passages, Bible-stories, and sacred hymns?

To help you find the Christian answer to any question

of home-life, the facilities of this radio system are at your disposal, and — more important — thousands of pastors and teachers throughout the country, joined with us in this Mission of the Air, are ready to help you. The one nearest your home will be grateful for the privilege of giving you counsel based on God's pure Word and Jesus' love. Let us bring His help to your family circle, and in return we promise that through faith your earthly home will be a foregleam of the heavenly mansions!

O God, save our Christian families in America, bless them with trust in Thy Son, our only Savior, and keep parents and children in the faith until we all reach the heavenly homeland. We ask this confidently because we plead in Jesus' name. Amen.

WHAT GLORY WITH JESUS!

"We know that, when He shall appear, we shall be like Him; for we shall see Him as He is." — Saint John, First Letter 3:2

Christ, Our Divine Redeemer:

Thou who didst come in lowliness to live on this earth of strife and turmoil, wilt soon return, but in glory and power to judge the world and take Thy ransomed believers to heaven. What reassuring promise to know that this greed-encrusted globe will not remain forever, that a better homeland awaits the redeemed in Thy presence! Help us prepare for Thy approach by watching in confident prayer! The predicted signs of Thy second advent are unmistakably fulfilled in this age of war, unbelief, immorality. Open our eyes to discern each token of Thy blessed closeness! May we always keep our lamps lit as we wait to welcome Thee. Make this the glorious climax of our faith: because Thou didst come to us, we, in trusting reliance on Thy grace, can always come, just as we are, to Thee! Do Thou therefore abide with us through Thy Word and sacred ordinances to strengthen our weaknesses, remove our fears, deepen our trust, change our lives, grant us soul-peace, refuge in the storm of life, blessing even in death! O come, Lord Jesus, come quickly! Amen.

OUR message today centers in the most glorious promise that God Himself can ever grant, the pledge of Christ's coming to us and our coming to Him, the divine comfort that has given children and world figures a holy readiness to face death. Our text offers heavenly hope in this harassed age, with its bloodthirsty hostilities, its heavy fears, its desperate need for spiritual strengthening. — When intrepid Missionary Morrison, translating the Bible into the Chinese language, came to this pledge in the words chosen as our text, his native helper cried, "Stop! That mercy is too great. The people of China can hardly believe such boundless love." Doubtless some of you, when you hear these words, will similarly wonder whether the American people will accept this magnificent grace. Yet, as Dr. Morrison told his Oriental assistant, "Write what God has written," so today I declare to you what God's Word declares in this priceless, peerless assurance of Saint John's First Letter, chapter three, verse two, only twenty words, the shortest and simplest our language contains, the conviction, *"We know that, when He shall appear, we shall be like Him; for we shall see Him as He is."* Imploring the Spirit's blessing on our study of this truth, we exclaim,

"WHAT GLORY WITH JESUS —

when He appears to us in His second coming or when we, resurrected in eternity, see Him before His celestial throne!"

I

THE GLORIOUS PROMISE OF HIS APPEARING

Saint John here speaks of the Savior's blessed return, for which millions have hoped and prayed ever since Christ's ascension, His glorious second coming "to judge the quick and the dead." This world of sin and sorrow, which God almighty created perfect, but which man has repeatedly turned into a madhouse, will not endure forever. This earth with its bloodshed, hatred, injustice, violence, oppression, cannot continue indefinitely. This race of passion-whipped, crime-bound men and women must come to its end when God's clock strikes the hour of doom for sin, but the hour of salvation for those who are Christ's.

"He shall come," the Christian Church throughout the ages declares in the Apostles' Creed, that statement of Bible truth accepted by all who follow Jesus, Protestant and Catholic, Lutheran and non-Lutheran. *"He shall come,"* the Gospel records assure us; for Jesus Himself said after His promise that He would go to prepare our

place in the heavenly mansions: *"I will come again and receive you unto Myself, that, where I am, there ye may be also."* *"He shall come,"* the epistles of the New Testament pledge repeatedly; as almost every sacred writer explains with inspired detail that He who once appeared in Bethlehem's lowliness to live His life of service and self-sacrifice will come again, radiantly majestic, the eternal, all-glorious Lord of lords.

"He shall come," the signs of our times insist, as they remind us that we are unmistakably in the last days, nineteen centuries closer to the world's end and Christ's reappearing on earth than were the apostles who wrote, *"The end of all things is at hand,"* and who prayed, *"Even so come, Lord Jesus!"* Consider carefully the startling present-day fulfilment of Scripture prophecies concerning the Lord's return; and even if you know nothing of Christ's death for your life, be honest enough to admit that God's Word foresees our own age! Preceding His coming, the Bible says, there shall be *"wars and rumors of wars,"* and no generation, even in savage lands and during the most barbarous eras, has witnessed the bloodshed of this age, called history's most cultured and advanced century, yet truly a brutal period, terrorized by the daily uncertainty that this war may eventually — O God, prevent it! — involve our beloved country.

During the last days, the Scriptures foretell, there will be *"famines,"* and this generation, which has seen millions die in a single Chinese famine, is now being warned that during this winter hunger and privation will visit war-gripped Europe, while diplomats prepare to keep milk and food from little children. The days before the Lord's return will be marked by *"earthquakes,"* and here is the present-day fulfilment: 1906, the earthquake in San Francisco, which killed 700 and caused a property damage of more than $200,000,000; 1908, the earthquake in Sicily, with 90,000 killed; 1915, the earthquake in Central Italy, with 30,000 killed; 1917, Guatemala, 2,500 dead; 1920, Mexico, 3,000 dead; 1920, China, 200,000 dead; 1923, Tokyo and Yokohama, Japan, 160,000 dead; 1929, Persia and Turkestan, 2,000 dead; 1934—1935, India, with 37,000 dead; and in more recent years Japan, Martinique, Turkey, and Rumania — more earthquakes than ever before recorded for a similar period.

"Pestilence," death-dealing diseases similarly are signs of the last times. Do you remember what happened in 1918, when a world-wide influenza epidemic dug millions of graves and the American death-rate was nineteen times higher than in 1917? Have you not heard experts predict that Europe is unmistakably doomed to suffer from the scourge of new plagues?

If you are still in doubt that Jesus is coming soon, think of the many signs (which I shall discuss next Sunday) foretelling moral and religious decline preceding His return.

Remember, however, this great sign of the last times: Before Jesus comes, the Gospel must be preached in all the world, and this is being fulfilled through world-wide missions and in the very invention by which I speak to you, the miracle of the radio, perhaps God's last great gift for the quick, wide spread of His Word. Our Gospel-message is now broadcast in a dozen countries outside the United States, in Canada, Central and South America, the Philippine Islands, even war-torn China itself. New and tremendous opportunities loom before us, not only in our land but also particularly in South America, where with Spanish (and, we hope, Portuguese) broadcasts we plan to start a mighty campaign for the Gospel, using scores of outlets in the Southern Hemisphere.

These tokens of Christ's return, fulfilled as never be-

fore, combine to preach one all-important message: Jesus is
coming! According to the clear Scriptures Christ will
return, not to build an earthly kingdom of glory (for He
Himself emphatically stated, *"My kingdom is not of this
world"*), not to rule in millennial reign over this sin-
saturated globe, but to judge the quick and the dead, to
pronounce the doom of all unbelieving, unrepentant sinners, to take His trusting followers home to heaven. How
much precious time is wasted in pulpit speculations which
seek to make Ezekiel's thirty-eighth and thirty-ninth chapters and similar passages predict the outcome of this war
and the detailed trend in tomorrow's political events —
employing the very passages for which ten years ago men
gave an altogether different interpretation and which
twenty, thirty, forty years ago, and so on, were given still
other explanations! When some of you preachers foretell
the world's end on a certain date and that time comes and
goes, just as a hundred contradictory dates selected for the
final moment of human history have come and gone, can
you not see that you are making men and women lose faith
in the Bible? You have never saved any one by insisting,
for example, against all evidence, that the Biblical Tubal
is the Russian city Tobolsk or that Meshech is Moscow.
You will not bring one soul closer to heaven by teaching
that Mount Zion in Jerusalem will be made higher than
the Himalayas, that the Jews in their entirety will become
Christians, and that all nations will stream to Palestine.
Stop this speculation! Preach prophecy and fulfilment as
the Scriptures and history clearly portray God's miraculous
power to foretell the future! Preach the Law and the
Gospel! Preach the blood and the cross! Preach the
atonement and the resurrection! Tell your congregations
that Jesus is coming for judgment on unbelief and for the
salvation of His believers! Tell them to watch for that
coming!

In that spirit I ask you, my fellow-redeemed, What would you do were Christ to come today? Would He find you in the only-saving faith? Or would He overtake you serving sin? Oh, while there is still time, prepare yourself! Come to that Savior — and remember, every one can come, for He knows no class distinctions. He imposes no conditions. You can come just as you are, especially if you feel that you are too unworthy, that you have sinned too frequently and repeatedly to be forgiven!

When Queen Victoria heard a sermon on the Savior's second coming, she was seized with such thrill of divine love that she prayed: "I wish I could be here when He comes. Oh, that I might lay my crown at His blessed feet!" I hope that hundreds of thousands in this audience will look forward to Christ's coming with the same eager joy that makes us pray, *"Even so come, Lord Jesus!"*

If His return, the time of which no man knows despite many mistaken predictions, is not marked for our generation, Saint John is still right when He says that Christ will appear to those who are His. Through faith we have the assurance that because He died for us, He is to every one who believes *"the Resurrection and the Life."* When we have acknowledged Him our God, our Lord, our Savior, our Redeemer, our Atonement, our Ransom; when we know with personal, trusting faith that Christ died for each one of us, so that, our transgressions removed, we might escape the terror of eternal destruction; when we believe that death is swallowed up in the triumph at the open grave, we have passed from death to life. We die, of course, and this body decays, but when the resurrection trumpet sounds over the world's graveyards, by Christ's promise those who are His will come forth in an indescribably blessed heavenly existence to be with Jesus.

Many of you, however, are ready to object: "Well,

how can there be a resurrection when some of our greatest geniuses insist that death ends all? How about the German refugee professor who recently announced that he has given up 'the doctrine of a personal God' and with it every thought of the eternal life?" — Do you think that because a physics professor has advanced a theory on relativity, he is entitled to speak with authority on the relation between God and man or body and soul? If an agnostic scientist declares that our people should "refuse military duty in time of war," do you red-blooded Americans agree with him? If the same scientist was divorced from his first wife, do you applaud divorce for that reason? If he has been a member of a World Congress convened in Moscow under the auspices of the Workers' International Relief, do you therefore approve of Internationalism? Why, then, in the name of all that is logical and decent, are you ready to follow that scientist in his religion, in his denial of God and eternal life? When you are stricken with a serious disease, you are not interested in any theories concerning your sickness that might be advanced by a plumber, an electrical engineer, a Latin teacher, certainly not by those who deny that you are sick. You want a doctor, and the most capable of physicians. Why, then, if your soul is involved, do you listen to men who, as proficient as they may be in other respects, are religiously ignorant, spiritually blind? I like the clear-cut rebuke by Sir Isaac Newton, whose fame will be remembered long after the twentieth-century leaders in these cut-throat attacks on Christianity are forgotten. Answering Halley, the unbelieving English astronomer and mathematician, Newton declared: "I am always glad to hear you when you speak about astronomy . . . because that is a subject you have studied. . . . But you should not talk of Christianity, for you have not studied it. I have and am certain you know nothing of the matter."

Mighty intellects, acclaimed throughout the world, have been humble believers in the Resurrection and the heavenly life. Michael Faraday, called "the greatest scientist experimenter the world has ever seen," proclaimed, "Our hope is founded in the faith which is in Christ. . . . I bow before Him who is Lord of all and hope to be kept waiting patiently for His time and mode of releasing me according to His divine Word and the great and precious promises by which His people are made partakers of the divine nature."

William Harvey, honored throughout the medical world for discovering the circulation of the blood, wrote in his will, "I do now humbly render my soul to Him that gave it and to my blessed Lord and Savior, Jesus Christ."

When Sir David Brewster, authority on optics, lay on his death-bed, he told Sir James Young Simpson, "I shall see Jesus, and that will be grand; I shall see Him who made the world." Simpson, brilliant scientist and anesthesia expert, who had these words carved on his tombstone: "Nevertheless I live," leaving that death-chamber, declared, "There is Sir David, resting like a child on Jesus and speaking as if in a few hours he will have all his problems solved by Him."

David Hayes Agnew, the distinguished American physician who attended President Garfield after an assassin had shot him, wrote in one of his last letters, "Christ is to me all, and my aspiration is for the immortality to come."

Other scientific leaders have expressed similar unrestricted faith in the resurrection of the body; so when our children come home from high school and quote their science teacher as declaring, "We, as animals, will end like the beast," then tell that would-be authority that he has no right to attack Christianity in a public school and remind him that his puny protest is lost in the mighty chorus to the praise of the Lord Jesus raised by the most noteworthy intellects. One of the world's greatest chemists was Frederick Woehler at Goettingen. Shortly before Christmas, years ago, when a few students in the laboratories at that university joined in singing the song which, I hope, will soon be in your heart and on your lips, "Silent Night, Holy Night," the aged Woehler entered their laboratory, removed his hat, folded his hands, and stood with bowed head while the students caroled their praise to the Christchild. If only every scientist would be guided by the same faith and thus reverently acknowledge Jesus!

Do not let your heart be turned from this resurrection promise by the thought that you cannot understand how your body, placed into the grave, covered with six feet of heavy earth, left to decay, can be restored. I am not asking you to understand it. Can you explain how you see? Can you account for the power that makes it possible for you to breathe? Can you solve the mystery of life itself? No scientist, not even the most astute Nobel Prize winner, can. But do you deny that you see, live, breathe? Why, then, reject the fact of eternal existence?

May God give you the grace to share St. John's certainty when he declares, *"We know"* that Jesus shall appear; *"we know"* that life does not end with the grave! Other basic facts may change; Detroit logicians may suggest an altogether new process of reasoning; but write this down as a verity that neither God nor man will ever alter: We can live again! Why? By this assurance: we have Jesus Christ, and He has promised us, *"Because I live, ye shall live also."* That truth is sealed in His blood. The Scriptures give us this guarantee, *"He died that we might live."* His cross, His agony, His wounded hands and feet, His thorn-crowned head, His riven side — all His suffering in my stead and yours, together with the open grave, gives us the pledge that through faith we shall survive the grave.

What about those who die without faith, who curse and reject the Lord Jesus Christ? Men try to build the hereafter according to human specifications. They want a second chance after death, a third place, other than eternal blessedness and everlasting damnation. They seek something besides the Savior's pledge — the prayers and the gifts of parents, friends, church officials. End that wishful day-dreaming! Be clear on this: You will never have another chance after this life. According to God's specific Word no intermediary stage exists between heaven and hell. Nobody can pay or earn his way to salvation. *"There is none other name under heaven given among men whereby we must be saved"* but the name of the Lord Jesus; no other faith, no other hope, no other promise, no other real comfort, no other way, except Christ, who says, *"I am the Way, the Truth, and the Life."*

II

THE GLORIOUS BLESSING OF HIS APPEARING

What blessing will be ours when Christ appears to us, either at His second coming or when we stand before His eternal throne! Because millions of people know the word "heaven" as just another term in a popular song, or a motion-picture title, it is a great privilege to present the Bible's promise concerning the life to come. This is the more necessary because deluded masses think they can secure information concerning the hereafter through spiritist mediums; but Scriptures are the only source of truth concerning heaven. If you are trying to speak to the dead through frauds and charlatans, stop! Your Bible gives all the facts concerning the next life that you or any one else can ever know on this earth.

My Prayer for Toda

For this cause I bow my knees unto
Jesus Christ, of whom the whole family i
that Thou wouldst grant me, according to
be strengthened with might by Thy Spirit
may dwell in my heart by faith; that I,
love, may be able to comprehend with all
and length, and depth, and height; and t
which passeth knowledge, that I might be
of God.

Now unto Him that is able to do exc
that I ask or think, according to the po
Him be glory in the church by Christ Jes
without end. Amen.

How marvelous, then, to read that, when Jesus appears, *"we shall be like Him"!* In our human weakness we have to reread these five short, simple words as we ask, "Can God really be as gracious to us as this? Dare we actually hope that in the hereafter we shall be like Christ Himself? We think of Jesus, the blessed, merciful, loving Savior; we contrast ourselves, with our impurities, unholy desires, selfish greed, and then we read that, when we appear before His throne, *"we shall be like Him."* If this were not the Almighty's promise, most of us, like Missionary Morrison's Chinese assistant, actually could not believe it.

It is God's truth, however, that in eternity, saved by faith, we shall be like Christ because we, too, shall have a marvelous resurrection body. As Jesus on the third day arose with a radiant body, so, when Christ released us from the grave for that new and infinitely better existence, ours will be a perfect body — never to be overtaken by sickness or disease, marred by spot or blemish, broken by accident or amputation, worn out in old age and infirmity — a glorious celestial body. With that promise, my fellow-redeemed whose cross in life has been one siege of illness after the other, a weary wasting away, a long, hopeless battle against an incurable malady, do you not now yearn to be with that Savior? Christ's arms are pointed especially to you when He gives His promise of rest; and though you have suffered to an extent that probably no person will ever know, your Savior understands and promises that *"the sufferings of this present time are not worthy to be compared with the glory which shall be revealed in us."*

"We shall be like Him" because with Christ in eternity our knowledge will be much stronger than it can be on earth under human limitations. *"Now,"* the Apostle says,

"I know in part, but then shall I know even as also I am known." In the radiance of that eternity, mysteries which baffled our earth-bound reason will be solved. God's unsearchable ways with us will be revealed as evidence of His love; afflictions which once seemed cruel will appear as divine blessings. Clear to our celestial vision will be God's marvelous love in calling to Himself dear ones whose death seemed unbearable or His wisdom in keeping us humble and closer to Christ through reverses and the collapse of long-cherished hopes. The fact that our knowledge in the next life will be unspeakably greater than now answers the question asked by thousands, "Shall we know our loved ones in the hereafter?" As the great scientist Priestley, the discoverer of oxygen, a clergyman (mark that, you who say that the Church is opposed to scientific development!), could gather his family and friends around his death-bed and in the Savior's name look forward to a blessed reunion; as Ampère, noted electrical scientist (keep that in mind, you who claim scientists must be unbelievers!) could ask God when his wife was taken from him, that he might be granted a reunion with her in heaven, so you, too, can be assured that in the homeland of light you will certainly know your best-beloved who here on earth worshiped the Savior with you. What joy in that comforting promise!

We who are Christ's *"shall be like Him"* because we, too, shall be stainless when we join the white-robed throng before His throne. No imperfections, however small, no greedy thoughts, no impure desires, no hasty words, no destructive action, will ever break the complete holiness of that new life which mirrors His perfection. Is not that the blessing which you crave, my brothers and sisters, when a sense of shame over sin rises up to break your peace of mind; when in your own lives you pay heavy penalties for transgression and in your homes faults and failures have wrought perhaps irreparable damage? Come now to the Lord Jesus, and when temptations too easily ensnare you, when your sinful heart keeps you from doing the good that you would, remember that through Christ you, too, can direct your pilgrimage toward the better land in heaven, where there will be no tears over breaking God's Law, no agony over sorrow, no terror of conscience over your misdeeds, nothing but absolute innocence, sinlessness, holiness, and divine righteousness. What glory in that celestial perfection!

Again, through faith in Christ *"we shall be like Him";* we, too, shall live eternally. What overflowing grace we can find in this assurance! It would be the purest mercy if the Almighty were to give us a lifetime of sixty or seventy years in heaven; yes, it would be nothing but grace if we were to have a year or even a day in that bliss; but by His immeasurable love these blessings will never end. Here on earth we see one friend after the other drop on the pathway of life's pilgrimage. We set our hearts on some plan or throw our energies into a project which soon collapses to leave us downcast and disillusioned; but in that spiritual grandeur we cannot begin to grasp there will be no farewells, no departures, no end of these heavenly blessings. What radiance in that eternity!

I can hardly tear myself from this promise, for though it contains matchless blessings, they are real and genuine. When you sing:

> I long to be like Jesus,
> Meek, loving, lowly, mild;
> I long to be like Jesus,
> The Father's holy Child.
> I long to be with Jesus
> Amid the heavenly throng,
> To sing with saints His praises,
> To learn the angels' song,

that longing can be fulfilled, for here is the promise of God Himself, *"We shall be like Him,"* our Jesus!

Now, Jesus might have granted all this and yet kept Himself distant from us in eternity; He might have reserved a special section to which the redeemed could have no access; but His Savior-love would not permit this, and so we read in today's promise, *"We shall see Him as He is."* In heaven we, the ransomed, shall behold Jesus in His radiance, the same Savior whom men saw beaten, bleeding, crushed into soul anguish, dying in unspeakable agony, dead in the punishment for our death; that Savior who, above the petty attempts of wilful, hell-bound men to deny His deity, is the true God and, together with the Father and the Spirit, the only God; that Jesus who, despite the futile attacks of unbelievers within and without the churches, is the Savior of our souls, the Redeemer, whose cross marks the entrance to heaven, with the gates of Paradise swung wide to welcome every penitent believer; that majestic, indescribable Christ — my fellow-sinners and fellow-redeemed, accept this truth: we who are His shall see Him face to face! We shall hear Him speak words of divine power that we could never endure or understand here on earth; we shall behold Him in the midst of cherubim, seraphim, and the heavenly hosts, praised by patriarchs and prophets, adored by apostles and evangelists, exalted by saints and martyrs, acclaimed by our own heavenly praise! Oh, what glory, what unfathomable glory, with Jesus!

Why, then, do we shrink from death? Why do we cling so desperately to life's trinkets and baubles, instead of praying, *"Even so come, Lord Jesus!"*? As we recall that even the murderous thief on the cross was granted the promise of Paradise because he turned to the Savior in faith, I ask you likewise to push all else aside now (in a moment which, as I have asked God, may bring you to Christ if you have never known Him or restore you to His grace if you have forsaken Him) and humbly pray: "O Lord Jesus, Thou who art come into Thy kingdom, remember me and preserve me for the heaven in which I can behold Thee and be like Thee! Lay on me in helpful trial every affliction which may keep me close to Thee! Take away whatever Thy divine wisdom may see fit to remove; but, O Jesus, by the cleansing of Thy blood, by the mercy of Thy cross, by the power of Thy resurrection, keep me, O Christ, for eternity!"

If Jesus is thus All in all for you, this Savior will fill your heart with joy even in your last moments because He promises you, too, " *'Verily, verily I say unto thee, Today shalt thou be with Me,'* to see Me, to be like Me, here *'in Paradise!'* " God grant that heavenly glory to us all for Jesus' sake! Amen.

JESUS, YOUR CHRIST AND YOUR SAVIOR

> *"We have heard Him ourselves and know that this is indeed the Christ, the Savior of the world."* — Saint John 4:42

Lord Jesus:

Enrich every one of us with the clear, unquestioning faith by which we acclaim Thee our God, our Savior, our King! Amid many denials of Thy deity and increasing attacks on Thy redemption draw us ever closer to Thee and sustain within us the unwavering confidence that Thou wilt remove our transgressions and graciously help us in each need or sorrow! May Thy Spirit fill us with gladness that we joyfully prepare to commemorate Thy coming into our flesh! By Thine abiding love in our souls and Thy power in our lives show that Thou art our Christ, the Savior of the world! Remind us how marvelously the Old Testament Scriptures predicting Thine advent have been fulfilled; and so direct our hearts that we may confidently face each day, experiencing in our personal destiny the glorious realization of Thine unbreakable promise! Stand at our side as we battle the temptation which would lure us from Thee and coax us to reject Thy mercies! May we joyfully receive Thee, our coming King, whose love always welcomes us! Answer us and bless us, Jesus, our only Savior! Amen.

"PROTESTANTISM as a Christian influence is almost dead." This startling charge was recently voiced by the Secretary of New York State. He deplored the fact that as a member of the Roman Catholic Church he was obliged to make this assertion, but he deliberately repeated, "Protestantism as a Christian force has lost its influence."

The Secretary of New York State is wrong! Real Protestantism, built on the Scriptures, with Christ's atoning love as the corner-stone and justification by faith its pillar doctrine, can never die. During the Thirty Years' War, with its religious butchery, the claim was raised that the cause of the Reformation was lost. Enemies declared that

French Protestantism had been destroyed after the massacre on Saint Bartholomew's night cut down 70,000 victims in a mass-murder that even the Russian atheists have not equaled for a short-time record. Fanatical explorers boasted that Protestantism was completely wiped out on this continent when the Huguenot settlement at the mouth of Saint Johns River in Florida was razed; but the protesting spirit of Martin Luther's Scripturally grounded trust will always live. Protestantism dead? As little as the legions of hell and the regiments of raging man can destroy our Bible, kill our Christ, and remove His truth, so little can they demolish any Church built on the Savior's faith.

Yet the Secretary of New York State is partially right; for thousands of American and Canadian churches are actually lifeless. They are constantly losing in members, in the support and regard of the masses, and in their spiritual usefulness. The last Government statistics record shocking membership decreases in every large Protestant denomination save one! Think of the 25,000 deserted churches in the United States! Examine the morning and evening church attendance in your community, and in too many instances you will find churches only half filled for a brief Sunday morning hour, closed and cold during the remainder of the week!

One outstanding reason explains this tragedy: The message of the world's Savior has been banned from those pulpits. The deity of our Lord Jesus has been forgotten under emphasis of His humanity. The cross of Calvary has been replaced by the double cross of doubt and denial. Preachers discuss, not heaven's glories but earth's blessings; not salvation with Christ but without Christ; not the redeeming Gospel of His atonement but the social gospel of man's attainment. When Jesus is thus banished, no power on earth can save the churches; and far from giving men

Heaven's answer to the problems of body and soul, these Christless churches in which the divine Savior has deliberately and systematically been hushed out of the sermons are as helpless as a corpse.

In protest against this rejection of our Lord and in preparation for the blessed day of His birth, I place before you the most vital fact you can ever know, with the greatest promise you can ever receive:

JESUS, YOUR CHRIST AND YOUR SAVIOR

This acknowledgment of our Lord is found in our text, Saint John, chapter four, verse forty-two: *"We have heard Him ourselves and know that this is indeed the Christ, the Savior of the world."*

I

JESUS IS THE *CHRIST* AND *SAVIOR*

The fourth chapter of Saint John tells the remarkable story of our Lord's conversation with the woman at Jacob's Well. When she testified publicly that Jesus had revealed her hidden sins (remember His penetrating power whenever you think that you have safely concealed your transgressions!), many Samaritans believed in Him, and, eager to learn more of the Messiah, begged Him to stay with them. Although the Samaritans were a despised, mixed-blood people, from whom all self-respecting Jews kept their distance, our Lord, for whom no one is ever too low or too far beyond the pale of decent society, remained in Sychar with them for two days. During those blessed hours their faith was so strengthened that they could declare, *"We have heard Him ourselves and know that this is indeed the Christ, the Savior of the world."*

The same divine influence of the Savior has been with this world, not for two days, but for almost two thousand years; and the tragedy that millions today reject Christ's

Gospel is to be explained by the fact that instead of asking Jesus to abide with them, they have spurned all contacts with His mercies. Often when skeptics or unbelievers take time to study Christ's Word and spend thoughtful moments in His presence, they likewise are converted. John Randolph, eminent statesman during the early nineteenth century, became an infidel. But in fairness to his God-fearing mother's teaching he decided that he would give God's Word a chance. He records: "I resolved to examine the question for myself. So I bought the Bible. I pored over it. I examined it carefully. When my labor was ended, I came to the irresistible conclusion: The Bible is true!" He heard Christ speak to him, and he believed.

When General Lew Wallace and Robert Ingersoll once approached Saint Louis by railroad, Ingersoll turned to his freethinking friend and said: "Wallace, you are a scholar and a thinker. Why don't you gather material for a book to show that Jesus Christ never lived, much less taught the things found in the New Testament?" Wallace readily accepted this suggestion. He spent years searching library after library for every scrap of information concerning Jesus' life. But before he had written his fourth chapter, truth convinced him that our Lord was as real and actual as any other historical personage. A few months later, after deeper investigation, came an unforgettable night in his Indiana home, when he learned to accept Jesus. For the first time in his life he fell on his knees and found forgiveness in his Savior. The studies in preparation for the book that was to destroy Christ helped to build his faith and later produced *Ben Hur.*

One of the most distinguished New Testament scholars of recent times was Sir William Ramsay. During his early life he had only a low regard for the Bible. He himself admits that he began his studies "with a mind unfavorable to" these Scriptures, particularly because of his radical university teachers. Yet the more deeply he delved into the New Testament, the stronger became his conviction that its record is true, historical, accurate. Christ spoke to him from its pages, and he believed.

If you, too, will study Jesus' Word, hear Him speak to you from the Scriptures, give the Bible a fair, unhindered chance to prove its truth in your heart, your doubts will be defeated. Like the Samaritans, you, too, will find personal promise and heavenly blessing in Christ's name, which, although blasphemously defamed in profanity and not fully appreciated even by millions of Christians, is the name above all names.

To be the Christ, God's anointed, long-promised Redeemer, meant, in the faith of the believing Samaritans, to be the Son of God. Because Old Testament prophets foresaw the coming Deliverer as divine (David calls Him *"God"* in the Forty-fifth Psalm, *"My* [God's] *Son"* in the Second Psalm, *"the Lord"* in the One Hundred and Tenth Psalm; Isaiah calls Him *"the Mighty God";* Jeremiah, *"the Lord Our Righteousness"*); because Jesus repeatedly claimed to be God (He said, for example, *"I and the Father are one"*); because His unnumbered miracles, evidences of divine power, proved Him to be God; because His own Father twice before human witnesses acknowledged Jesus His Son with the words, *"This is My beloved Son";* because the infallible Scriptures, in scores of convincing passages, call Christ our God — believe with reverent acknowledgment that Jesus, despite present-day contradictions, is your God! Do not try to understand this glorious doctrine! When some one asked Daniel Webster whether he could explain how Christ was both God and man, he replied: "No, sir! Such is my sense of sin and the consciousness of my inability to save myself that I need a superhuman Savior, one so great and glorious that I cannot comprehend Him." Jesus had to be God in order to achieve what men and angels combined could never accomplish: conquer sin, defeat hell. He had to be God to produce the miracles in human history that make us date our modern era from the year of His birth. He had to be God to give you Heaven's unfailing assurance of His power and love. Instead of quibbling, quarreling, questioning, come to Him in His Word, attend a Scripturally grounded church to hear Him speak to your soul, and may the Spirit help you declare, "I have heard Him myself and know that this is the Christ!"

Since Jesus was sinless and perfect, it was necessary that He be born, not as you and I, in sin, but that He enter the world in a miraculous manner. Therefore, seven centuries before the first Christmas Isaiah foretells the Virgin Birth, and the Church through all the ages declares Jesus to be "born of the Virgin Mary." Again, if your reason protests, "This is impossible!" stay with Christ, listen to His message, as the Samaritans did, and the Virgin Birth will offer no difficulty whatever. Learned minds have welcomed its truth. The verdict of physicians, particularly in obstetrics, should be valuable to you in this connection. Listen to this statement by one of the nation's outstanding medical men, a doctor who has written many text-books on the subject of gynecology, an authority honored by scientific societies and by governments throughout the world, Dr. Howard A. Kelly of Baltimore! That Johns Hopkins University professor states: "The Virgin Birth is the great key to the Bible storehouse.... The Virgin Birth is a fact fully established by competent testimony and abundant collateral evidence." If Dr. Kelly meets no difficulty whatever in accepting this article of our faith; on the contrary, if he finds this truth comforting and sustaining, will you not follow his example and have your doubts removed by meeting your Savior through the constant reading and hearing of His Word?

Part of the Old Testament picture of Christ was drawn in darker lines: He who was true God, the Son of the Almighty, and true man, born of the Virgin, was to be *"wounded for our transgressions"* and *"bruised for our iniquities."* Eleven times in the short fifty-third chapter does Isaiah foresee the coming Christ as one who suffers, not in consequence of His own sins, for He has none, but under the burden of our total iniquity. When Jesus came, He lived on earth for one purpose — not primarily to usher in a new age, to dispel superstition, to promote international understanding, to improve working conditions, to help establish better homes, schools, nations; He did this, but primarily He came to save souls, and especially — so let every one of us say! — to rescue me from sin for a blessed eternity! He had to save us since we could not deliver ourselves from the tyranny of our own transgressions. He had to cleanse our stained souls because no human process can purify them in God's sight. He had to die in our stead on the cross because it was ordained by the Father that all sin must be punished by death, and so Jesus Himself — O the depth of this divine, immeasurable love! — had to suffer, as our Substitute, the agonizing punishment of every wrong-doing, the damning death of all transgressors. This is the most important truth you have ever heard or can hear: Christ died for you, the Innocent for the guilty, the Sin-free for the sin-burdened, the heavenly Pure for the earthly impure, the holy Creator for His unholy creatures.

If you have doubted the supreme truth of your redemption, ask Christ to abide with you as He remained with the people at Sychar; and when you study Calvary's cross of self-sacrifice; when Jesus speaks to you personally, you, too, will join the Samaritan converts in declaring, "I have heard Him myself *'and know that this is indeed the Christ, the Savior.'* " You will understand why John Ray, botanist and zoologist, after years of intense Scripture study, could declare: "That the eternal Son of God, equal with His Father, should so highly advance our nature as to unite it to the divine in one Person, so that He might be qualified by the sacrifice of Himself to expiate our sins, to make an atonement for us, and to reconcile us to God — the greatness of this love, together with the freeness and unmeritedness of it, there being not any, even the least, motion on our part to invite Him to it, is so matchless and stupendous that it challenges the highest degree of reciprocal affection and gratitude."

Yet, not His crushing sorrow on the cross nor death itself was to be the end of the promised Christ. The Sixteenth Psalm predicted that His body would not decay in the tomb, as our remains will, but that He would be resurrected. When this and other promises were fulfilled on the first Easter, His victory over death became the seal of our own triumph over the grave through faith in His promise, *"I am the Resurrection and the Life."* Take Jesus at His word! Let the Holy Spirit show you that, though unbelief may invent a dozen theories to disprove the Savior's resurrection, the Holy Spirit, who speaks to you on every page of the Bible, will convince you, *"He is risen!"*

The final picture of Christ, the Deliverer, in the Old and New Testaments describes Him as seated at God's right hand in heavenly power and glory, prepared to return to this earth, not as He came in His first advent, a helpless Babe, but in the might and majesty of divine omnipotence. Read the Word of God, and you will under-

stand that Jesus is the Christ because the predictions concerning His coming are fulfilled in the signs of the last
times which we witness now. Preceding His return, the
Bible says, there shall be *"wars and rumors of wars";*
and no generation, even in savage lands, has recorded the
bloodshed of this age, called the most cultured and advanced period in human achievement, yet in truth brutal
years, in which rumors of increasing bloodshed keep us in
the daily uncertainty that this war may eventually —
O God, prevent it! — involve our beloved country.

If, after my remarks a week ago, you still doubt that
Christ is coming soon, then consider in addition the predic-
tion concerning religious conditions in the last days. *"False
Christs and false prophets shall rise,"* we are forewarned.
And the fulfilment? A young Hindu called "the Messiah,"
a Negro worshiped as "God," and lying prophets in unparalleled numbers.

Again, it is stated, Christians are to be afflicted. The
short lapse of twenty-one years has witnessed terrifying
attacks against Christianity, with Communism persecuting
believers by hundreds of thousands and totalitarianism
restricting Gospel-preaching.

We are also told that *"the love of many shall wax
cold,"* a definite description of the worldliness which is
ready to quench the burning zeal for Christ, the willingness
to testify, the readiness to sacrifice and give.

In the next place, there will be little faith in these
end days. Jesus asks, *"When the Son of Man cometh,
shall He find faith on the earth?"* And His question is
answered by Modernism's denial, which drives the Lord
Jesus and the message of the atonement from pulpits,
Sunday-schools, theological seminaries, church-papers, religious books, from the hearts and lives of its preachers and
its laity.

Churches of the last days are described as *"forbidding to marry and commanding to abstain from meats."* Need I remind you that this is literally true today of several religious groups?

Before Christ returns, churches, it is predicted, will have *"a form of godliness but deny the power thereof."* Is not lip-service, mouth-worship, one of the curses in present-day Christianity? Outward religion builds mighty churches, flaunts costly vestments, and elaborate ceremonials, while impoverished millions, receiving scant attention from many rich churches, can easily be led to oppose Christianity as capitalistic and unconcerned about the working-classes. Churches that have spent vast sums for recreational activities, theatricals, socials, too often are spiritually dead.

The Church in the last days will be marked by Antichrist, a mighty power within outward Christianity which parades under Christ's name, even places itself above God as it prohibits the reading of the Bible, exalts human delusion over divine truth, consorts with kings and nations, persecutes God's children, practices abominations, and denies the saving doctrine that we are justified only by faith in the Lord Jesus Christ, not by our own good deeds or by the prayers and accomplishments of others.

Think of these additional signs, foretelling moral conditions previous to His return. Men will be *"lovers of pleasures more than lovers of God."* Inspect your own community tonight! Most of the churches will be closed. The few still open generally will be attended by only a handful, while the motion-picture theaters will cater to crowds. Men, it is predicted, will be *"without natural affection,"* *"incontinent,"* *"walking after their own lusts."* If you don't believe me, write to the Government offices in Washington, and they will send you Federal statistics showing that this nation has more illegitimate children, more transgressing the commandment *"Thou shalt not commit adultery,"* more divorces, sex crimes, bestial perversions, than ever before, despite our boasted progress. In these last times men will be *"blasphemous scoffers,"* and I challenge anybody who doubts the Lord Jesus' imminent return to show any previous period in which blasphemy was spread throughout the world as it is today, with uprising against God in schools, religion, politics, business, in the home itself. Before the final Judgment comes, men will be *"truce-breakers"* and *"false accusers."* Think of the broken peace treaties, the breach-of-promise suits that clutter our courts! Men will be *"covetous,"* *"boasters,"* *"proud"* — three rampant evils of our day! Men will be *"fierce"* — the screaming horrors of Europe's warfare! *"Incontinent"* — the growing drunkenness! *"Despisers of those that are good"* — the present-day sneering at Christianity! *"Disobedient to parents"* — juvenile crime higher than ever before! Men will be *"unthankful."* Despite two Thanksgivings, how much of real gratitude is there in our land? *"Unholy"* — that is the blanket charge against our generation, with more non-Christians in the United States and therefore more breaking of God's Law and of man's than at any previous time in our history! Convincing proof that Jesus is the Christ! Clear and unmistakable are the signs of His coming!

Thus I have laid before you five fundamental facts regarding the Lord Jesus: His deity, His virgin birth, His atonement on the cross, His resurrection, and His coming to judge the quick and the dead. If Christian bodies preach these truths clearly and unmistakably, they will never die; but because many American churches have turned from Christ and featured negative, impracticable theories and platitudes, let me warn you that the hope of American Christianity is not to be found in any modern denial of Christ, wavering emotionalism, or pulpit speculations concerning the roles that Hitler, Mussolini, Stalin, are falsely said to play in Biblical prophecies. The Church's power tomorrow will come not through the emphasis on an earthly millennium at the expense of the Bible's chief doctrines on heaven and salvation, not through question-mark preaching, the compromise with modern unbelief, nor the silent approval of worldliness, but through positive, convincing proclamation of Jesus Christ as God's Son and the world's Savior.

Churches should use every possible opportunity to train their members in this Biblical faith. Records of the past show that spiritually ignorant churches cannot overcome the attacks on the Gospel; and for the future, in which the foundation truths of the Christian faith will be assailed with a hatred never before known in this age, churches should adopt far-reaching programs for religious instruction and home guidance. During continued bombardment the destruction of British buildings has prevented people in many communities from worshiping in sacred edifices; instead, English Christians are following the example of the first Church by conducting services in their homes. America needs far more of Christ in its families, and it may yet be that Modernism, combined with outspoken unbelief, will help to make many homes, as among early believers, "houses of God."

II

JESUS IS *YOUR* CHRIST AND *YOUR* SAVIOR

More important, however, than the attitude of the churches or the homes toward Christ is your personal faith in Him as your own Savior. These outcast Samaritans at Sychar had this confidence; they knew more than many twentieth-century doctors of divinity or theological pro-

fessors. They acclaimed the Lord as their Redeemer because they recognized in Him the Savior *"of the world,"*
and I have prayed that God would similarly strengthen
your hearts to accept Jesus as your own atoning Christ.

Every one of us needs Jesus with increasing urgency
as cruel godlessness heightens its rebellion against the
Almighty. No one except Christ can bring us back to God.
Nothing but His blood can cleanse us from the guilt-stain
of our sin. No other word can gain entrance for us into
heaven beside this declaration, "Jesus is my God and
my only Savior!" A few moments before Nurse Edith
Cavell was executed in Belgium during the first World
War, she told the chaplain: "I have no fear or shrinking.
I have seen death so often that it is not strange or fearful
to me; but this I will say, standing as I do before God
and eternity, I realize that patriotism is not enough." In
this day of intensified Americanism, with all the commendable zeal shown for the defense of this God-blessed
nation, we must understand that the highest degree of
patriotism is not enough for your soul, not sufficient to win
God's grace and keep you in His mercy. Nor are culture,
college degrees, refinement, pleasing personality, faithfulness in your duties, courage in your afflictions, striving after
honesty, decency, purity — these and whatever other virtues
you may find in yourself — enough to answer the voice of
your conscience, not to mention the charges by the holy
God. For pardon, life, salvation, heaven, eternal blessing,
you need Christ. You must feel the conviction of your
own unworthiness; you must hear the Advent cry *"Repent ye!"* be moved by a genuine, deep-rooted sorrow over
your sin, confess your transgressions without any excuse,
and then turn to the Lord Jesus Christ for this promise,
*"Though your sins be as scarlet, they shall be white as
snow; though they be red like crimson, they shall be
as wool."*

All this is necessary, but nothing else. You do not have to wait until you feel worthy of coming to Christ. He wants you, even though you consider yourself the chief of sinners. You do not have to delay until you can pay your way to Christ or learn the approach to your Savior through complicated lessons. His mercy is free. You require no human guide to Jesus; the Holy Spirit will lead your contrite, trusting heart directly to His blessed grace.

We need Christ, too, because crushing perplexities can arise overnight. Sudden deaths, unpredictable disasters, unforeseen sorrows, such as last week again brought misery into thousands of American homes, should direct our hearts to Him who *"changeth not."* Where, in the swiftly changing scenes of the present, can there be any promise of help for our war-crazed age or our own heavy problems if not in the love of the Lord Jesus Christ and the hope of His coming that Christmas again emphasizes?

Make these days before that festival of the Savior's birth a glorious, Spirit-filled time of preparation, though the world around us has lost the Christ-centered message that gives us Christmas. As you read your holiday newspapers and magazines, you witness the complete neglect of Jesus during the season when the very mention of Christmas should make men think of Him. One weekly news magazine, for example, has page after page of liquor advertisements in which special brands of whisky are recommended as outstanding Christmas gifts; yet not one of its pages even mentions the Lord Jesus Christ — as though He never existed, despite the fact that His birth gives us the year's outstanding celebration, when men spend hundreds of millions of dollars and the festive spirit reigns supreme.

During the dark days of the first World War, a Swiss professor at the University of Zurich, Dr. Ragatz, looked from his classrooms upon an earth torn with strife; and as he heard the cannon boom across the border, it seemed to him that God had forgotten His world; that Christ's promises were not to be fulfilled. The foundation of his faith, he thought, was being destroyed. In his doubt he turned to the Old Testament prophets and learned that, although these inspired writers had seen even wider devastations sweep over their country, they could discover a remedial, helpful purpose in such sorrows for God's children: the strengthening of their trust and the purifying of their purposes. Through the Bible, Professor Ragatz found his way back to God and Christ. This pre-Christmas period can bring the happiest days you have ever known if you, too — surveying both a world of turmoil, hatred, killing, and examining your soul, heavy with distress as it may be — declare in the immortal confession of Martin Luther (which I ask all Christians to adopt as their own and a copy of which I shall be happy to send any of you on request) : "I believe that Jesus Christ, true God, begotten of the Father from eternity, and also true man, born of the Virgin Mary, is my Lord, who has redeemed me, a lost and condemned creature, purchased and won me from all sins, from death, and from the power of the devil, not with gold or silver but with His holy, precious blood and with His innocent suffering and death, that I may be His own and live under Him in His kingdom and serve Him in everlasting righteousness, innocence, and blessedness, even as He is risen from the dead, lives and reigns to all eternity. This is most certainly true." With this faith no church can ever die; with the trust which declares, "I have heard Him myself and *know that this is indeed the Christ, the Savior of the world,*' my own Redeemer," you have the most blessed certainty that Heaven can give you. God grant it to all of you for Jesus' sake! Amen.

THE LIGHT OF LIFE AT BETHLEHEM!

"I am the Light of the world: he that followeth Me shall not walk in darkness but shall have the light of life." — Saint John 8:12

Christ, Thou Light of Life and Love:

Raising our hearts in humble praise to thank Thee for the unspeakable gift of Thyself at Christmastide, pardon for all our sins, life everlasting, and heavenly reunion with Thee, the Father and the Holy Comforter, we also implore Thee to show Thy tender mercies to those who suffer from war — the wounded and crippled, the hungry and destitute, the widowed and orphaned. Let them know in their hearts and experience in their lives the peace of which the angels sang at Thy nativity! What cruelty and poverty men inflict upon their fellow-men! Yet what overflowing compassion Thou didst reveal to this earth with its iniquity and hatred when Thou wast born to bring us the triumph of inner joy through Thy redeeming love! If it be in accordance with Thy will for a world that has forsaken Thee, O Christ, Thou Prince of Peace, stop this war and help the nations live in constructive harmony instead of murderous enmity! If, however, we are not now to enjoy outward tranquillity, give us calm, serene souls that find their rest in Thee! This we ask by Thy Christmas promise, O blessed Babe of Bethlehem. Amen.

"MORE light for Christmas!" a New York publisher asks as his eight full-length-column advertisements in the nation's leading newspapers plead for a blaze of illumination in homes, factories, business offices, public buildings, on Christmas Eve. Europe is darkened by blackouts, he reminds us, and America should show the world our free way of life by turning on a flood of Yuletide brightness.

No one should oppose his appeal, especially not under present conditions. This may be the last peace-and-prosperity Christmas America will celebrate in our generation;

so let us enjoy light and laughter while we can. We do, however, object to the fact that this light campaign is being waged without a word about the Lord Jesus Christ, whose birth gave us Christmas. It is the old hush policy: Keep Christ out of Christmas! Forget that He was born! Question it! Deny it! Belittle it! Above all, don't speak a syllable concerning His claim to be the Savior of the world!

Particularly, however, must we disagree with the proposal to make these lighted homes what the imposing newspaper advertisements want them to be: evidence of "our faith in the decency and dignity of man." "Decency," in this carnally minded age, when the United States prints more filthy books and salacious magazines than any other country on earth; when every form of indecency that perverted men have ever been able to invent is widely practiced? What about the "dignity" of man? Was there ever an age in which less value and dignity was attached to men's lives than in these breakdown years, with the mass destruction of human beings in two World Wars and the startling increase in race as well as individual suicide? Human life is cheap today, when Europe's youth can be mobilized for fresh slaughter; when a single Japanese bomb made of American materials can blast a hundred Chinese into eternity! "Faith in the decency and dignity of man"? I for one, and millions of Christians with me, place no reliance on our own decency and dignity. At Christmas we want to reaffirm our trust in God, our confidence in the Christ-child, Son of the Almighty and Son of the Virgin, the Savior from sin, the Destroyer of death. We need much more than brightly illumined dwelling-places, shops, and factories. Confucianists in China, like many other heathen, have festivals of light such as this plan proposes, but of what good are they? And what benefit comes to us if our houses are aglow yet our hearts are black with sin, distress, hatred, ignorance? We want an unfailing beacon that will shine into our souls, a heavenly brilliancy to brighten life's darkened pathway, dispel sin's black night, remove sorrow's gloom.

That guiding Beam, the only *true Light,* men can ever follow is given us by God's mercy in the promise of His Word, and especially during this joyful Christmas season, in the Gospel of the new-born Savior. So let your homes gleam radiantly on Christmas Eve! But if some of you must watch every penny and cannot burn an unnecessary bulb or candle; if sickness or bereavement in your home demands subdued illumination; if, above all, you feel that Christmas Eve demands a light-blessed heart before a light-swathed home, be sure that you know

THE LIGHT OF LIFE AT BETHLEHEM,

the radiance of which Jesus Himself describes in these words, *"I am the Light of the world: he that followeth Me shall not walk in darkness, but shall have the light of life"* (Saint John, chapter eight, verse twelve).

I

HOW NECESSARY THIS CHRISTMAS LIGHT!

When the President of the United States can accept engagements only three months away with the express condition, "if the world survives," we certainly should agree, that at this Christmas the world needs light.

We customarily refer to the Middle Ages, with their superstition, ignorance and tyranny, as a dark era, but at least in one respect, despite their cruelties and vice, those medieval centuries were in advance of ours. They instituted what was called "The Truce of God," by which, on special week-days and during festival seasons, all warfare ceased. The recent refusal of the belligerents across the seas to declare a Christmas armistice showed that our generation, despite its culture and achievements, sometimes exhibits less humanity than that shown in the benighted, barbarous years before the Reformation. Not only does the darkness of the European conflict overcloud our world, but the lengthening shadows of a closer struggle into which our country is being pushed step by step looms heavy before us. Make no mistake about this: The United States today is directly headed for war, and the consequences in the aftermath will be terrifying. This may be the last Christmas season in which I am allowed to address you; for if a state of emergency is declared and the radio is put under Government censorship, I have no delusion about the fact that the religious programs permitted to continue will be those featuring the messages of modern unbelief, which even now, through the support of American millionaires and discriminating church federations, has secured all but a stranglehold on religious chain broadcasting. If that hour should come and darkness deepens in America because the Gospel light is hidden, I hope that every one of you will join in a mighty protest which must be heeded.

While we still have freedom of speech (for which, together with the liberty of worship, we in America should ceaselessly thank God), I raise my voice to indict the tactics of certain prominent educators and particularly clergymen, too old to fight themselves, who, as fear-fomenters, warmongers, hate-hucksters and pied pipers of propaganda, now openly demand, without the deceptive phraseology which marked their earliest tactics, that during this season, when the world hears the Christmas carol "Peace on earth!" we declare war, send our youth across the seas, and devote our vanishing billions to bloodshed. Of all the criminals showing human degeneracy in its most dangerous form, few are more brutal and perverted than the men who for selfish reasons of blood profit eagerly work to have America fight again in Europe's age-old battles. Among the blind leaders of the blind none causes as much confusion and chaos as the preacher who, without knowing the facts of history, tells his congregation that we must enter this war for Christ and Christianity, as though the Lord Jesus, who said, *"Put up again thy sword into his place; for all they that take the sword shall perish with the sword,"* would ever need an earthly army to defend His kingdom! Some day, when the terrors of new battles have piled higher ruins in America than during the last World War, we shall realize that, if it is wrong for an individual to circulate false rumors and deceive his neighbor, it is a million times worse to use malicious falsehoods in steering a nation toward war. Some day, perhaps not until America's church-buildings have been torn down by Red-minded mobs, certain religious leaders will understand that the Church is not here to preach hatred nor desecrate its pulpits with poisonous propaganda but to proclaim the blessed Gospel. British authorities are now measuring the war cost in terms of religious loss. Work in every department of the Church of England, the number of baptisms, confirmations, ordinations, Sunday-school pupils, the amount of contributions, dropped drastically during the first four months' fighting. What must the subsequent terror and bombing bring? Every mission-field in the far-flung frontiers of Christ's kingdom has already sustained lamentable reverses through these hostilities. If our country, too, is embroiled, the spread of the Gospel will suffer its most severe setback in modern times. You need not be gifted with second sight to realize that, if the United States, the last great bulwark of peace and democracy, becomes a belligerent, finally none but the atheistic Communists can win; that in our own land during war emergencies the very influences which we justly condemn will attempt to assume control and deprive us of our liberties. You need not be a prophet to foresee the financial chaos, industrial collapse, moral breakdown, social unrest, that can rule within our boundaries in the awful aftermath, if we enter war. As American Christians we utterly reject the principles and practices of all tyranny in Fascism, Naziism, totalitarianism, Communism; but we can best build democracy and Christianity by constructive peace. Because it is our Scriptural duty to promote such honorable peace, I ask you especially in this Christmas season to plead with fervor and faith in Christ that the wickedness of this war be stopped.

We may soon enter the decade of darkness, these night-filled 1940's. Besides the murk of war, other black clouds encircle us: the gloom of godlessness, for while the angels carol, *"Glory to God in the highest!"* the American way of living often defames the Almighty; the intellectual darkness in some of our largest and respected schools, where teachers deliberately assail Christ's glorious Gospel; the spiritual darkness in certain church groups where, incredibly enough, the medal for distinguished religious services is awarded a man who even denies the existence of a personal God. Government leaders are concerned over the slow tempo of our defense program, but the spiritual defense program has not even started in many churches. At a time when men need the light and soul-comfort found only in Christ, many modernist churches have failed to meet the emergency. Add to this the lengthening shadows of suffering across our country: sickness, poverty, disappointment, and, more distressing than what I have listed, the engulfing gloom of sin, responsible for all darkness, the cause of each sorrow, the root of every war — sin in my life and yours, sin in our hearts and on our hands, sin weighing heavily on our souls and our minds, sin to separate us eternally from the Father.

Thank God, however, we are too close to Christmas not to see and feel this warm, glorious truth that the Christ-child cradled in the manger, Son of a Palestinian virgin, yet Son of the almighty God, a helpless Infant, though the all-merciful Savior, is *"the Light of the world"* that can send its bright beams of love into every heart; a Light that cures with a heavenly healing incomparably stronger than the most helpful rays of science; a Light to guide us from earth to heaven with greater accuracy than the most powerful beacon or airbeam can have; a Light to banish gloom more completely than any sun can disperse the sullen storm clouds! Men have followed other lights: reason, superstition, human theory, their own achievements; but all this never so thoroughly resembles passing sparks or the fitful flare of dying embers as on Christmas, when we compare man's candle with Christ's brilliance, *"the Light of the world."*

Do you know the splendor of His grace? Is your heart brightened by that light of Christ's love? Do you believe that Jesus came to save you from your sins, deliver you from death, and give you in your faith a guiding lamp from time to eternity? Do you realize that, once your sins are forgiven, you can find — even if war comes to our shores — inner peace through the Christ-child and His soul-strengthening love? Whatever the Christmas season may mean to you, be it joy or sorrow, Christ wants the anniversary commemorating His birth to linger in your life as a day of divine light on which, having beheld the bright mercies of God born as your Immanuel, you join the ageless procession to Bethlehem with the resolution, "God helping me, I will *'walk in the light!'*"

II

HOW BLESSED THIS CHRISTMAS LIGHT!

What heavenly happiness the Christmas light gives those who follow Jesus! If with the shepherds' eagerness and Mary's reverent trust we acclaim the Christ-child our God and Savior, then His exalted truth promises us, *"He that followeth Me shall not walk in darkness."* You want proof that these nine words, the pledge of guidance and comfort which our groping age needs above everything else, are true? Each page of the past since the first Christmas proves our Lord's power to dispel gloom. It was Jesus who scattered the murky clouds overshadowing family life and marriage by elevating womanhood, stopping the sale, exposure, or murder of children, demanding personal purity, damning fleshly lust, and mightily blessing home-life. Christ's Gospel brought light in place of the ignorance and superstition which held the world shackled before the first Christmas, as faith promoted education, helped to establish the first schools for public training, and founded our best universities. It was Christ who pleaded for peace and put a curb on bloodshed by restricting personal feuds and private wars, denouncing torture, supporting humane movements like the Red Cross to relieve suffering, giving the impulse for international law and arbitration. It was Christ who brought love into the chaos of our selfish world by His pleading for the poor, His rejection of ill-gotten riches, His ennobling of labor, the abolition of slavery, and the more equitable division of property which sprang from our Lord's new commandment, *"Love one another!"* These and a hundred other blessings have come, not through any supposed evolution and self-improvement of our race (who can believe in that today?), not as a result of men's endeavors during long centuries, not through human processes of trial or experiment; every one of these benedictions on the race comes ultimately from the Christ-child and the new age beginning with His birth. If even intelligent unbelievers have repeatedly admitted that Jesus brought light into every dingy corner of our social relations, why should any one today, after nineteen centuries with Christmas, require proof for the Savior's words *"He that followeth Me shall not walk in darkness"*?

You yourself, however, can have much more glorious and personal testimony for Christ's gloom-destroying power. When you accept the Babe of Bethlehem as your Savior, you will still meet darkness, of course, but you need not *"walk"* in it. Because this is a practical, materially minded age; because a Minneapolis newspaper, for example, editorially demands that the churches show specifically what help the Christ of Christmas can extend in our crisis, let me outline this clear program of His light-giving love. First of all, Jesus offers His guidance to all the confused and bewildered who have lost their bearings in life. They do not know where to go nor what to do. They wonder why they are still here. They complain of becoming a burden to their family or to society at large. As a Hartford, Connecticut, woman who wrote me recently that, unless I can help her, suicide is the only way out of her dark despair, they think that life is not worth living. Now, the trouble with most of you whose thoughts I have described is basically this, that you have not fully heeded Christ nor completely taken Him at His word. You have not unreservedly said, "Savior, I follow on, Guided by Thee." Therefore, you especially should take heart this Christmas and accept the caroled invitation, "Oh, come, let us adore Him!" issued directly to you. If only you will permit the Spirit of God to lead you from dismal thoughts and depressing doubts to *"the Light of the world"* cradled in the manger; if only you will fall on your knees to acclaim Mary's Son God's Son and your Savior, you will understand that, no matter how little love there may be for you here on earth, you have a God who loves you with such inconceivable intensity and immeasurable depth of devotion that on the first Christmas He sent His own Son into the lowliness of Bethlehem for all the world, yes, but particularly for you. God grant that in this blessed Christmas season yours will be a real determination, with the Spirit's help, to follow the unfailing Gospel gleam, which outshines every overclouded moment, and in Christ to find a new joy, a real purpose in life and an abiding peace triumphant over every difficulty. Oh, pray that the light of the Infant Redeemer will lead as long as life is yours!

Others are beset by the darkness of destitution. They have been fighting losing financial battles. They hear about high wages and plenty of work, good business; yet somehow all this has passed them by. Then they pick up the newspaper to read the claim of a professor at New York City College that poverty in the United States is psychic. That is a fancy word for "imaginary." Poverty "psychic," unreal, in the United States, with about 20,000,000 people so poor that the Government has to support them? Tens of thousands of you Americans know better than that. Federal relief has not given some of you a penny; and you are unable to buy the bare necessities, not to speak of a few Christmas presents for your children. But do not let this banish your inner Christmas joy! Do not turn to those who seek to promote discontent among the poor and disheartened! Few follies are deeper and more tragic than this, that men pin hopes for improvement on Communism and its atheistic cruelty. Rather join the pilgrimage of Christian faith to Bethlehem, to remind yourselves that Christ was poor, more completely

impoverished than any of you! His first bed was a manger
full of hay and His last a borrowed grave. His first
shelter was a lowly stable, and during His entire life He
held no title to real estate and had *"not where to lay His
head"* until, wounded and bleeding, it bowed into death on
a crude cross; His first garments were common swaddling-
clothes; His last, the blood-stained apparel of mockery and
anguish. Yet through sincere Christmas faith the poverty
of Jesus can make you rich — rich in hope, courage, and
love; rich in contentment and the confidence that *"God
will provide,"* that above your powers of understanding the
Savior *"shall supply all your need according to His riches
in glory."* So trust the Christ-child completely, without
question or misgiving, and in the light of His festival you
will be able to exult, *"He that spared not His own Son
but delivered Him up for us all, how shall He not with
Him also freely give us all things?"*

Other afflictions may darken your hopes and at Christmas time lay their particularly heavy burden upon you.
It seems that everything has gone wrong in life. The plans
for which you prayed incessantly have been completely
shattered. Some — and I always hesitate before taking
a text which mentions light when I think of you — will
never see the day's brightness; God's inscrutable ways
have permitted you to be deprived of your sight. But the
same Savior who in the days of His flesh restored vision
to the blind can grant every one of you a holy insight into
His love and self-giving, with the personal promise that
when this period of your sightless pilgrimage is over, you
shall behold what no eyes today have ever seen, the rap-
turous glories of heaven, face to face with Him. Sufferers
at Christmas time, believe as you kneel before the Christ-
child that affliction overshadows you only to make God's
grace the brighter and Christ, the Light of the world,

more radiant for you! If you are misunderstood and persecuted; if pain and sorrow dwell in your home as love's ideals crash under the weight of cruelty or unfaithfulness, remember that the Lord Jesus understands your personal troubles since He endured hatred and enmity incomparably greater than any malice which may afflict you. No room for Him in the crowded inn! No room for Him in Judea over which hate-filled Herod held his murderous sway! No room for Him in the hearts of His own countrymen whom He had helped in their needs! But by His Christmas love His heart has room for you, refuge in every trial that may burden your life! No matter what your afflictions may be or how boldly they stand out against the background of Christmas rejoicing, follow Jesus! As you recall that He Himself was *"a man of sorrows and acquainted with grief,"* the five glorious names with which the prophet Isaiah beheld Him from the distance of seven centuries, *"Wonderful, Counselor, The Mighty God, The Everlasting Father, The Prince of Peace,"* combine to assure that in the Christ-child lies the heavenly answer to every problem. The course of our Lord's life and the repeated promises of His grace prove that *"all things work together for good to them that love God"* in Christ. If doubt lingers in your mind as to the Savior's power to help, give yourself wholly to Him now, and a light, brilliant and penetrating beyond expectation, will stream from Bethlehem. Only Christ can send that brightness. When Jean Henri Merle d'Aubigné, author of a comprehensive history of the Reformation, which can still be read with profit, found himself harassed and opposed, he went to an older pastor for assistance in solving a perplexing difficulty. The venerable minister of God replied: "Were I to succeed in ridding you of this problem, others would arise. There is a shorter, deeper, more complete way of annihilating them. Let Christ really be to you the Son of God, the Savior, the Author of eternal life! Only be settled firmly in His grace, and then these difficulties of detail will never bother you. The light which proceeds from Christ will disperse all your darkness." Blessed counsel for you, too!

We think particularly of homes overshadowed by the sorrow of bereavement with its loneliness — and does death ever seem harder than during the radiance and laughter of Christmas? To you, friends of this Bringing-Christ-to-the-Nations crusade, who during these days have laid the lifeless form of a beloved one into the silent grave, I bring no human balm for your heartache, but I remind you that our text promises those who walk in Christ's faith *"the Light of life."* Because our merciful Savior came into the world on the first Christmas; because He lived His life of unsparing devotion and died His death of limitless love; because He rose again, He is *"the Resurrection and the Life."* He has the *"keys of hell and of death"* itself. He, but only He, the divine Conqueror of the grave, *"brought life and immortality to light."* Push every other consideration and false comfort out of your mind, for nothing else can help you. Last year at this time a Long Island cult proposed to prove that men can live forever if they eat vegetables, abstain from meats, surround themselves with lofty thoughts and good music. So they took a new-born child, placed her in a mansion, gave her the prescribed diet, the happy surroundings, and called her "Baby Sunshine." She was to live forever. Last week, however, the newspapers told us that the demonstration would be discontinued. Baby Sunshine was sent back to her mother; no proof of immortality will be given. Of course, a demonstration of that kind can be only a failure. Yet in Jesus and through unwavering faith in the love of which Christmas is the first chapter, Calvary the climax, and the open grave the blessed ending, we can have eternal life now. The death we all must face brings only a temporary separation for those who are Christ's. In His time and by His mercy a glorious reunion with the faithful will follow, where even the Christmas joy will be immeasurably intensified by the eternal rejoicing and celestial carols.

Thank God especially that the darkness of sin in your life will disappear under the brilliance of Bethlehem's glory! For some the joy of this Christmas season is marred by a deep-grooved transgression, a breaking of God's law, that gives no rest. There is too little of preparation for Christ and too much of indecency and drunkenness in many of the social and business parties at Christmas where the sacred name of the Lord Jesus is defamed; and it may be that during these pre-Christmas days some evil has slipped into your life which will haunt you with regrets and, far worse, seek to estrange you from God on the day when of all days you should be closest to Him. Your emotions may be tightened and torn by covetous desires, unholy impulses; your heart may be filled with hatred, while the message of peace and love is proclaimed. But don't let Christmas come and go with sullen gloom beclouding your home and happiness! Here is the angel's glad cry on our Savior's birthday: *"Unto you is born this day in the city of David a Savior, which is Christ the Lord!"* Come contritely to Him and realize that for your transgressions He left the indescribable glories of His heavenly throne to be born in a darkened age and an enslaved country. For your pardon He shed His own blood and died on the cross so that you, *"being justified by faith"* — that means, completely saved from your sins by the free, unmerited mercy of Jesus Christ — may have *"peace with God."* For your complete victory Jesus gave you His Word, the sacred ordinances of Baptism and the Lord's Supper, the power of faith, and the answer to prayer, so that, having beheld the Christ-child, you resolve — and what better birthday gift can be brought the Lord of light and love? — to follow Christ's truth and holiness in a consecrated battle against sin.

Once you have seen Christ's light, you yourself must become a light-bearer for Him. About twenty years ago a Russian physicist proposed the theory that certain vegetables emit supposedly ultra-violet rays. American scientists have developed the theory that the human body has mysterious radiations. Whether or not this is true, one fact is certain: We who know the Christ-child as our Savior must bear in our lives the reflected light of His peace. As Moses could not leave Mount Sinai after his forty days in Jehovah's presence without having his countenance reflect the light of God, so those who are close to the Savior must shine forth gloriously in this old, corrupt, sin-cursed world to help banish its darkness and heal its myriad sorrows. *"So let your light shine before men,"* Jesus earnestly exhorts, *"that they may see your good works and glorify your Father which is in heaven."* Saint Peter echoes, *"Ye are a chosen generation, a royal priesthood, an holy nation, a peculiar people, that ye should show forth the praises of Him who hath called you out of darkness into His marvelous light."* If any of you who pretend to be Christians, far from serving as beacon-lights to guide others, have been misleading lights; if instead of radiating the brightness of Christ, you have let your lamps go out, the loving Savior, whose grace is endless and whose mercies are renewed every morning, but doubly renewed with this Christmas season, asks you to come back, in contrition over your sins, but with the joy and triumph of your salvation, to hold high over this darkening world the light of Christ's love.

A fisherman was once overtaken by a sudden storm off the coast of Scotland. Night soon fell, and there was no light by which he could safely direct his course. Besides, his small boat was leaking badly. In that fateful hour he prayed, and in God's quick answer his son cried out, "Father, I see a light!" In a manner that could not be explained, an unknown beam guided the fishing-smack back to its own harbor. It proved to be a lamp accidentally placed in the window of his own home. Out of gratitude the fisherman afterwards kept a beacon there, and when he died, the British government erected the Rocky Shore Island Light. You have been saved, brought out of a sea of darkness to the light, not by an accident but by God's eternal plan of your redemption. That deliverance came to most of you through the Christ first taught you in your homes by a believing father or mother. Will you not on this Christmas say, "O God, help me to follow that light!"? Will you not, however bright your homes may otherwise be, keep them illuminated with the light of the Lord Jesus, so that they may shine as beacons of hope to others?

If I had my way, every Christian home in America on Christmas night would have these words in their lighted windows, on the decorated walls, and especially in the hearts of every member in the household: "Christ, the Savior, is born!" "O come, let us adore Him!" "*Glory to God in the highest and on earth peace, good will toward men!*" What blessings would come from that true Christmas light! If we cannot give such wide demonstration of our faith, we can pray as we look in spirit to Bethlehem: "O Father, help us to give glory only to our Triune God! O Jesus, grant us soon a Christmas peace and, if it be Thy will, break the tyranny of bloodshed! But whatever happens, send Thy blood-bought peace into our hearts!

O Holy Spirit, give us Thy good will toward suffering, wounded, dying humanity; good will toward those who are still in the darkness of unbelief; good will toward our enemies as the light of Thy good will toward us has brightened our path!" Then, indeed, will Christmas bring Christ's *"light of life"* and love into our hearts. God grant you all a Christmas bathed in this brilliance of Bethlehem's Babe! Amen.

THE MIRACLE OF THE MANGER: GOD WITH US

"They shall call His name Emmanuel, which, being interpreted, is, God with us." —Saint Matthew 1:23

Thou Christ of Bethlehem's Crib:

W*hat limitless love, what unfathomable depth of devotion Thou didst show for us through the mystery of Thy blessed incarnation! O Jesus, our God and Savior, how can we in our sins, coldness, and ingratitude ever thank Thee worthily for Thy matchless mercy, the gift of Thyself? Despite our pitiful blindness and wilful rebellion come to us again as in this vast congregation of the air multitudes in America and Canada join to acclaim Thee their Christ, their God, their Redeemer! Send the Spirit of love once more into our war-racked world to teach us what a wonderful Savior Thou art and how gloriously Thou, our Brother, didst make us God's children through Thy Sonship! On Thy birthday comfort all who are ground under the heel of tyranny, bleeding from the wounds of war, made destitute through man's inhumanity, or dying with no one to help them but Thee! Jesus, our Prince of Peace, if it be Thy will, put an end to the devastating conflict that rages across the seas! O Babe of Bethlehem, on this day of Thy birth our hearts plead: Give us peace, blessed peace! Amen.*

THIS is a Christmas of contrasts, almost the best holiday season American business has known, yet the heaviest in poverty and indebtedness we have ever witnessed, a Christmas with Bethlehem, birthplace of the Prince of Peace, darkened by the first blackouts in its annals. While we repeat the angels' carol, *"Glory to God!"* millions of Red, atheistic blasphemers chant, "Away with God!"; while we join believing Christians in all creeds to sing and pray, *"On earth peace!"* the United States feverishly prepares for what, if it comes, may be the most destructive war in its history, and tyrannized millions in Europe have lost their real peace for years to come. Though we chant *"Good will toward men!"* one statesman broadcasts threats to grind a hostile nation to sand and the diplomats on the other side answer with embittered taunts that they will wage total war such as the world has never known.

On this crisis Christmas, when the world, if it only trusted Christ's promise, would have unspeakable blessings, but when, instead, it sees bloodthirsty men bent on destroying each other in deep-rooted hatred, let us pray God that shadow-haunted multitudes in these fear-filled forties may recapture the surpassing comfort of the first Christmas glory. During these nineteen centuries mankind has traveled fast and far from the meaning and spirit of that first hallowed night; and many of you have succumbed to the subtle campaign which would make this anniversary of Christ's birth not the year's holy day but just another holiday; not Christmas but "Xmas"; not a festival for the soul but a feasting for the body; not a season for Christ's carols but for carnal carousals; not a time of giving but of getting. A few nights ago I read to a group of women business executives in St. Louis the translation of an account written by Libanius, a fourth-century Latin author, describing a certain celebration in Rome. As I asked them, so I now ask you to identify the holiday which the Latin writer pictures in these words: "The festival . . . is celebrated everywhere. . . . The impulse to spend seizes every one. . . . People are not only generous toward themselves, but also toward their fellow-men. A stream of presents pours itself out on all sides. . . . The festival banishes all that is connected with toil. . . . From the minds of young people it removes . . . the dread of the schoolmaster. . . . Another great quality of the festival is that it teaches men not to hold too fast to their money, but to part with it and let it pass into other hands." Those business women answered — and doubtless most of you would agree: "Christmas." But that is wrong. No!

Libanius referred to a heathen festival called the Saturnalia, the pagan period for unbounded excesses in eating, drinking, and sensual pleasures. The point I wish to make is this: How tragic that the observance of the blessed Christ's birthday is often so worldly and tinseled that the account of an ancient heathen holiday depicts many a modern Christmas celebration in the United States.

Therefore I speak particularly to you who are overbusy and overburdened with Christmas preparation, irritated by loss of sleep, dejected when you should be happiest, inwardly troubled when your heart should exult with joy, distressed of soul through want when you should be rich in rejoicing, bowed by bereavement during the sacred season that promises the joy of life. For the real, basic, heavenly comfort of this blessed day we turn, not to Dickens' *Christmas Carol* but to the angels' carol; not to Adolph Hitler's *Mein Kampf* but to Christ's battle against sin; not to Karl Marx's *Das Kapital* but to Jesus' poverty; not to the *New York Sun's* widely quoted letter, "Yes, Virginia, there is a Santa Claus," but to our heavenly Father's Christmas message: *"Unto you is born this day in the city of David a Savior, which is Christ the Lord."* If we reverently study the Christmas Gospel (it takes only three minutes to read St. Luke's account of the most sacred story ever told, and you parents will certainly find time after our broadcast to read that record in your family circle, will you not?) as we join the shepherds in the resolution, *"Let us now go even unto Bethlehem and see this thing which is come to pass,"* how blessed to know the cradled Babe, the Christ of Christmas, the Savior in swaddling-clothes,

THE MIRACLE OF THE MANGER: GOD WITH US!

This is the Christmas truth expressed in Saint Matthew, chapter one, verse twenty-three, *"They shall call His name Emmanuel, which, being interpreted, is God with us."* May this divine Christmas radiance be gloriously impressed on your souls! To that end, kneel in spirit before the manger as you hear the meaning of these three words, *"God with us,"* in the holy Child's name, Emmanuel.

I

THE CHRIST CHILD IS OUR *GOD*

Judged by human standards, all the circumstances of our Savior's birth were poor and disappointing. He was born, not in the capital but in a village six miles to the south, which, even in its heyday during Old Testament prophecy, was *"the least among the thousands of Judah,"* and which, in the time of tyranny, when Judea bowed before Caesar's legions, was a straggling, squalid, unnoticed hamlet, quite different from your dream of Bethlehem or the artists' idealization. God often chooses the weak, the insignificant, for mighty, earth-moving purposes. You are not beyond His notice or reach if you live in a small community or in isolation beyond country crossroads! His love recognizes no distance or barriers. With faith, you in your out-of-the-way, beyond-the-beaten-path home can be closer to your Father than those who without faith live in Europe's castles or America's penthouses.

Christ was born, not of a royal princess but of a plain Palestinian maiden. This, too, runs counter to all human expectations. Yet what comfort this fact implies! Don't think that the almighty and all-loving God is unconcerned about you because your ancestors came over in the steerage of an immigrant ship instead of on the *Mayflower* or because your mother, without a college degree (since her life was devoted to you, instead of business or professional interests), may never have her name listed among America's outstanding women! God has a far higher reward. As He exalted Mary, humble and modest in her virginal purity, to be the greatest of women, so in our country He has made Christian mothers like Abraham Lincoln's in pioneer Kentucky the most eminent among this nation's women.

Jesus was born in a stable, the last place where men should expect to find the Prince of Peace. Since God never moves by accident, trial-and-error methods, chance or change, He chose the manger as the first cradle of His Son, to proclaim during all cold and selfish centuries that He befriends the homeless and helpless. Take heart, you in the submerged sixth of our American population who often by no fault of your own have been driven to poverty, who have endured long unemployment (despite the lavish emphasis on our present artificial industrial prosperity), who have been discharged at forty-five despite your increased ability and experience, — all of you should remember that Christmas, to whomever else it may belong, is your day, in which God's love for the poor, His understanding of their problems, is convincingly demonstrated at Bethlehem.

I repeat, everything about Christ's birth was disappointing, judged by men's standards. Another child was born — that was all. Bethlehem was unconcerned, the villagers unsympathetic. Live or die, the new-born baby made no difference to them. Whatever happened to that infant, affairs in blighted Bethlehem would go on as before — so they must have thought, had they even taken time to think of the Galilean strangers, outcasts in the stable with the lowing cattle. In contrast, while men were silent, angels cried out; though earth was indifferent, heaven itself throbbed with joy. One angel was not enough to celebrate this day of days; *"the multitude of the heavenly host"* announced God's message to earth.

For, however lowly and poor the Lord Jesus' birth may have seemed, one eternally triumphant truth of divine majesty rings throughout the ages to make Christmas the most magnificent event in history, and it promises the most glorious grace God Himself could bestow. Here it is, foretold in the voice of ancient prophets, announced by the angel Gabriel, proclaimed to the shepherds by the celestial messenger, recorded by evangelists, affirmed by apostles, declared by Jesus Himself, assured by God the Father, attested by the Holy Spirit, proved by the conquering faith in billions of Christian lives, manifested in every blessing that saved our world of selfish men from itself. The Christ-child cradled in the manger is our God! In the complete, unreduced sense of that glorious word Jesus Christ is very God of very God. He is not only a godly man, a God-like leader, a God-sent teacher, a God-directed prophet; today we testify to America He is all this, but infinitely more: that Child, the promise of the ages, the center of our hopes and fears, the climax of divine love and wisdom, is our true and only Lord. Isaiah foresaw Him as *"the mighty God"* and as *"Emmanuel,"* the Hebrew of which means *"God with us";* and in fulfilment the angel in the annunciation to Mary declares, *"His name shall be called Emmanuel . . . God with us."*

He is called *"God with us"* because He is *"God with us."* Listen to the angel's proclamation, the message that makes today Christmas: *"Unto you is born this day in the city of David a Savior, which is Christ the Lord."* From these first pages until the last of the New Testament, as the Savior is acclaimed *"over all, God blessed forever,"* you will find such unquestioned, repeated testimony to Christ's Godhead from His own lips and His own works, from the testimony of God and His holy angels, the acknowledgment of the apostles and their epistles, the confessions of converted enemies and reconciled rebels, that today you ought to believe rather than belittle, to follow faith before reason, to acclaim instead of disclaim, to exalt rather than question.

Can you not see that, if you contradict the truth of Christ's deity, you take away from this holy day and season the supreme blessing which separates the Christian Church from the Roman winter holiday, the rejoicing over the Nativity from the sensual Saturnalia? We need a Savior who is more than man or superman, higher than angels or archangels, greater than lords or overlords; we must have God Himself, who alone can forgive our sins, remove our guilt, cancel our punishment. We look up to the mysterious night skies strewn with heavenly bodies (in comparison with some of which this earth seems only a grain in our universe), and we ask ourselves, "Where can we find the God who made this majestic marvel, the only God who can save us?" We look down to the ground on which we walk, as every step we take on Mother Earth reminds us of our temporal destiny, *"Dust thou art and to dust shalt thou return,"* and we ask, "Where is the God who can deliver us from the doom of death and the gruesomeness of the grave?" We look out on a world torn by turmoil and suicidal struggle as nations grow more cruel with their advancing culture, deadlier with their progress, and we plead, "Where is the God who can bring peace on earth and stop this slaughter of youth?" We look into our own hearts, to the conflict of the selfish, covetous, impure emotions that surge within us, and exclaim, "Where is the God who can cleanse my heart, speak pardon to my soul, give peace to my rest-robbed spirit?" These questions as well as Job's plaintive plea *"Oh, that I knew where I might find Him!"* are answered at Bethlehem. Your search is ended there, for in Christ, God is cradled in the manger. Whatever else Christmas may have brought you of good or grief, may every carol you hear sing into your heart the glories of Christ as your God! May every light, in the words of the Nicene Creed, accepted by all Christians —

we seem much closer to each other on Christmas Day! — remind you that Jesus is "God of God, Light of Light," in the mystery of His incarnation that Heaven alone understands but that we can *believe* with our whole hearts.

II
THE CHRIST-CHILD IS *WITH* HIS OWN

With the Christmas marvel comes this message of mercy: The Christ-child is *"God* WITH *us."* He lived with sinful men, walked with them, talked with them, abode with them in their homes, ate with them at their tables, mourned with them in their sorrows, and died with mocking men around His cross — despite their blasphemy and brutality, for He was their Savior. His life among God's enemies proclaimed the promise that this Christ was to be the sinners' Savior, the royal Redeemer, the eternal Atoner for the whole race estranged from God, perishing in its own sins. He humbled Himself so that we might be exalted. He became the Son of Man so that by faith we might be the sons of God. He was born in a stable so that by grace we could be born again in Him.

Because He was *"with us"* in the flesh, even though despised and rejected; because He stayed with this world even when it nailed Him to the cross, His Savior love pledges all who accept the Christmas promise that He will be with us on this earth, come what may. How soul-strengthening is His valedictory assurance, *"Lo, I am with you alway, even unto the end of the world"!* The newspapers report that when King George visits Britain's bombed cities, the cry goes up, "The King is with us!" and immediately the hearts of those harassed people — O God, give every war-sufferer Christ's comfort this Christmas Day! — leap with joy. If the presence of an earthly monarch can bring a thrill of courage, how much more should the fact that our King of kings wants to be *"with us"* in His Word and Sacraments embolden us to face the hardships confronting us and meet bravely whatever these overclouded years may bring!   *"God with us"* in Christ to forgive us, redeem us, restore us!   *"God with us"* in Christ, to strengthen us against our sinful selves, fortify us against our own flesh, steel our resistance against temptation!   *"God with us"* in Christ, to walk by our side and help us carry the weight of worry, to share our burdens, to turn afflictions into advantages and make every blow a blessing!   *"God with us"* in Christ, to remove our fears, dispel our doubts, wipe away our worries!   *"God with us"* in Christ, to push through the wilderness of our misspent years, the jungle of our jumbled lives, the frozen terrors of our fear-filled days!   *"God with us"* in Christ — who, as the apostle challenges, *"shall separate us from the love of Christ?   Shall tribulation or distress or persecution or famine or nakedness or peril or sword?   Nay"* — and this is the Christmas assurance — *"in all these things we are more than conquerors through Him that loved us.   For I am persuaded that neither death nor life nor angels nor principalities nor powers nor things present nor things to come nor height nor depth nor any other creature shall be able to separate us from the love of God which is in Christ Jesus, our Lord."*

III

THE CHRIST-CHILD CAN BE WITH EVERY ONE OF US

If ever you feel inclined to doubt whether these Nativity blessings extend to you; if in dark moments, when at Christmas the world around you seems light and you see only disappointment in yourself, perhaps even death in your own home; if you are ready to charge God with cruelty, remember that the Christ-child's name, His love and His mercy, combine to prove that He is with *us*, every one of us.   No soul has ever been too heavily loaded with sorrows, too completely crushed by sin, outcast too harshly by self-seeking friends, or opposed by bitter enemies, to be deprived of Jesus' soul-sustaining presence. The radiance of our Redeemer's birthday reminds us that, the farther we are removed from human help, the closer our faith can bring us to our Savior.

God wants to be with every one of you in Christ today. Oh, believe that! Push all else aside to trust this truth and build on His promises! Every scene in the Nativity cycle emphasizes that He is the Savior of *all* men. Jesus was born as a child so that He might redeem, bless, protect childhood. Treasure this truth, you boys and girls throughout the land, and come lovingly to Him who in His youth proved that you have no sincerer Friend than the Savior! Give our American youth higher education, better recreation, more opportunities for development; but be sure to give them Him whom they need the most and who can give them all they require — Jesus, the Christ!

He was blessed by elderly Anna and Simeon (and these stories are recorded to encourage you, my aged friends, for whom this may be the last Christmas, that Jesus was taken into the arms of a venerable, world-weary believer), so that you, too, can depart in heavenly peace once the eyes of your faith have seen His salvation. You who have passed the threescore, fourscore, and higher mile-stones in life's uphill pilgrimage, come to this Christ-child now, before it is too late!

His birth was first announced to the shepherds, to show those who have not had the opportunity of higher education that He is the Redeemer for the plain and unlearned folk. Yet, among His early worshipers were the Wise Men, intellectual leaders of that day. What promise of power our twentieth-century wisdom and learning can find in the Savior, who alone answers the vital questions that no laboratory or scientific research can ever fathom, the problems of sin and salvation, death and the grave, life and eternity!

He grew up in a carpenter's home, and early He learned that trade. How essential that we preach to a world torn with industrial strife the Christ who is the working-man's Friend, the laborer's Comrade, the Champion of the down-trodden! Yet angels higher than human potentates bowed before Him and showed that the mighty from the far corners of the earth can find in Him what royalty's pomp and circumstance can never grant: light, life, and salvation; pardon, peace, and paradise.

He was born into a middle-class family to give us the assurance that our every-day family life can always be blessed by His presence. In Bethlehem He suffered humiliation such as today even those in the lower classes do not know, so that He could be the Deliverer of the under-privileged and suppressed masses. Yet by the miracle of divine grace the first tributes laid at His feet were lavish, perhaps royal, gifts, examples of the devotion monarchs and millionaires should show Him. Lower class, middle class, upper class — all are Christ's.

Join me, then, whoever you are, whatever you are, wherever you are, as we now declare in a mighty confession of Christian conviction: "O Christ-child, blessed Babe of Bethlehem, Thou art 'God,' almighty, all-knowing, all-merciful, 'with us,' every one of us, despite our wickedness and weakness, 'with us' for our salvation, 'with us' for our strengthening, 'with us' for our blessing. O Christ-child, grant us as the greatest Christmas gift even Thou canst give us, the assurance that we in Thy time, by Thy mercy, and with Thy conquering power will be with Thee in ever-lasting joy!" That Christ-centered Christmas blessing I wish to every one of you, my friends, and to every one of you, my enemies, through Jesus, the Christ, the Savior, the Emmanuel, the *"God with us!"* Amen.

WE WANT PEACE!

"I am for peace!" — Psalm 120:7

O God, Our Past Help, Our Future Hope:

The relentless flow of time reminds us that soon another year will have slipped into the unchangeable past, and we are all twelve months nearer the final moment of our lives. Help us cling more closely to Jesus Christ, our only Savior, the same yesterday, today, and forever! Reviewing our own frailty as we prepare to close the declining year, we ask Thee to remove every unholy thought and action in our lives! Pardon us for every selfishness by which we withheld reverence, prayer, and praise! May the love of the Christ-child, incarnate in Bethlehem's manger, be born again in us! Our sins forgiven by His matchless mercy, may we have Thy peace in our hearts and be peacemakers for a world of sore strife! Be with us during the new year, Father Almighty and All-knowing! Walk by our side during the burden-heavy days before us, O Jesus! Keep us in the faith, O Holy Spirit, and fortify us for the reverses and sorrows that may confront us! Go with us, O Triune God, particularly with the destitute, the suffering, the dying, and make the coming months fortify us with greater grace and deeper devotion to Thee! We prepare to close the old and begin the new in Jesus' precious name. Amen.

LAST Sunday our Christmas-message asked you to hear the angels sing, "Peace on earth!" accept the Christ-child as your Savior, and then work for peace. As a consequence of this plea, my fellow-countrymen and fellow-Christians, I was bitterly attacked, and deliberately cut off the air by a Detroit station. While broadcasting time is granted speakers representing the Communist party, organized to overthrow our Republic; while indecency, attacks on the Scriptures, and ridicule of religion have been featured on the radio without rebuke; while those who plead for our country's active entrance into the war use network time often without any charge, I have been denounced and threatened because this Mission of the Air (which pays for every minute of its hook-up time at full commercial rates), in exalting the new-born Prince of Peace, also indicted war propaganda and profiteering.

Such appeals, it was charged, are controversial. But is it controversial to pray for real, honorable peace? Is it controversial to ask that our youth be spared war's horrors? Is it controversial to express the hope that our country, the last stronghold of democracy, may be protected against Communist or Fascist uprisings and the social upheaval which may follow any World War with its gigantic destruction? Is it controversial in Christ's name to follow the Bible's direction, *"Seek peace and ensue it!"* when you feel that armed forces, once loosed in the fury of a world-wide conflict, can cripple the work of Christian churches? If this is the prevalent attitude in our country today, all I can say is, "God help America!" and then ask you who love Christ and who are ready to lay down your lives in our country's defense, should this nation be invaded or attacked, to continue your protest. The encouraging response to last Sunday's broadcast in many ways is unprecedented (more than 5,000 letters and telegrams were received on one day), and while I thank certain labor leaders, many clergymen of all denominations, and the mass of intelligent American Christians for their support, I ask the aid of all Scripture-loving friends in a spiritual preparedness program to protect our vital constitutional right of free worship which may be threatened by the continuation of the European war and its after-effects.

Particularly, however, do I invite you on this last Sunday of a year with many failures to hear King David, oppressed and persecuted, cry out in our text (Psalm 120, verse seven): *"I am for peace!"* and on the basis of these words, looking toward the problematical new year, to declare: "WE WANT PEACE!"

inner *"peace with God through our Lord Jesus Christ"* and
honorable peace with our fellow-men through that Savior's
blessed power.

I

WE WANT PEACE WITH GOD!

The fundamental truth, often disregarded in our
present-day striving for peace, is this: We can expect no
rest or quiet for ourselves, our homes, our churches, unless
with a living, trusting faith we have Jesus Christ as our
own personal Savior. Woodrow Wilson would be eighty-
four years old today if he were alive, and the World War
President, who saw more bloodshed than any other American chief-executive, asserted shortly before his death that,
if we would have real peace, above wars and treaties and
leagues, we must grope our way spiritually back to God.

For peace in your own lives, with the heaped regrets
of the old year and the fears of the new, where can you
find pardon for the past and pledge for the future unless
in a repentant return to Jesus Christ? If you have thought
that money could assure calm but now know that it only
increases your problems; that love would offer you happiness, yet now find that it has grown cold, its promises
broken, its attractions vanished; if you have been blind
enough to believe that by eating sin's forbidden fruits, your
eyes would be opened to life's full verve and tang; or if
you have concluded that you could think yourself into
security apart from God and Christ, you should be ready
for a rude awakening. Nothing in our modern age so
emphatically recalls the Old Testament warning against
crying "Peace!" when there is no peace as the deep-rooted,
insistent efforts to find assurance without Jesus. My earnest
appeal, therefore, directs every fear-weighted, trouble-
burdened soul to behold the Savior of all mercies as in this
moment He stretches His divine arms toward a war-

wrecked world and promises, *"Come unto Me, all ye that labor and are heavy laden, and I will give you rest!"* *"My peace I give unto you; not as the world giveth, give I unto you. Let not your heart be troubled."*

Jesus extends a divine pledge of peace because He removes sin, the destructive evil which takes away all calmness, placing men at war with God and their consciences. In your home, family relations, business associations, you can see how directly the transgression of the divine Law produces disturbed hearts, disquieted moments, distracted fears. But remove sin, and you have peace! Put Christ into your own life; enthrone Him in your home as your only Savior, your true God, your King of grace and power; let Jesus be All in all for you; and as you declare, *" 'I am for peace'* with my God," you will witness that, your transgressions canceled, a blessed joy will dawn to give you calm and quiet in any chaos of confusion.

Many of you do not really trust the Lord Jesus. You hear about His grace, but the seed, God's Word, falls on rocky soil of doubt and never produces complete trust, full reliance on our Savior. You cannot find peace through half-hearted interest in Christ. He must have mastery over your soul! You must accept Him as your *only* Redeemer, knowing that no one else can remove your sins. You must welcome Him as the *complete* Savior, believing that He has *fully* atoned for every transgression in your life, and you can bring nothing, sacrifice nothing, contribute nothing, earn nothing, to secure your redemption, but need only come in repentant faith and acknowledge: "O Lord Jesus, You are my Redeemer! You came into this world as the Christmas Christ-child for me, so that I can be born again in You. You died on the cross as the Good Friday Lamb of God for me, to save me from my sins. You arose as the Easter Victor over the grave to give me everlasting life.

You ascended to the eternal glory-crowned throne, there to intercede for me and prepare my place in the heavenly mansions." You must welcome Jesus as the assured Savior, not because you think that He may be your Christ and that His promise deserves at least a trial, but because He *is*, beyond every doubt, your own Savior and His Gospel the everlasting truth, which can never pass away, though mountains depart and hills be removed.

In that faith we have peace with God. We who were once estranged from our heavenly Father, enemies of His holy love, mockers of His majesty, have become His children, heirs to salvation. The warfare between Heaven and earth is over for us; His grace assures us, *"Being justified by faith, we have peace with God!"*

The reason some of you are still restlessly torn by conflicts is this, that you have kept yourselves away from Christ and wilfully banished His mercy from your hearts. If only you would find time for Jesus, so that His Word could prove its truth! Many an infidel or skeptic has been brought to repentance and faith through a closer study of His Word. The same divinely dynamic Scriptures can remove your doubts, build your faith, strengthen your certainty by keeping you close to Christ, constantly near His mercy!

If you have Jesus, you need no one else, least of all the soothsayers and astrologers who flourish in times like these. Recall how the rose-hued, honeyed predictions made by fortune-tellers a year ago were ironically turned upside down by subsequent events, and come penitently to Christ, the only Help for a world suffering by its own violence and unbelief, the only Help for your soul! Do not lean on the arm of flesh and try to find peace in the futile theory of a steady forward march by which the human race is said to be advancing with constant moral gains toward a state of perfection! The closing year offers a striking argument to discredit such claims of human evolution. It is a *lost* year, in which sin and war have caused a drastic setback in religious, humanitarian, cultural, educational, and social progress. The greatest need in your life, the supreme necessity for every American, is repentance and the faith in Christ, which reunites us with the Father.

Blessed by this divine peace with God, you can face even the dangerous, unmarked paths of the critical months ahead with the firm conviction that, come what may, Jesus' promise *"Neither shall any man pluck them out of My hand"* will be fulfilled. The Savior does not tell those who are His that the coming fifty-two weeks will offer uninterrupted prosperity, unbroken happiness. The future seems to forbode the opposite for masses of American people. In this uncertainty our heavenly Father does not guarantee us steady work, bulging bank accounts, new automobiles; He does not pledge earthly peace, business booms, social advancement, but He does assure us of peace, radiant harmony, with God. As you remove one page after the other from the new calendar, you may lose your money, but you need not lose Christ. Your friends may forsake you, but His promise reads, *"I will never leave thee nor forsake thee."* The devotion of loved ones may disappear, but of Jesus it is written in the Book of Truth, *"I change not!"* Enemies may assail you, but Jesus comforts you. As reverse piles on reverse and your burden becomes so great that you sometimes join unbelievers in wondering how you can bear it, He will still give you, in answer to your childlike trust, the spiritual courage to find the warrant of His love in the cradle at Bethlehem as in the cross of Calvary and to rejoice even in your afflictions. By following Christ, and only in this way, will you have the serene outlook on life which understands that, no matter how rough the road may be, how often the blows may fall, how deep the depths of anxiety, how frequent the fears of pain and sickness, how lonely and misunderstood your life, all this is but the plan of Christ's peace, the design for a spiritually beautiful life, the pattern for a victorious faith, which can overcome the world.

Whatever else, then, the new year may bring, once your trust in Jesus exclaims, " *'I am for peace'* with my heavenly Father through Christ," that Savior will walk by your side as the shadows lengthen over the untrodden paths before you. Livingstone declared that Christ was with him in Africa's jungles. Sven Hedin testified that the Bible was his constant companion during the dangerous travels in Tibet. Professor Piccard, who ascended high into the stratosphere, writes me that as a believing Christian he was aware of divine companionship even in those mysterious heights which he penetrated for the first time in history. A noted diver, obliged to descend into the depths of the submarine world, states that even in those black, death-filled waters he had the consciousness of God's living presence. You can have the same assurance that *"neither height nor depth"* can separate you from God during the coming twelvemonth. Through trusting faith Christ will walk by your side on the darkest days that men's hatred and blindness may bring, to give you this gracious promise, *"Lo, I am with you alway, even unto the end of the world."*

II

WE WANT PEACE WITH OUR FELLOW-MEN

The peace with God which is ours through Christ must show itself in our daily lives and in our contacts with our fellow-men. The Christmas love which brought the Lord Jesus from heaven's holiness and its glory to earth's sin and misery; the devotion by which He lived His life of limitless self-giving and then died His all-atoning death at Calvary, is so forceful and penetrating that, once we know this grace, we must be ready to reflect its sustaining comfort by our peace-filled lives.

Declaring with David, "*I am for peace!*" we can, through Christ, have this quietude to bless us where it is often needed most but found least — in our homes. As we approach the New Year, the annual inventory of our family life reveals that in far too many American homes, which should be havens of happiness, miniature warfare rages. During the last year more than 71,000 American husbands deserted their wives. This means that almost 200 families, on the average, were broken every day because married men ran away from their pledged responsibilities. Many of these fugitives from the home could have spared their family and themselves sorrow and suffering if they had known the Savior's peace. Last year, too, about 290,000 marriages were dissolved by divorce. If these husbands and wives had sincerely served Christ and daily made their dwelling-place a church of God through family devotion and prayer, most of their troubles would never have led to this fatal disruption. Divorces and desertions may be computed statistically, but who knows the vastly greater number of instances, not argued before court nor recorded on social charts, in which happiness has been banished by constant quarreling, continued selfishness, drunkenness, profanity, cruelty, or even unfaithfulness to marriage vows? Only one remedy can cure such sin-sick homes, and that involves much more than plans for the financial, psychological, or physical side of marriage; it asks for Christ in the home circle to stifle selfishness and strengthen mutual love. If some of you, as the old year tapers into the new, look regretfully back over long months of unhappy home-life, with heated words, tense situations, protracted sullenness and coldness, nervous, high-tempered bickering or even more serious sins and you face the future with the dismal feeling that all this will increase, remember, your home can enjoy peace and quiet as soon as it has Christ! Whatever else you intend to do when on next Wednesday we write January 1, resolve that in your strife-torn family and for divine blessing on the marriage which seems to have crushed your ideals, you will take Christ as your own personal Savior and employ His help in improving these distressing conditions. Whatever else you may write on the first page of the new annual life-volume, inscribe it with your own determination to practice Joshua's resolution, *"As for me and my house, we will serve the Lord."* Then come what may, you will find in Christ, through family prayer, Scripture-reading, hymn-singing, devotional exercises, His sustaining presence for calm and joy.

We say with David, *"I am for peace!"* also in our other human relations, notably in the struggle between the employer and employee, that bitter, destructive feud which, despite labor laws and Federal boards, puts the business men and the working classes into opposing trenches and prolongs the labor war with its toll in both money and lives. How can our strife-torn industrial world find an armistice for such hatred if not by closer conformity to the example of the Lord Jesus, Himself a working-man, and through His Gospel, which helped raise labor to its present level and dignity? If in American industry there were more acknowledgment of the Savior and less covetous greed; more of Jesus' Golden Rule and less of the rule of might; more New Testament and less radical philosophy; more Christ and less Communism, we would witness harmony and cooperation rather than hardship and competition. To actualize this peace, workers of America, we want you *for* Christ, not against Him; *with* Jesus, not without Him. Employers, business men, industrialists, capitalists of America, during these critical years, when the alternative may be Christ or chaos, give yourselves wholly to your Savior and, as He points you to His cross, find in His love the assurance for your personal redemption and the power of self-sacrifice and self-denial required for co-operative effort and success in solving our social problems!

"We want peace!" our age chants as it witnesses the disheartening and destructive results of class warfare. Let no one self-righteously think that our country is innocent on this charge, when in some sections Negroes are still treated as the scum of the earth. If only half the reports concerning the lot of the red men in the United States are true, even our advanced age has added injustice to the frequent inhumanity of the pioneers, some of whom defrauded the Indians and taught them the white man's vices. An undercurrent of agitation against the Jew is felt, not only among radical, anti-Semitic groups, but even within circles of polite society. Under the financial and economic pressure exerted by war, this bigotry may break all bounds — and this more quickly than we realize! Class hatred will be strengthened. Never before was Christ's presence in the lives of America's millions more necessary for our national well-being than during this era of racial hatreds, with its emphasis on the haves and the have-nots, the upper 400 and the lower 20,000,000, the Aryan and the non-Aryan, the Jew and the Gentile, the white and the black. The age that has discarded the Saviorhood of Christ to emphasize the brotherhood of man has created class antagonism such as we have never dreamed possible, with men who call themselves God's priests serving as rabble-rousers, and politicians becoming demagogs who thrive on class appeals. Pray the Almighty that before it is too late and this country becomes a house class-divided against itself, professional venders of social venom may be converted to the Savior of love and peace! If your hearts and lives are swayed by rancor, think of our Lord's surpassing devotion to men of all colors, climes, and conditions! Recall His love, even for those who crucified Him, when He pleaded, *"Father, forgive them, for they know not what they do!"*

"We want peace!" the cry of Christian hearts continues, particularly among churches that bear Jesus' name. More than 200 religious groups in the United States alone claim to follow our Lord's teachings. What the one affirms the other denies, and the distinctive teachings of one denomination are emphatically contradicted by the doctrines of another. Yet all of these claims, the pros and the cons, the we-teach-this and we-deny-it, assert that they find reason for their position in the Scriptures. As a result, churches which should be completely united by God's one truth are torn by dissension, often thrown into opposing camps, employing attack and ridicule, when they ought to seek doctrinal agreement and concentrate especially against the common foe of atheism and materialism. Our age is still not so enlightened that the fires of intolerance and religious persecution which flared up during the past centuries may not break out again. A host of twentieth-century martyrs may be added to the hundreds of thousands who during past years died under excruciating agonies because they were Christ's or belonged to a certain church. It is a source of great encouragement for us in our radio mission with its plain statement of the Biblical principles and their application to our modern problem-filled times to receive wide-spread support from the clergy and the laity of various churches. Under God we can find some reason to hope for a degree of deeper Christian unity (and I mean genuine fellowship, no setting aside of God's Word, but a complete agreement in every Bible doctrine) in the fact that regardless of denomination you love this old Gospel and agree with me when I testify that within the covers of the Bible we have God's own Record, every page the heavenly guide. Besides, we have its gracious assurance that we who bow before the Lord Jesus as our only Savior and before His Word as the complete truth are members of Christ's Church Universal, united by bonds of faith stronger than the differences which keep us apart. Pray God that our love for real unity — not the pomp-and-circumstance idea of making Christianity outwardly impressive, politically powerful, socially decisive, but the humble, Christ-centered trust which first of all seeks God's kingdom — may increase and the fellowship of our holy faith be continually enlarged!

"We want peace!" our whole soul cries out in this war-wrecked world, "blessed peace among the nations!" I have been warned not to make this appeal today.—A confidential service to American investors states that the odds favoring war are continually increasing. What if they are? There is still time to avert bloodshed by the prayers of righteous men and women, — intercession that even today avails much. — "A plea for peace will make your broadcast unpopular," we are told! Suppose it does? A minority with God on its side can go farther than any majority without Him. Besides, the people of the United States by every poll show overwhelmingly that they do not want war. The President himself has repeatedly promised to avoid military entanglements. — If I, a minister of the Lord Jesus Christ, who said, *"Blessed are the peacemakers; for they shall be called the children of God!"* cannot use the radio to speak for peace, I would rather raise my voice, free and unrestricted, on some street corner. If we have consistently denounced every form of tyranny over men's consciences in Naziism, Fascism, Communism, certainly we should be permitted to apply God's word *"Scatter Thou the people that delight in war"* to all war-mongers, even in this country.

We want peace, because Scripture has commanded Christians to *"seek peace and ensue it!"*; because we regard war as among the most grievous and destructive of all earthly sins, often a visitation from God Himself in punishment for pride and unbelief. While the Christian Church cannot endorse pacifism and the refusal to bear arms in national defense, it dare not hesitate to raise its voice against the savage sins often associated with war, the madness of militarists who want to create right by might, claiming that conflicts are necessary since they remove weaknesses or stimulate strength. We must protest against scheming politicians and diplomats who in the past, as history testifies, have often been moved by personal gain rather than patriotic impulses; against international bankers and munitions-manufacturers who waxed wealthy as the yoke of poverty was placed on the neck of ever larger masses. Whatever else the World War brought the United States, it gave us a total of 21,000 new millionaires. Stock which previously sold for twenty dollars a share sky-rocketed to $1,000. A New York banking house, among other profits, made $30,000,000 on a 1-per-cent commission for war orders. The dividends paid during 1917 and 1918 on certain securities was 458 per cent of their face value — all this while American boys were laying down their lives on Flanders Field and in France! We want helpful, constructive peace — such as the British clergymen, Protestant and Catholic, outlined last week — that will guarantee every child, regardless of race or class, adequate educational opportunities; a peace that will safeguard the family and protect and exalt labor; a peace that will use the earth's resources as God's gift to the whole human race and — as far as possible — abolish the extremes of poverty and wealth.

We want some such equitable, humane, far-sighted program lest the lives taken in the present war be lost in vain and the scene be set for another catastrophe once this exhausted world has received its second breath and begins to hurl itself headlong into the next, far deadlier conflict. We want peace particularly because the kingdom of Jesus Christ must flourish, and we know that conflict can be one of the Church's worst enemies.

As the new year beckons us, we come to God with the plea that, if it be His will, not only this country may be granted continued peace, but also the belligerent nations may lay down their arms, halt destruction, make an honorable peace, by which Christians can work together, live in harmony, build happy homes, labor with industry and frugality, and enjoy constructive achievement. To that end, heavenly Father, bring many to Jesus! Bless us individually as peacemakers for Christ, with the *"peace of God, which passeth all understanding"*! Enrich us with the faith which, beholding the crucified Savior, declares, *"He is our Peace!"* and, strengthened by His courage, proclaims, *" 'I am for peace'* with God and with my fellow-men"! Amen.

WORSHIP THE WORLD'S SAVIOR

*"When Jesus was born in Bethlehem of Judea in the
days of Herod, the king, behold, there came Wise
Men from the East to Jerusalem, saying, Where is
He that is born King of the Jews? For we have
seen His star in the East and are come to worship
Him."* — Saint Matthew 2:1, 2.

Christ, Our King:

As a bright star once directed learned worshipers from the distant
East to Thy cradle, so may the Holy Spirit lead many to a firm
faith in Thy guilt-removing mercy! Help us to discover ourselves
as we are without Thy love, hopeless and forever helpless; but
then, accepting Thy promises, teach us that through Thy life and
death for us we can conquer sin, sorrow, temptation, death itself!
How can we sufficiently show our gratitude for the compassion by
which Thou didst leave the celestial glories to become the Savior of
all men, Jew and Gentile? Oh, make our lives memorials to this
magnificent mercy, which in its timeless sweep has no respect for
person, race, or position! Bring us humbly, trustingly, to Thee,
our only Savior! Give us a childlike confidence, unmoved by the
attacks of reason, always contrite in its approach to Thy mercy!
Encourage us, especially all who suffer for Thy name's sake, in our
fears, pains, and afflictions! With Thy love shall we be truly
strengthened, for Thou art our God, the Sovereign and Savior of
our souls. Amen.

IS atheism to control America? Shall the sneering ridicule of God and the boasting rejection of the Bible
become outstanding features of our education, culture, and
life philosophy? Must our youth be trained in an academic
atmosphere that dethrones the Almighty, denounces the
pure, the honorable, and revels in lewdness? These were
the questions I asked myself when I saw the Christmas
number of a magazine issued by students at a Pacific Coast
State University, typical of certain other college under-
graduate publications throughout the land. With crude
vulgarity and outright blasphemy, recalling the worst that

Russian atheists have ever produced, this campus paper caricatured one of the most sacred scenes in our Savior's life, the Lord's Supper, substituted politicians for Jesus and His disciples. The three Wise Men were represented as reeling drunkards. The refrain "Noel, Noel, Born is the King of Israel" was changed to "Born are the Kings of Buy and Sell." John the Baptist and Saint Peter were pictured in mockery. The Savior's own words were brazenly changed, prayer belittled, Christian faith derided. As every attack on God involves an assault on morality, so also in this sacrilege virginity and virtue were derided, drunkenness exalted, sex sins glorified, marriage lampooned, unfaithfulness championed, profanity applauded — by students of this large State university and with the sanction of the United States Post Office, which permitted copies to be sent through the mail. Every war tears down decency and brings out the viciousness of the human heart; so we, too, must be prepared for the fact that when by international upheaval Christian standards are abandoned, certain liberal American colleges will promote moral decline in the nation's youth, encouraging them to think it is smart and modern to vilify religion and show contempt for morality. In opposition I ask for Christian *vigilantes* throughout the country who will watch every attack on our holy faith made in State-supported schools and effectively protest against each violation of the constitutional principle prohibiting the use of public facilities for assaults on Christianity.

American churches must do their share in a spiritual defense program. Side by side with national preparedness, we need an aggressive, militant Christianity to fight skepticism, materialism, atheism, on all fronts, through the preaching of Christ's pure, powerful Gospel. Because this swelling chorus of unbelief will continue to increase as the war menace grows stronger; because these student publications, their dirty jokes, and boasting sacrilege, are but the products of their time, in which teachers and educational leaders often declare, "We can't believe in God or Christ!" "We don't believe in heaven or hell!" "We won't believe in the Bible or the Church!" I want to use this broadcast at the beginning of the Epiphany season, when the Wise Men from the distant Orient bowed before Christ, to raise the counter-appeal:

WORSHIP THE WORLD'S SAVIOR!

Following the Magi's example, of whom we read in Saint Matthew, chapter two, verses one and two: *"When Jesus was born in Bethlehem of Judea in the days of Herod, the king, behold, there came Wise Men from the East to Jerusalem, saying, Where is He that is born King of the Jews? For we have seen His star in the East, and are come to worship Him!"*

I

WORSHIP HIM, AMERICA!

A deep-rooted, driving desire to acclaim Christ sent these leaders of learning on their momentous journey to Bethlehem. They were ready to travel great distances, devote months of their time, undergo hardships, overcome national pride, if only they could *"come to worship Him"* whose star they had beheld in their far-off homes. With a holy earnestness, which was to disregard the command of a hostile ruler, they were determined that in the deepest joy and most sacred privilege of their lives they would kneel before the new-born Sovereign.

The same desire to find Jesus, bring Him the tributes of reverent love and proclaim Him Lord of lords, King of kings, should grip your hearts today and move particularly the indifferent and undecided, who up till this

moment have never given themselves to Christ. Without
Jesus you not only lose the best with which God Himself
can strengthen your soul, mind and body, but you also
reject His promise of a glorious eternity in heaven. Recall
the blessings which the Savior brought you. I repeat them
each Sunday, but they always seem so new and impelling
that, if it were not for the depraved side of every life, it
would be most difficult to understand why throughout
all Christian history a single unbeliever has ever risen up
against our Lord. He is the Savior, not of a small, select
group, but the Redeemer of the race, the personal Deliverer
of every man, woman, and child during the past, present,
and future of all centuries. Therefore, He is also our
Christ! — He brings complete forgiveness, absolute pardon
for every sin. You can fall so low that polite society casts
you off and the Government revokes your citizenship; but
Jesus is always ready to receive you and help you retain
your heavenly citizenship. Though we reject His love, the
most magnificent mercy men can ever know; though we
ridicule the grace that brought Him to the poverty of the
manger and to the agony of the cross, such blasphemy —
terrifying as it is — should not keep us from Christ. He is
eager to remit even the blackest vice, for He loved every
lost soul so intensely that He, without sin, assumed our
sins. Our iniquity was transferred to Him in a very real
substitution by which our condemnation, guilt, punishment,
and death became His, His alone and His entirely. *"Christ
died for us"* — so the Scriptures summarize this supreme
truth — to remove the shackles of our transgressions, free
us from hell, break the power of the grave, swing wide
the portals to the heavenly Paradise.

All this the precious Savior offers you freely. You
need only believe, only come with the Magi *"to worship
Him."* Approach Him penitently — not concealing, dis-

guising, disregarding, excusing, or, worse, denying your iniquities — but confessing them contritely, declaring with sorrow-crushed hearts and Christ-centered souls, "O My Savior, Thou *'Lamb of God, which takest away the sin of the world,'* have mercy on me! Grant me Thy peace!" Then your forgiveness is a divine certainty that neither human power nor aging centuries can ever alter. Here in Christ is the highest, heavenliest love, mercy, grace, compassion, that the almighty God can bestow. In addition, through faith, Jesus gives you the strength not only to resist temptation, reject evil, but also to grow in holiness, find contentment in a discontented world, peace in a war-wrecked age; the ability to fight fear and win victories over your worries.

Every time the message of Christ's mercy is proclaimed, we ought to be stunned by its fulness, overcome by the glory and grandeur of His grace. Once when the great evangelist Moody preached to the inmates of the Colorado State Penitentiary, the governor permitted him to announce at the close of his sermon, "I have a pardon here for convict ——," and he mentioned the number and name of a prisoner in the audience, a woman criminal, who, hearing of her release, fainted. It was such unexpected, undeserved joy! Yet the pardon that Christ grants you is incomparably greater, its pledge immeasurably more precious in its freedom for your soul and its forgiveness for eternity.

Now, what happens in many instances when this Gospel grace is offered? Jesus is rejected, His Word ridiculed, His cross contemptuously pushed aside! We hear a chorus of unbelief chant: "We cannot believe in your Savior!" "Christianity is contradicted by science!" "We won't accept anything we cannot understand, any doctrine the great thinkers have rejected!" How we need the Magi mind today in its reverent worship of the Christ-child! Since our Lord's infancy mighty intellects have been among the foremost in acknowledging Jesus. Christianity, far from being the hopeless refuge of ignorant and dwarfed mentalities, has been the religion of the world's leading thinkers. Take only one scientific field, the most widely effective discovery and invention of the last decades, the radio! Do you know that practically all the men who pioneered in this present-day miracle (which makes it possible to spread the Gospel more quickly, widely, and inexpensively than ever before) have been stalwart Christians? James Clerk Maxwell, classed among the greatest scientists of the nineteenth century, discovered mathematically the waves which were later to be used in radio. He was a devout Christian. Even when occupied by serious problems he had time for family devotion, regular Sunday worship, and frequent attendance at Holy Communion. An elder in the church, he had unshaken faith in our Lord's incarnation and atonement. He declared, "I think that men of science as well as other men need to learn from Christ." Sir Michael Faraday helped develop the condenser now used in radio. He, too, was an active church-member, a lay preacher, an elder in his congregation, called "a just and faithful knight of God." He freely confessed his sins and his complete confidence in Christ. Samuel Finlay Morse, inventor of the telegraph, who introduced some of the principles directly employed in bringing you this message, was a humble Christian, with unshaken reliance on his Savior and full trust in the power of prayer. Sir William Preece was one of the first to transmit messages from stations unconnected by wires, and this eminent authority, member of many learned societies, asserted, "I have never run across a single fact in science that is opposed to the teachings of the Christian religion." Profiting by his labors, William Marconi received the first wireless signals ever to be transmitted across the broad Atlantic. He declared, "Life would be truly frightening were it not for faith." He was always a church-member and died in the faith. Sir Ambrose Fleming, whose discoveries helped develop the thermionic valve (without which this broadcast would be impossible), asked all doubters: "Let me invite you to study at your leisure the records in the four gospels, . . . and you will see that nothing in the certainly ascertained facts or principles of science forbids belief in those miracles. . . . The Christian Church is not founded on fictions or nourished on delusions, . . . but on historical and actual events, . . . the greatest events which have happened in the history of the world." Reginald Fessenden — who developed an entirely new system of radio transmission, effected the first two-way trans-Atlantic short-wave telegraph service, invented the wireless telephone, secured more than 500 patents, especially involving the transmission of light, sound and electric waves — was so convinced of the Bible's truth that he devoted a large part of his life to prove the accuracy of the frequently attacked Old Testament chapters, those dealing with Noah's Flood. Plainly did that master mind write: "I have attempted to show on geological evidence that the Deluge *was* an actual, geological fact and occurred . . . exactly as described." Thus these mighty intellects which helped produce the radio: Maxwell, Faraday, Morse, Preece, Marconi, Fleming, Fessenden — follow in imposing procession, every one a Christian, convinced of Scriptural truth, loyal to the Lord Jesus. I have been able to find only one man in the entire roster of radio research leaders who discarded our faith, and he was one of the lesser lights. Yet in his diary he confessed, "This new position [of skepticism] is painful; at times I feel hopeless."

Similarly in other branches of related endeavor the

most eminent scientists have often been the most devout
Christians. The atheists, the antireligious, are frequently
the second-rate minds. Recently a distinguished St. Louis
surgeon, who does not hesitate to admit that he prays
for Christ's presence and blessing at each operation, told
me, "When unbelief can create part of a little finger,
I will be ready to consider its claims. Until then I will
bow humbly before my Savior, the Friend of sinners."

If only that modest reverence would guide all American
culture and education! Instead, however, we have traveled
far and long on dangerous roads. One of every five
children receives real Christian training. Only schools
with systematic religious instruction — like those supported
by my Church to which I again invite your boys and
girls — can have a Christ-centered curriculum. You parents ought to realize that God has been eliminated from
most education, Bible principles have been barred from
much of our modern life. The Constitution of the United
States recognizes God and His sovereignty, but often the
tendency in cultural and political circles is to discount the
divine and banish the Almighty.

Where is the humble, penitent mind of America's
yesteryear that brought many in our country to their
knees before God in remorse over their sins? Where is
the emphasis on repentance in an age with dangers ad-
mittedly greater than any since the days of Jamestown
and Plymouth? When John Adams, second President
of the United States, saw this country imperiled by the
war in Europe, he asked — and these are his words —
"that all religious congregations . . . with the deepest
humility acknowledge before God the manifold sins and
transgressions with which we are justly chargeable as
individuals and as a nation, beseeching Him at the same
time, of His infinite grace, through the Redeemer of the

world, freely to remit all our offenses and to incline us by His Holy Spirit to that sincere repentance and reformation which may afford us reason to hope." When the Civil War began, Abraham Lincoln declared, "It is the duty of nations as well as of men . . . to confess their sins and transgressions in humble sorrow, yet with assured hope that genuine repentance will lead to mercy and pardon, to recognize the sublime truth, announced in the Holy Scriptures and proved by all history, that those nations only are blessed whose God is the Lord." Underscore that in your devotion to this God-blessed country, *"Those nations only are blessed whose God is the Lord!"* and hear Lincoln continue: "We have been the recipients of the choicest blessings of Heaven; we have been preserved these many years in peace and prosperity; we have grown in numbers, wealth, and power as no other nation has ever grown. But we have forgotten God. We have forgotten the gracious hand which preserved us in peace and multiplied and enriched and strengthened us, and we have vainly imagined, in the deceitfulness of our hearts, that all these blessings were produced by some superior wisdom and virtue of our own. Intoxicated with our success, we have become too self-sufficient to feel the necessity of redeeming and preserving grace, too proud to pray to the God who made us. It behooves us then to humble ourselves before the offended Power, to confess our national sins, and to pray for clemency and forgiveness." My fellow-citizens and fellow-Christians, the people of our country, as a whole, were closer to God during the Civil War than they are now, overshadowed as our nation is with the possibility of a World War which by comparison can dwarf Lincoln's struggle. Yet where are the voices in America even in churches, pleading for a return to God? How often do you hear anything about our sins and moral responsibilities?

Instead we sit back arrogantly and pride ourselves on the American way of life. What is this American way? Is it seen in empty churches and overflowing penitentiaries? Can it be found among our 70,000,000 unchurched, our 4,000,000 criminals, in our $15,000,000,000 annual crime bill, or the masses of our destitute countrymen? Is our American way signalized by the 1,000,000 illegitimate births and abortions every year and the 1,000,000 divorces every three years? Let us realize immediately that, if we are to retain our country's blessings through the decades before us, we must have a humble, repentant spirit! "On your knees, America!" must be the cry for this crisis hour. If the Federal Reserve Bank officials this week proposed steps to stop the possibility of inflation, you will agree that we require more than reliance on dollars and cents. If the Maginot Line, called the most impregnable fortress in the world, fell with hardly a struggle, you will concur that America needs more than fortifications, as essential as our defense program is. In this momentous hour you can individually do nothing better than follow the sacred reverence of those Oriental leaders and acknowledge the Christ-child your Savior! The best you can possibly contribute to lighten this distressed day is the determination to put your own house in order, turn penitently to your Father, acknowledge your own guilt, your personal responsibility, and, bringing Christ the treasures of your faith, find in Him the salvation of your soul together with the power to work and pray for national progress.

II

ALL THE WORLD, WORSHIP HIM!

Zeal for Jesus, however, must go far beyond self and country. The visit of the Wise Men, Gentiles from distant heathen lands, was to show from Christ's infant days that

His kingdom is not restricted to one people. He is the Savior of all men. His missionaries are to go *"into all the world."* His kingdom shall embrace the very ends of the earth.

For the darkened years before us the world needs the blessed Gospel-message. Whatever the outcome of this war may be, whether the United States is dragged into the conflict — which God may prevent! — or not, a testing time lies ahead for the Savior's Church. Christianity has already received one blow after the other. A thousand church-buildings have been destroyed in England alone! Mission-fields are abandoned and restricted! The distribution of the Bible is curtailed, since three fourths of the financial support for agencies publishing the Scriptures has been cut off. The youth in a dozen foreign countries is being torn away from Christ. Economically difficult days will come, for every shell exploded, every piece of property destroyed, every life taken adds to the money burden already crushing millions of men. It seems inevitable that a social reorganization must follow the war, among both the victorious and the defeated peoples. As the one means of helping in the readjustment and bringing comfort, peace, and pardon to sorrow-swept souls, we need a wide-spread missionary campaign, dedicated to bring Christ to the nations.

Have you ever pictured what this weary world could be with Christ universally accepted? Love would rule instead of hatred, peace in place of war, cooperation rather than cutthroat competition. If every idol throne were broken and Jesus could reign in each heart, all that is ugly, criminal, destructive, would be checked, and progress promoted. The earth would be changed; for it is a truth proved throughout history that, *"if any man be in Christ, he is a new creature."* When a sinner is born again in

Jesus, he enters a new spiritual life, by which, as far as possible, he tries to follow his Savior's footsteps, live in harmony with his God, and serve his fellow-men. You skeptics and editorial writers for radical newspapers who ask me, "What can Christ and Christianity do for us?" should find the answer in the history of missions. Jesus can save your soul, and then, as a secondary blessing of His power, He can advance everything good and restrict everything evil. When James Chalmers began his work in the South Sea islands, the people he found were distressing combinations of ignorance, fear, vice, superstition, cruelty. Once while visiting a native hut, drops of liquid fell down near him from a bulky package overhead. Inquiry revealed that it contained the remains of a grandmother stored there by her savage grandchildren. But James Chalmers preached Christ to those cannibals, and on a glorious night, as he proclaimed the Gospel in their pagan temple decorated with human skulls, converts, who had been brutal man-eaters, came to him after long, serious questioning and expressed this unanimous resolution: "No more fighting! No more man-eating! We have heard the good news, and we shall strive for peace." Even Charles Darwin gave unstinted praise to the miraculous transformation of these islands wrought by the Gospel, recounting how he had seen former cannibals kneel and pray to Christ.

On the other side of the globe, Iceland, Lutheran for long centuries, with more than 99 per cent of its population church-members, has almost no jails nor police officers, no divorce nor juvenile delinquency, no unemployment nor deficit, practically no crime and, in general, none of the distressing signs that mark a people's rejection of Christ.

If you want to help make a better world, incomparably more vital, if you want to direct men to their souls' salvation, spread the Gospel! Work for Christ! Give for Christ! Testify to Christ! America is to be an arsenal for democracy throughout the world, we are told; but let those who believe in Jesus make it an arsenal also for the extension of the Savior's universal kingdom!

This broadcast, which under God's blessing has been built through your gifts and prayers, now seeks to win men far beyond the United States for Christ. Seven years ago we employed only two stations; today we use more than 260, and with the continuation of God's grace will soon take another mighty forward step in foreign broadcasting. Outside the United States and Canada our appeal "Worship the World's Savior!" is broadcast in Spanish and English in forty-one programs, long- and short-wave, in Cuba, Puerto Rico, the Dominican Republic, Costa Rica, Nicaragua, Panama, Bolivia, Chile, Colombia, Ecuador, and Uruguay. Stations on the Rio Grande River bring the message into Mexico, where the restrictions against religious broadcasting may soon be relaxed. Stations in the Philippine Islands and Shanghai, China, help us proclaim Jesus to the masses in the Far East, with audiences thousands of miles apart in war-torn China, India, New Zealand, Australia, and the islands of the Melanesian seas. The response to our broadcasting from the Spanish-speaking people in Mexico, the West Indies, Central and South America, is so encouraging that a campaign has been inaugurated to use many additional stations, employ other languages, invade new strongholds of spiritual ignorance with the promise of our Savior's pardon. This must be only the beginning, however. With your help, prayer, interest, gifts, we can send these messages around the world in scores of different languages and reach the six continents and the islands of the seven seas. We want war-torn Europe to have Christ's message, especially in the reconstruction days, which, we pray God, may soon come. Will you help us?

With belligerents constantly inventing new techniques for destroying men's lives in war, what greater task can the Church have than to devise ways of helping save their souls for peace in Christ? If the Savior's followers fail in this crisis, we shall face chaos. But they must not and will not fail, under God, if you, clergymen of America, preach the crucified Christ and every word of His truth; if you, parents of America, teach your children the saving Christ; if you, the believers in America, live the victorious Christ — if, in short, from coast to coast and from continent to continent a truly repentant people returns to its God and resolves to walk in His ways! May that resolution grip your hearts from this first Sunday of the new year until its close, for Jesus' sake! Amen.

TRUST CHRIST IN EVERY TRIAL!

"Though He slay me, yet will I trust in Him." — Job 13:15.

Jesus, Friend of Sinners, Heavenly Helper in Every Need:

Grant us all that contrite, trusting faith by which we daily look to Thee and Thy blood-sealed mercies for pardon and unfailing guidance! Since we can be more than conquerors through Thy love, endow us with the courageous trust which rejoices even under crushing sorrows! Send the Holy Spirit to all who suffer! Show Thyself the Friend of the poor, the Companion of the lonely, the Champion of the distressed, that, knowing Thee, the broken-hearted may find healing for their wounds and light in their darkness! As we behold the horrors which may descend on this generation during the overclouded years before us, remove all doubt by bringing us ever closer to Thee and the heavenly help which is ours when faith rules our hearts! Turn the frightfulness of war into advantages for Thy Church and if it be Thy will, call a halt to this destruction of human life by bestowing, although the world has not deserved it, a real, honorable peace! Bless the preaching of Thy Gospel over the earth, wherever faithful servants of Thy Kingdom, showing men sin's folly and its fearful punishment, also exalt Thy greater grace and all-redeeming love! Hear us, O Christ, and save us from ourselves and our guilt! Amen.

THROUGHOUT our war-swept world haunted men and women grope for an unfailing answer to the sorrows of modern life. While some restudy ancient, outworn superstitions, others feverishly invent creeds in the baffled attempt to solve their suffering and build happiness amid hardships. Missionaries returning from Japan report an average of one new religion each week in that country, where masses, dissatisfied with the crumble and collapse of paganism, have tried to discover new escapes from their personal pain. In Europe desperate victims of the war see a single bomb demolish their home or destroy their family, and, discontented with the cold stones of modern thought, they go far back into the records of sixteenth-century fortune-tellers for comfort concerning the future. In our own country misguided multitudes likewise search restlessly for the assurance either in hoary heresies or in spiritual innovations. A California court is trying for charges of fraud the founders of a cult which, it is claimed, promises to remove all trials and sorrows, even offering its supporters gold from a secret lake hidden in the earth's core; according to newspaper accounts a half million people have been won for its teachings.

What stark tragedy must follow blind reliance on human guess-work and stupid fraud! In this fear-filled hour give us loud, clarion-clear voices throughout the land which will warn every grief-gripped soul against the delusion of obeying deceptive teachers or priests of error-laden cults promising freedom from life's hardships. More than ever before this uncompromising cry must resound over the United States: For strength during trial, for comfort in adversity, for peace under the pressure of pain, we must go back to God and His Word, back to Christ and His Church, back to faith and its fearless power! You need to be reminded that your personal problems, your intimate sorrows, the grief that tears at your heart while the world laughs in unconcern — the weight of past, present, and future burdens will never be lightened until you turn to God through your Savior Jesus Christ. The desperate "Why?"—"Why must I suffer in this way?" "Why does God permit this shattering sorrow?" "Why this staggering loss?" "Why this desertion?" "Why this forsaken loneliness?" "Why this accident and injury?" "Why this heart condition, this tuberculosis, this cancer?" "Why this bitter bereavement and the approach of quick, inescapable death?" — that "Why, why, why?" voiced daily in your letters and asked continually by millions throughout America can be answered only in God's truth, when you come to the cross and believe that the Christ who loved you there died for you.

His all-comforting truth I present, not only to sufferers in hospitals, sanatoria, public institutions, prisons; not only to the sick and crippled, the poor and destitute, the forsaken and deserted, the heart-broken and soul-sick, but also to you, the secure, the self-sufficient, who may think that trouble will never darken your door, but who, despite learning, wealth, personal courage, may almost in a split second find yourselves crushed beneath an avalanche of misery. For comfort in life's cruelest moment, for reenforcement when you are ready to surrender, for light when everything seems dark, I point you to the Savior and say:

Trust Christ in Every Trial!

I base this promise not on my own opinion nor on any human theory, but on God's truth and, in His Scriptures, on a passage representing the highest heroism of faith despite deepest distress, the cry of afflicted Job (chapter thirteen, verse fifteen), words so sacred that we ought to bow every time we hear them — this death-defying confidence by which that sufferer says of God, "*Though He slay me, yet will I trust in Him!*"

I

BE PREPARED FOR MANY TRIALS!

Think of the besieging sorrow and the testing trials Job had endured before this cry of trusting faith left his lips! Here was a man who feared the Lord, hated evil, and walked uprightly before his Maker, who conducted family worship, offered morning sacrifices, and continually sought to keep his ten children with God. Yet he was

crushed by a series of blows such as none of you has ever
known. In the first place, he experienced the loss and
the destruction that come with war. Murderous enemy
hordes swooped down on his pasture lands, stole his cattle
and camels, massacred his men. The forces of nature
combined against him. Fire from heaven flashed over
his farmlands, struck his 7,000 sheep, and killed his herds-
men. A tornado swept in from the wilderness, destroyed
his home, and in its collapse crushed his children to death.
Has any one in this audience ever endured a comparable
ordeal? Today, at the smallest reverses, people blow out
their brains, jump from sky-scrapers, drown themselves in
rivers, suffocate themselves in garages. But not Job! When
the news came that he had lost his property and his children, he bowed down, without question or protest, and
prayed with the faith I want every one of you to have,
*"The Lord gave, and the Lord hath taken away; blessed
be the name of the Lord."*

Still his torture increased. He was overtaken by a
loathsome disease that ate his flesh and bone, covered
him with festering boils, and almost drove him mad with
its burning, itching, aching, the most terrifying and
repulsive form of leprosy, for which the doctors of that
day could offer no cure. Now, if you say, "That must
have been the limit of Job's endurance," you are wrong.
His unbroken trust was put to new tests. In his pain he
turned, as every husband should, to her whose companionship and love can share every burden — his wife. Imagine
the unspeakable grief that must have gripped Job when
his wife screamed, *"Curse God and die!"* Still he had
not reached the depths. He looked to a few lingering
friends; perhaps their sympathy could sustain him. But
they were so overwhelmed by his torment that for seven
days they sat in a circle, speechless, unable to utter a word

of comfort — a telltale picture of all worldly counsel when it is asked to heal sorrow.

Only then does Job's faith begin to waver, and he curses the day on which he was born. Soon, however, he regains his confidence in God. His possessions may be lost, his children dead, his health ruined, his home happiness destroyed, and only his breath — his very existence — remain! Nevertheless, with a heroism that I hope the Spirit will implant into your heart today, Job says in effect: If God wants the last thing I own, my life, He may have it, and I will still cling to Him. Hear this triumphant cry, ringing through the ages, *"Though He slay me, yet will I trust in Him!"*

How, you ask in awe, could Job have such immovable confidence despite all he had endured? He knew what some of you do not realize, namely, that whatever happened to him as a child of God came not by accident or the whim of fate but from the Almighty — not from His wrath but His mercy. He understood the radiant comfort which too many of you have never believed: *"Whom the Lord loveth He chasteneth."*

Without Job's faith you must view your sorrows, sickness, family trouble, money losses, repeated reverses, only as a punishment for your refusal to accept Christ's grace. If you boast that you can defy God and denounce His Church; if you have seen the Savior's hands stretched toward you but continually spurn His mercy; if once, in a God-fearing home and under Christian training, you were *for* Christ, but are now ungratefully *against* Him, accuse no one but yourself and your stubborn unbelief when afflictions are heaped upon you! There is only one explanation for grief in your life: It comes directly as God's punishment, the penalty which the Almighty both here and hereafter places on unforgiven sin. Every

time you are crushed to the earth in consequence of rejecting Christ, blame yourself! Charge your own denial of
the Lord Jesus with the agonies which leave many of you
battered and bleeding! Fall on your knees in remorse
over your sins but with the repentant trust that declares:
"I have sinned against You, my Savior, against my fellow-
men, and against myself. I am not worthy to receive
anything but Your rebuke and rejection. Be merciful to
me, and by the promise of Your blood, Your cross, and
the dark anguish of Your death forgive me!" And the
blessed Savior, whose grace draws the sinner to the cross,
will pardon you fully, freely, finally, and by His mercy
change life's wretchedness into its blessings. Then you
know that, since God loved you with the immeasurable,
incomparable love which sacrificed His own Son on the
world's gory altar at Golgotha, His only thoughts are
endless compassion for you, a life's program in which each
moment of the twenty-four daily hours is marked by
your heavenly Father's ceaseless protection of your soul.
Everything that happens to you as Christ's — and now
think of the heaviest burdens you may be called to carry —
comes from divine love, not hatred, from heavenly grace,
not anger.

Standing in faith beneath the cross, you will not be
troubled by the claim of contradiction in the fact that
God is indescribably merciful, yet you must suffer! Look
at it in this way: We are all weak, frail, faulty, easily
misled, and the Lord of grace cherishes us too much to
grant us unbroken prosperity. The human heart is so
forgetful and unthankful that often only a tinge of success, the first flush of prosperity, are required to make us
pat our own shoulders and completely lose sight of the
fact that without Christ we are miserable, envious, selfish
creatures who, were room given to our ambitions and lusts,

would destroy our own souls and wreak endless suffering on our fellow-men. Now, our heavenly Father, who gave His Son for our salvation, loves us too dearly for that; so He permits sorrows to overtake us. Unexpected reverses check and change our plans. But here is His glorious comfort: As Christ's, all this, even death itself, comes to us from His love!

You can see, then, why suffering plays a perpetual part in Christ's kingdom and why in these peace-robbed years we repeatedly preach on the text, *"We must through much tribulation enter into the kingdom of God."* Some insist that this generation will never know any real peace, that we are witnessing the first stages of another Thirty Years' War. If you know from history what those three decades of bloodshed meant to Europe, as marauding armies slashed back and forth across the continent and by their devastation stopped the clock of history for at least a century, you will pray God that men and women may have Christ to sustain them. In our country artificial prosperity, then deep poverty, may be the trend during the next years. The problems of large-scale unemployment have not been solved. War business and defense orders can offer only temporary relief. Warning voices tell us that, if the war spreads over time and territory, a new social and industrial order may rule vast sections of the globe, with repercussions producing radical changes in the United States. It is not easy to speak in protest against those who picture the future gloriously filled with achievement, progress, and higher standards of living; but who can seriously survey the multiplied perils surrounding us from without and assaulting us from within and still keep his eyes closed to the fact that dangerous days are in store for America, that only God's grace can prevent disaster for more millions than have already experienced increasing hardships? Last week the President asked for sacrifice, the self-denial which every American Christian will gladly give. But will sacrifice be enough? We ask ourselves: May there not be added much suffering, such as the Scriptures predict for the last days, when *"men's hearts"* shall fail *"them for fear"*? Let us be clear on one basic truth: Our country must expect trouble. I say this not from any economic point of view, with reference to national finances, staggering indebtedness, the question of inflation; nor do I refer to the complicated issues which war would create. I do point, however, to the moral and religious issues with which alone the Church is concerned to remind you that because masses in America have forgotten the Almighty; because much of our education and culture is godless; because many American churches have forsaken the Lord and His Word, we are producing a situation which cannot be removed by American flags in pool halls, "God Bless America" signs in taverns, or politicians singing "The Star-spangled Banner." Only a repentant America can have the assurance of Heaven's blessing.

Since we must be prepared for adversity and especially in these overclouded days restudy the Savior's command, *"If any man will come after Me, let him . . . take up his cross and follow Me,"* we must also learn the advantages of adversity. Clinging to Christ through every trial, we can make this declaration of Job's faith ours: *"He knoweth the way that I take. When He hath tried me, I shall come forth as gold."* Through Jesus the chastening hand becomes the caressing hand, our sorrows signs of love.

Some of you, however, are at the point of shouting back: "How can the ordeal through which I am now groping be of any possible benefit to me? What good can result for me if I am to lose my money? What can anything in the world ever mean if my dreams of love are shattered? What purpose can God possibly have in permitting me to suffer a nervous breakdown or battle terrifying doubts and agonies?" In homes where bereavement has brought fresh wounds some of you are saying, "He dare not apply Job's words, *'Though He slay me, yet will I trust in Him'* to us and say that death can be part of God's gracious plan."

In Christ's name I will dare to do that and more. Through Jesus your sufferings are purifying, remedial, restorative. What seems to be an unbearable blow becomes unlimited mercy. When the British artist Thornhill was painting a picture under the dome of Saint Paul's Cathedral in London (which recently was barely saved from destruction by bombing), he stepped backward for a better view of his work. It was a dangerous step, for it took him near an unguarded edge of the high scaffold and might have cost his life, had it not been for a friend, who, fearing the artist would lose his balance if suddenly warned of his precarious position, quickly threw a wet paint-brush at the finished picture. Thornhill was dismayed by his friend's action and could not fathom his purpose, until later he learned that the smear on his painting brought him away from the edge of the scaffolding and helped save his life. This illustrates, in a crude, yet true-to-life manner, the way our loving Father deals with those who are His in Christ. Like Thornhill, we are perplexed when the things for which we yearn and strive are suddenly marred, until we see God's high purpose and realize that He has used afflictions to save our lives or, more important, to rescue our souls. Even if we cannot understand on earth, we shall be able to fathom the Lord's unsearchable ways when we have full knowledge in heaven. It is marvelous grace when God often permits us to discover the answer to that restless "Why?" but it is greater grace that for every adversity we can have the Savior's assurance, *"What I do thou knowest not now, but thou shalt know hereafter."*

If your husband has left you, try to believe that this may be part of a blessed plan for you, which ultimately will help produce repentance in him. Don't charge God with unfairness if you have been prevented from marrying and having a home of your own. By faith you can be just as happy and useful unmarried. As your heavenly Father's child you know that *"all things work together for good to them that love God."* Perhaps you are being spared the multiplied agonies of a maladjusted marriage. Many of you can testify that protracted illness is often a means by which God produces spiritual health. You may have lost your business so that you would not lose your soul! Even war's horror can serve a helpful purpose if proud nations are humbled before God; and if from this turmoil of ruined cities, ruined churches, ruined morals, ruined men and women, we can, through contrition and trust in God, build better than we have in the past, these millions of lives will not have been lost in vain nor the engulfing hardships endured without blessing. Pray God for His benediction, for a wide, repentant return to His mercy! Pray God for His help, without which we can do nothing!

In a textile factory, where cloth with intricate designs and decorative pictures is made, spools with many threads of different quality, color, thickness, and material are fed into a complicated machine. You cannot understand how exquisitely designed cloth is fashioned from these varied, separate threads. Yet look on the other side of the machine, and there you see a flawlessly woven design! Between these spools and the finished texture is the heart of the mechanism, which, unseen by you, produces the artistic tapestry. Will you not believe that, if an automatic loom can shape disconnected threads, many of dark and somber hues, into a beautiful pattern, the God of all power and love can take the detached, contradictory forces in your life, the sorrows and the joys, the black moments as well as the light, and weave them into the fabric of glorious certainty in Christ?

This blessing of affliction is so complete through Jesus that in the eyes of faith even death, no matter how unexpected and unfair it may seem to us, comes from divine love. Christians are often disturbed by the unqualified ring of Job's triumphant *"Though He slay me, yet will I trust in Him,"* and some preachers have sought to explain away the full force of these words. Let us accept them as they read. Should God take his life, so Job exalts, even this would be evidence of His mercy, additional reason to trust Him. Nor is Job alone in expressing this truth. I have told the students at our Seminary that as future ministers of Christ their faith and resolution must be satisfied with nothing less than complete dedication to God which declares, *"Though He slay me, yet will I trust in Him."* Every prophet of God who has been struck by the stones of hatred and bigotry, every martyr who entered the blood-stained Roman arenas, every true Gospel missionary tortured by pagan brutality, must have said in one form or another, "Even if devotion to my God brings me death, *'yet will I trust in Him!'* " The Savior Himself lived and died these words: *"Though He slay me, yet will I trust in Him!"* When He hung on the cross, broken not only by the torture of the crucifixion, the burning of His five wounds, the exposure, thirst, fever, and bodily agony, but weighed down by an incomparably greater anguish, the hellish heaviness of all sin, God then *"spared not His own Son but delivered Him up for us all."* Not once did Christ, innocent, yet suffering as the whole world through its heaped centuries has never suffered, lift His voice in protest or charge God with cruelty. For a moment that disconsolate "Why?" pierces the rumble of Calvary as His parched lips plead, *"My God, My God, why hast Thou forsaken Me?"* but that was followed by the cry of victorious resignation, *"Father, into Thy hands I commend My spirit."* His last words are the triumph of exulting trust, *"Though He slay me, yet will I trust in Him!"*

As faith increases strength for life's trials, so God can gloriously enrich His children through death. Pain-racked Job recognized that truth; his faith in the coming Deliverer triumphed. *"I know that my Redeemer liveth and that He shall stand at the Latter Day upon the earth. And though after my skin worms destroy this body, yet in my flesh shall I see God."* If, when you breathe your last, you, too, commend your soul to God through Christ, you will see Jesus face to face, and your death, far from being cold, ugly, terrifying, can be God's supreme blessing. I have often thought that, if heaven could have any regrets — we know, of course, that in its perfection it cannot — most of us, enraptured by the blessing of beholding our Triune God, would feel regret over every day of earthly life which kept us from His glory.

Death may also help bring soul-life to others. Has it not frequently happened that parents who lived in God-forgetful carelessness were brought to their senses and on their knees in grief when their only child was called home to Christ? Those who have thus been fortified by faith in Him who alone is *"the Way, the Truth, and the Life* can adapt Job's declaration, *"Though He slay me, yet will I trust in Him,"* by asserting, "God's love and wisdom has employed even death for the highest purpose — the return of my lost soul to the Savior!"

II

BE STRONG IN TRUSTING FAITH!

God grant you whole-souled reliance on Jesus! When John Paton, Christ's ambassador to the South Sea Islands, was translating the Bible into the language of New Hebrides, he searched long but futilely for a word expressing "faith" and "trust." One day a worker, visiting the missionary after a hard day's labor, leaned on a chair and said in his own tongue, "Oh, I am so tired; I feel I must lean my whole weight on this chair." That was what Paton wanted. "Praise God," he said, "I have my word," and he translated, "*'God so loved the world that He gave His only-begotten Son, that whosoever' leans his whole weight 'on Him should not perish but have everlasting life.'*" Lean your whole weight on the Lord Jesus, and with Saint Paul you will be able to "*rejoice*" in afflictions!

If trusting God blindly and unfalteringly along the steep paths of suffering seems difficult, turn to Christ! He not only sanctifies our suffering; He also lightens our burdens and clears the way before us. It is told of good King Wenceslaus of Bohemia that one winter's night he went barefoot through a raging snow-storm to pray in the royal chapel. His servant tried to follow him, but the drifts were high and heavy, and soon he began to sink exhausted. The king directed the weakened man to walk exactly behind him, to place his feet into the very footsteps which he, the king, had made. By a much higher truth Jesus, our King, has blazed the way for us from cross to crown, and the path of sorrows along which we may be led has been clearly marked by the wounded feet of God's own Son. A strong consolation in adversity is the assurance that, since Jesus sustained such deep sorrows, His heart can sympathize with us. Nothing can ever assail you that has not assaulted Him. Suffering of body, mind, and soul, the loss of every possession, rejection by enemies, desertion by friends, ridicule, scorn, and hatred, this Jesus suffered to lighten the blows which descend on your life and turn them into blessings. When everything else fails, when family ties are broken, when the love of husband or wife is chilled in death, when friends forsake you and you try to brace yourself against the onrush of new anguish, remember that in Christ, God is at your side, and He says, *"I will never leave thee nor forsake thee."*

In His merciful power God can bring an end to your trials and, if it be His will, restore your losses, gloriously compensating you for each moment's misery. Job received twofold for all he had lost. Health, long life, riches, friends, beautiful children, were given him by divine direction. God can do even more for you! But show your trust by praying, *"Thy will be done!"* If Saint Paul made a prison-cell ring at midnight with hymns of praise; if Jesus, only a few hours before the ordeal of the ages in Gethsemane, sang a hymn, let your resolution, *"Yet will I trust in Him!"* overshine every pain! Associated with our Library for the Blind, whose facilities I again offer the sightless, free of charge, is a dear Christian soul who, deprived of her eyesight, experiences more happiness than many others possessing full use of their senses. She testifies that blindness has been her blessing because it enables her to serve the Lord in a greater capacity than she might ever have enjoyed otherwise. As man's extremity is God's opportunity, so your trial may be your triumph. Moses, barred from the Promised Land, wrote his books on desert wanderings and foreign soil. David, man-hunted, composed some of his vibrant psalms in Judah's stony wilderness. A few of Saint Paul's epistles were dictated in a Roman prison. The last New Testament book, Saint John's

Revelation, was finished while that exiled apostle languished on the lonely island of Patmos. Who knows, perhaps the crush of sorrow may press down on you, so that you can write, in words or in actions, your book of faith, *"Yet will I trust in Him"?* Florence Nightingale organized the hospitals of England from her invalid bed. Louis Pasteur, Christian genius, to whose discoveries many in this audience, humanly speaking, owe their lives, was paralyzed on one side and threatened by apoplexy when he did his epochal work. Thank God, if He permits you to use the time of your trials for similar triumphs!

Trust your heavenly Father to limit and restrain your afflictions, for He has promised that we shall not be required to endure more pain than we can bear. His merciful wisdom will use your sorrows in opening your heart and hands more widely for your afflicted fellow-men! "Sympathy" really means "suffering together with others," and once you have endured the agony which racks the minds and bodies of others, your own love is deepened and intensified. God can employ continued hardships in producing penitence, humility, patience, deeper devotion, higher gratitude for your benefit! Commit your destiny to Him, and He will transform fires of affliction into lamps lighting your way to heaven. There — blessed promise! — we shall know that *"the sufferings of this present time are not worthy to be compared with the glory which shall be revealed in us."*

What more do we need than this faith? Beholding the cross and our crucified Savior, raising our hands in the oath of renewed allegiance to Him, we cry out in a world filled to overflowing with grief, a world of unbelief and misery, a world of attacks on God and assaults on His truth: "That crucified Sufferer, that Man of Sorrows, is my God and my Savior! I give myself to Jesus with renewed faith and reliance, since He is my only Redeemer and help. If it be God's will, and for my chastening, let days of darkness and weary years of war come; let hell's hatred rage against me as I have never known it; let death take this earthly life, I will still say, " *'Though He slay me, yet will I trust in Him!'* " God grant every one of us that all-triumphant trust for Jesus' sake! Amen.

———————

FAITH FOR THE FAMILY!

*"Daily in the Temple and in every house
they ceased not to teach and preach Jesus
Christ!"* — Acts 5:42

God of Mercy and Might:

We commend unto Thy loving care particularly the nation's
families. In these dark days, reechoing with wars present and
rumors of wars approaching, we humbly beseech Thee, almighty
Father, if it be Thy will, to keep the terrors of bloodshed from
our shores! Oh, that we could truly thank Thee for Thy vigilant
care by day and night which has watched over our dwellings and
averted disaster! As we read of the ruined homes in the war-torn
nations across the sea, we acknowledge Thy great goodness in sparing us such horrors. Give this wounded world a just peace! Let
our hearts rejoice through faith in Thy Son, the Lord Jesus Christ!
Show us daily and with ever-increasing clearness how much we individually need the Savior for the cleansing of our souls, how our
families require His presence for the strengthening in every weakness
and sorrow! Send us Thy Spirit that throughout the land many
groping for light in sin's darkness, for comfort in the apparent
hopelessness of affliction, may receive the Lord Jesus for themselves
and welcome Him into their homes! We ask this abiding family
blessing in His precious name. Amen.

FOR the first time in modern warfare battle-lines are
drawn at the very doors of civilians. There is no
trench-fighting, no infantry nor cavalry clash in England
and Germany today; instead, hundred thousands of destroyed homes. The worst that twentieth-century military
technique can devise now brings its devastation to the
tenements and cottages of the common people. When you
see pictures of destitute grandmothers and wide-eyed orphans weeping before the blackened shells and smoldering
walls of their homes; when you read how unnumbered
families night after night sleep in shelters and subways,
how in our own country, preparing for hostilities, people

are being instructed in air-raid drills, remember that the highest price for war is paid, not by statesmen who declare it, newspaper men who publicize it with inflammatory editorials, columnists and radio commentators who support it; not by preachers who are unwilling to send starving children food, but would send our troops to Europe; nor by international bankers and blood profiteers (we had too many in the last war, and human nature has not changed). No, the highest cost of conflict (I mean any war, right or wrong) is paid especially by the homes of the masses, by gold-star mothers, by fathers whose property is bombed to bits, sons, hideously maimed and crippled, children buried in mass graves.

It is easy to make war attractive, and dictators are past masters in this deception; but before we travel too far along their path, we should erect somewhere in this country a peace pavilion with exhibits to strip war of its glamor and reveal how militarism can destroy family life. As you read of bombed, homeless, destitute sufferers, no matter how repeatedly world leaders reject the proposal for an armistice, pray God on your knees for a just, honorable, cooperative peace that will end aggression and place the belligerents shoulder to shoulder for reconstruction!

More than the absence of war is essential for home happiness, since prosperity can likewise bring a destructive decline in family morality. Two days ago the Agricultural Bureau predicted that the next twelve months will be the most prosperous period in American history — far exceeding even 1929. This means that we shall face new assaults on Christian marriage. With increased wages, overtime work, wider employment, come more secret, sordid affairs, more broken marriages.

What, then, do our homes need for war — which God may prevent! — or for peace? As a citizen I answer:

Stronger marriage and divorce laws, financial aid for deserving engaged couples, a movement to stem the declining birth-rate, a check on immoral motion-pictures, filthy films, sex magazines, and suggestive broadcasts. As a Christian, however, I say: The American families should have the Lord Jesus to preserve faithfulness between husband and wife, provide a loving, constructive influence for children, offer domestic harmony and a divine solution for family problems; but first, last, and forever uppermost, American households should have Jesus Christ, the Redeemer and the Sanctifier of the home, to grant each member His blood-sealed promise of heaven.

Today I offer, under the Holy Spirit's guidance, as

FAITH FOR THE FAMILY

loyal trust in our Lord. That Savior can help us and our homes today, just as in the early Church when, so our text testifies, *"Daily in the Temple and in every house they ceased not to teach and preach Jesus Christ!"* (Acts, chapter five, verse forty-two.)

I

FIRST-CENTURY APOSTLES BROUGHT CHRIST TO THE HOME

An outstanding miracle of history is the growth of the Apostolic Church. If you want proof of the Gospel's power, see how those first-century groups flourished in the face of deadly opposition. Their members were man-hunted, martyred, murdered. It cost something to be a Christian in those days! One had to pay a price — sometimes even life — for acknowledging Jesus! Yet, the more determined the priests to wipe out this new faith and the sharper the sword of pagan persecution, the stronger became the Church, the wider its boundaries.

How could those humble Christians thus triumph over

tyrannical empires and ruthless religions? They listed no multimillionaires who financed their work. They never thought of raising money for Christ as modern congregations often do, by raffles, lotteries, bazaars, buncos, and — this is the latest — by sponsoring championship prize-fights! They numbered no lobbyists, politicians, public figures, social leaders in their membership; no famous musicians or acclaimed soloists beautified their service. They did not have even churches in which they could meet. But what heroic faith they had! They were guided by the Holy Spirit! They trusted God!

Because these primitive Christians built no assembly places, they turned their homes into churches and brought Christ's message directly to the family. After the Resurrection New Testament leaders made it their practice to gather families and friends in any available home; and, with the same spirit, throughout history, whenever Christians were persecuted, they rallied in their dwellings, no matter how small or despised, and by the Spirit's blessing transformed the chambers into glorious temples of Christ. That is happening now in England, where believers whose churches have been bombed are finding spiritual strength in home worship. Similarly, after this broadcast is over, every father who has neglected his responsibilities as priest to his own family should resolve: With God's help I will make my house a church of Christ!

The apostles followed the same plan in our text. They had been prohibited from preaching the Gospel but deliberately refused to stop. While I have the opportunity, let me urge you for the stormy years ahead to repeat with these first witnesses to Jesus: *"We ought to obey God rather than men."* If in your own home you are forbidden to confess the Savior, God wants you to disobey! If you pastors find yourselves in denominational groups where the higher-ups demand that you stop publishing the full message of atonement and the plain denunciation of sin, in Christ's name refuse, and God will compensate you in heaven for any loss you may sustain! If ever in this blessed nation, founded by Christians and built on the privilege of free speech and free worship, it should occur, particularly under the stress of war hysteria, that blasphemous hands are laid on the holy Gospel or restrictions placed on its proclamation, let us declare with these first witnesses, *"We ought to obey God rather than men."* It will cost much to do this, far too much perhaps for many Americans; but I pray God to awaken the first-century fire and loyalty in this spiritually anemic age that calls for a vital transfusion of Christian courage.

With unbroken zeal the apostles went from house to house, not only because they had no larger meeting-places, but also because they realized the basic importance of domestic ties. Win the whole family for Jesus! Start with the children! Convert the parents! Bring the home to Christ and Christ to the home! Have the household read the Scriptures and daily turn to God in prayer! — that was the apostles' program. They recognized that, if the family, the divinely ordained unit of human society, could be enlisted for the Lord Jesus, the Church would have a powerful support for its work.

Besides, they knew that homes required spiritual guidance. Then, as always, even the Christian family circle, where the binding tie of love should be the strongest, was often marred by selfishness. In those early households, now so far from us that we do not see their weaknesses, husbands were sometimes unfaithful, wives neglectful of their duties, children rebellious toward their parents. God was often banished under the reign of lust. More than anything else every one in those first-century families needed to know sin's destructive terror and secure the power to repel its attacks.

In addition, the Christians visited by the apostles were prevalently poor. These first ministers of Christ did not hesitate to enter the meanest hovels (what an example for present-day preachers!) nor speak to slaves, outcasts, and all who groped for a sustaining light in the gloom of many sorrows.

So by divine providence we find the apostles not only at the Temple each day, but particularly *"in every house."* They went from family to family. "With what?" we ask. If you think they preached politics, social reform, new methods of home-life, sex facts, domestic budgets, and finances; if you imagine they promised their hearers an easy religion, with the vision of comfort ahead, you are wrong. These apostolic messengers to the home, whether in Jerusalem, Joppa, Philippi, Colossae, Athens, or Rome, had only one theme. Our Scripture expresses it in this way: *"In every house they ceased not to teach and preach Jesus Christ."* Their Savior's love was so inexhaustible, His mercy so magnificent, His blessings so immeasurable, that they found time for nothing else. The Lord Jesus had so completely become All in all to them that they lived for a single purpose: to help spread His kingdom. They started where Gospel sermons should begin, with every man's need of a Deliverer from the terrifying penalty of unpardoned sin. Wherever they went, to whomever they spoke, whatever else they may have said, they always told the small household groups what I now say to you in this mighty international audience: Repent! Confess your sins! Get right with God!

For that reconciliation they pointed their hearers to the cross and the crucified Redeemer, the one altar and sacrifice by which the sins of men in all centuries and continents can

be removed forever. They preached — and these broadcasts try to echo their sermons — *"Jesus Christ"* as the
divine Savior, Son of the Almighty and Son of the humble
Virgin. To them, as I hope to you also, Christ was
nothing less than "very God of very God," together with
the Father and the Spirit the one true Lord. They exalted
"Jesus Christ," not primarily as the divine Teacher, Leader,
Master, Guide, Example. He was that for them, of course,
but much more; first He was their Savior from sin,
Deliverer from death, Redeemer from the ruin of hell.
They preached *"Jesus Christ"* as their only atonement.
To them — and may you agree! — the Christian faith was
not one of many creeds deserving men's attention. In these
hearthside gatherings they never stated what millions hear
in many fashionable churches today, that you can believe
anything you want as long as you follow some kind of
creed; that Christians, Jews, pagans, are merely taking
different routes to the same goal. Shortly before the
record of our text Peter had declared: *"Neither is there
salvation in any other; for there is none other name under
heaven given among men whereby we must be saved."*
They proclaimed *"Jesus Christ"* as the *merciful* Savior
who offered His heaven-granting grace freely, unconditionally, as the *complete* Savior, whose blood can cleanse
every iniquity and purify every sinner. They revealed
"Jesus Christ" as the *assured* Savior, whose redemption
is not a trial-and-error theory, a hit-or-miss promise, a per-
haps-if-and-maybe theory, but positive, unquestionable
truth; *"Jesus Christ"* as the *all-transforming* Savior, who
through His Holy Spirit makes His followers new creatures
with a reborn love for everything right, true, helpful.
Christ, the whole, redeeming, transforming Christ, and
nothing but Christ — that was the center of their message.

Note also that *"they ceased not to teach and preach*

Jesus." Sound doctrine, clear instruction, personal guidance — that was their method. Too many call this old-fashioned today. For solid teaching they substitute wild speculation, and in these hours when the clouds of sorrow hang over our land, far too much time is spent — always at the expense of the pure Gospel — in expounding favorite but unfounded theories of prophecy, ill conceived and ill executed. Nor did the apostles rely on emotional preaching and seek to sway only the feelings of their hearers. By slow, methodical instruction they worked for a firmly rooted faith, by which the believers could defend the Lord Jesus and confidently exult, *"I* KNOW *whom I have believed."* We must deeply regret that often churches neglect this apostolic method of teaching and sometimes admit as members people who actually have not grasped what Christianity is. While they look down condescendingly on churches which demand clear-cut catechism instruction, the memorizing of God's Word, a public examination in Bible doctrine, they are satisfied with a superficial smattering or a vague emotional agreement.

With such marvelous loyalty to Christ, then, the apostles went from house to house, as the New Testament records show, always with this message to the family circles and its friends: *"Repent ye!" "Believe on the Lord Jesus Christ!" "Be baptized in His name!" "Whatsoever ye do in word or deed, do all in the name of the Lord Jesus!"*

II

THE TWENTIETH-CENTURY FAMILY NEEDS THE SAVIOR

No long argument is required to show clearly that twentieth-century homes should follow the Savior's appeal, *"Repent!" "Believe on the Lord Jesus Christ!" "Be baptized!"* Ours is an age of advancing immorality, uncleanness, and pagan vices. To read some modern magazines, and not only the ten-cent sort, but the fifty-cent kind with two thirds of a million circulation, particularly among American men, one gets the inescapable impression from the lewd pictures, dirty jokes, and suggestive stories that today America laughs at purity, glorifies adultery and fashionable prostitution. Formerly France was considered the headquarters for vile, pornographic printed material. This unholy stigma has now been removed, and Vichy authorities have taken stringent precautions to prevent its return. The spirit of lechery has crossed the ocean to invade our shores, supporting in a marked measure certain vicious conditions in American family life.

Survey homes throughout the States, and you will find seven deadly family sins. Here they are: Number 1: Incontinence before marriage. Judge Lindsey claims that "more than 40 per cent of the boys violate the moral code before they are past school age, and at least 75 per cent of our girls do so." That is wrong. More than one of every four girls is still a virgin when she leaves high school! However, we dare not close our eyes to the shocking menace before us, nor put the entire blame on these young people! By example and negligence their elders have made immorality easy. The fear of dire results has been reduced by materials accessible to your sons and daughters in thousands of drug stores, shops, department stores, even from street venders. The dread of disease is destroyed by the advance of medical science, so that for the first time in our history young people have the means of escaping consequences. Do you doubt, then, that with popular entertainment, fashionable but questionable morals, and public attitudes condoning illicit relations, with college professors and sociologists championing them and even urging premarital experiences, our young people should be given reenforced help in guarding the most precious human possession they have, their purity and honor?

Family Sin Number 2: Unfaithfulness after marriage, usual consequence of premarital impurity. Again the spirit of our age often smiles at secret affairs, picturing people as smart and sophisticated when they deceive their husbands or wives and succeed in leading double lives.

Family Sin Number 3: Divorce, with wedlock regarded as such a temporary arrangement that third, fourth, fifth, and even more multiple marriages are no longer rare. It is not surprising that last week the newspapers printed the charges of a Utah authoress who pictured the old Mormon polygamy (the Brigham-Young-with-his-twenty-five-wives kind) as more decent and honest than the hypocrisy and collusion of modern divorces.

Family Sin Number 4: The avoidance of parenthood and the hatred of childhood. This may take the hideous form of prenatal murder — is abortion anything less than murder? — or it may be the sinful but wide-spread practice of artificial birth control that regards children as burdens instead of blessings, only often to bring heaped misery. It may be — and I am told this is on the increase — the return to the old pagan sin of voluntary sterilization. These practices have helped make the American birth-rate drop 60 per cent since 1810, brought the size of the average family, including the parents, down to 3.8 — a new all-time low, and caused other indescribable sorrows and loss.

Family Sin Number 5: Drunkenness and cruelty. Our broadcast loses some financial support every time I touch on this subject. People connected with breweries say we are Prohibitionists. This is not true, for we know what the Bible teaches concerning alcohol. But we also recall Scripture's repeated warning against overindulgence; and we have read too many letters from spirit-broken, beaten wives and cowering children, trembling before a drunken brute of a father, not to use the radio in the effort to put the fear of God into their hearts.

Family Sin Number 6: Quarrel and strife, the dividing of the house against itself, the sullen opposition between husbands and wives who ought to live together in the closest devotion, the changing of affection to anger, love to hatred, harmony to hellish discord.

Finally, Family Sin Number 7: The friction and enmity between parents and children, sons and daughters selfishly forgetting, deserting, and despising those who gave them life and sustained them; fathers and mothers so completely wrapped up in their own selfish interests that their children are neglected and deprived of the essential parental companionship.

These transgressions invade the American home today, and I picture them to you, not primarily because they provoke bodily suffering and mental misery, constituting a menace to good government and national welfare, but especially because these family failings, often associated with the rejection of Christ, bring down God's wrath, usually in this life, always, if they are not forgiven, in the next. The wages of all sins — domestic sins not excepted — is death, everlasting separation from God.

What do our homes need, then? Doctors on domestic questions answer, "Easier divorces, trial, temporary, or experimental marriages, vacations from wedded life, education in the physical, financial, social side of the home." In the name of Jesus, however, I offer you God's prescription for every family ailment, the supreme necessity of the American home: a firm faith in the Savior. A thousand times more than anything else give us the teaching and preaching of our Lord, which strengthened the first Christian dwellings for adversities greater than any we may face.

With this cry, "Christ for the family!" every one of you who still spurns the Savior's love should realize that this is a personal appeal to find forgiveness through penitent faith in Him. I have been preaching to some of you for eight years, and in each sermon I have asked you to accept Christ. You cannot expect God to repeat His invitation indefinitely. You do not know whether you will even hear another Gospel-message. In this moment — and I pray many will make this a day of decision for Christ — Jesus Himself is knocking at the door of your heart and home eager to gain entrance. Don't stifle that inner urge (it comes from the Holy Spirit) which would lead you to welcome Jesus! Let me send one of my fellow-pastors who, as he brings the Gospel across your threshold, can say, "*This day is salvation come to this house!*" If you have never been baptized, then God directs this appeal particularly to you, marked personally with your name, into your home wherever you are and whatever that dwelling may be, "*Repent ye and be baptized, for the remission of your sins.*"

We also ask Christian pastors to follow the apostolic example in bringing Christ to the home. Definite records in the past (I am thinking of Richard Baxter, Thomas Boston, and others who built their churches by building the homes of their members) show that family worship can offer powerful support for the Gospel. If only half the interest sometimes put into theatricals and the social side of the congregation could be directed to strengthening the spiritual foundation of the home, we would experience an outpouring of blessing such as churches in America have never experienced.

Fathers of America, this is your task, or rather, your sacred privilege, this teaching and proclaiming Christ in the family. Therefore, if some of you have turned from

Jesus, for the sake of your own souls and those of your children who may be kept from the Savior by your destructive example, ask God to forgive and restore you! Push everything else aside — I do not care whether it is business, politics, culture, education, or service to those outside the home — and do what God expects of every father: bring up your sons and daughters in the nurture and admonition of the Lord! Lead them closer to Christ! Teach them the Scriptures! Build up the family altar! Become the messenger of God to your own dear ones! What a terrible thought that a child of yours may be lost forever because *you* did not show it the way to the Savior and by your unholy living and blasphemous sneering kept it from God! Jesus may have been thinking of your sin when He wrote: *"Take heed that ye despise not one of these little ones. . . . Whoso shall offend one of these little ones which believe on Me, it were better for him that a millstone were hanged about his neck and that he were drowned in the depth of the sea."*

You mothers, into whose hearts and hands the almighty and all-wise Creator has placed great power and blessing, follow the apostle's instruction *"Learn first to show piety at home."* Take as your example Lois and Eunice, Timothy's mother and grandmother, who taught the illustrious disciple the Gospel truth in his early youth and helped pave the way for his glorious career in Christ! Learn of Lydia, who opened her whole house to their preaching! Understand that God has given you special endowments, so that your mother love will help put first things first, see that the family finds time for worship, that the little ones learn the Bible and selected hymns, that your household never forgets to thank God for His blessings at meals, to start or close each day by invoking His protection!

Children of America, Christ wants you particularly!

Through this broadcast He is calling you to enlist your youthful zeal, determination, optimism, energies, to make your home His church, your family His congregation. The world also calls you, trying to win you away from Christ or, if you have never acknowledged Him, to keep you from Him. May the Holy Spirit descend with a double measure of His power to convict and convince you, make you valiant disciples, who before anything else will try to win your family for the Savior! As you plan your own home, resolve that your life partner will be a disciple of Jesus, who can worship with you in the same true faith. Avoid mixed marriages! Plan married life with Christ and for Christ!

Come then what may, as dark clouds gather on the unformed horizon of America's tomorrow, we can all have peace in our hearts and, thank God, in our homes, if fathers and mothers, together with sons and daughters, looking only to Jesus, declare: "God helping us, in prosperity and adversity, in peace or war, in health or sickness, we will not cease '*to teach and preach Jesus Christ,*' our only Savior!" God strengthen you to give yourselves wholly to Him! Amen.

IS OUR AMERICAN YOUTH SAFE?

"Is the young man Absalom safe?" — 2 Samuel 18:29

Our God, Lord of Light and Love:

Teach us all to understand in a personal, intimate way that, since Thou art our Father through Jesus Christ and we Thy redeemed sons and daughters, our earthly homes should be blessed by a holy, happy relation between parents and children! For Jesus' sake and by the reconciliation of His cross forgive us our transgressions, particularly the family sins and the deeper evils which break Thy laws of purity. O Father, behold with Thy sustaining grace our American youth, surrounded by concealed temptations, facing a future heavy with increased problems! Show them that through faith, the study of Thy Word, the power of prayer, they have a heavenly defense against every treacherous enticement! Bring them to Jesus, their Savior, for pardon, guidance, strength! How reassuring that Thy Son in His limitless devotion loves every young person; that He was young Himself and understands youth's problems! Keep our families safe in and for Christ! We ask it in His blessed name. Amen.

I MAKE no apology for devoting this message to the nation's youth. Never before have our country, its churches, and homes more imperatively needed a mighty group of Christ-consecrated, Christ-strengthened, Christ-exalting young men and women than in these days of impending crisis. Never before has the love for American youth demanded so urgently that we give every means of helpful guidance to equip these young people for that complicated tomorrow in which they will be not only the builders, but also the burden-bearers, weighted down by the heaviest load any generation has ever received from its predecessor. If this country is maneuvered into war, youth will pay with its life and limbs, its blood and broken bodies. If we keep out of war, youth will pay the largest part of the $65,000,000,000 soon to be set as the new debt limit, plus the bewildering billions which, it is predicted, will still be added. Christian youth will pay for the sins of its fathers in opposition and persecution, as it strives to spread Christ's kingdom and valiantly proclaims the cross in a hard-hearted, unrepentant age.

With radical forces working overtime and double time to enlist the rising generation, we would be untrue to the responsibilities imposed by this mighty coast-to-coast broadcast if we would not, with all the power God gives us, seek to win America's young manhood and womanhood for Christ and with His leadership guide our youth safely through the perils of this uncharted future.

What issue could be more pointed and pressing than our question for today:

Is Our American Youth Safe?

Are your sons and daughters safe in their bodies and souls, safe for heaven and safe from hell? Are the young men and women of America shielded from the temptations surrounding them, safe from the unworthy coaxings assailing them from within? Are the boys and girls of the country protected against the faith-destroying forces, as vicious as the brutality of Herod, who murdered the innocents at Bethlehem? What question indeed could be more timely than this searching inquiry suggested by the Bible itself, in the impressive passage chosen as today's text, Second Samuel, chapter eighteen, verse twenty-nine, where the father heart of King David, crushed by fears for his son, cries, *"Is the young man Absalom safe?"*

I

MANY OF OUR YOUNG PEOPLE ARE IN DEADLY PERIL

In this eighteenth chapter, which should be read repeatedly in every home, discussed in every church, studied by every young person, we meet the tragic story of David's third and thankless son who had treacherously undermined his father's reign and planned a large-scale uprising against him. Because the king does not know where rebellious Absalom is or in what condition he may be, he asks a breathless messenger, not for a report on the victory just won nor for a list of the losses sustained by the loyal troops and the enemies. He sweeps these mighty national issues aside to ask, *"Is the young man Absalom safe?"*

Would it not likewise be true of many parents today that if God should now ask them, "Where are your children? Are they safe?" they could not answer. Too frequently fathers and mothers do not know where their children are, what they are doing, with whom they associate. The keeper of any city morgue will tell you that whenever a fatal midnight automobile accident occurs and the bodies of unidentified young people are left in his charge; whenever a night-club burns and charred corpses are placed in rows to await recognition, terror-stricken parents soon crowd the morgue and in dread-filled anguish draw back the shroud-sheets to see whether their own child lies there, cold and silent in death. As David's only question to his messenger was not: "Has our army won?" "What strategy did General Joab follow?" but, *"Is the young man Absalom safe?"* so for unnumbered parents in our country the subjects of prime importance are not: "How will the war turn out?" "Will the United States be drawn in?" — These vast issues are overshadowed by that disconsolate lament: "If only I knew where my son is!" "Oh, that I could be sure my daughter is safe!"

Had Absalom understood long before this the pain he planted in his father's heart, and had he repented, how different his life might have been! Similarly you young men and women away from home should relieve your parents of the heavy anxiety many of you are causing!

Even if your fathers and mothers know where you are, an unmistakable restlessness often comes with separation. Remember that, especially you men in the naval, military, and air-training camps throughout the land! At this moment your God-fearing fathers and mothers are thinking of you, praying for you, asking our heavenly Father not only to make you brave soldiers, good sailors, skilful air-pilots, but also to strengthen you for life's hardest battle: the defeat of evil. We are glad to hear that barracks' radios and ships' receivers are regularly tuned to this broadcast. In the name of your Christian parents and in the name of Jesus Christ, their Savior and yours, I ask you to continue this public testimony as you *"fight the good fight of faith"* and stand up for Jesus. When President Garfield attended college, he camped one night on a mountain top with a group of fellow-students who sang college songs and generally enjoyed themselves. Before retiring, Garfield took a Testament from his pocket and explained, "Boys, it is my custom to read a chapter before going to bed and offer a prayer. Shall we have this together?" A hush fell over the gathering, and every one remained, listening intently. When it was over, there was not one lad whose esteem for Garfield had not been heightened by this loyalty to Christ. Soldiers, sailors, aviators, defenders of America all, with such faith in your hearts, your parents will not have to ask, as David did, *"Is the young man . . . safe?"* Without that faith you will never know the agony you have caused.

You may want to know why David lost track of his son. For the same reason, I suppose, which frequently estranges parents and children today! David had spoiled Absalom, and the pampered youth became a haughty, overbearing young man. — Don't let any one tell you that discipline, sometimes severe discipline, is not necessary for proper child-training! Our advanced age, of course, likes to speak of self-determination. Certain psychologists warn that parents who punish their children retard their individuality, destroy their independence. Some forms of progressive education have the motto, "Let the child do as it pleases!" See where this has taken us, this frowning on discipline, this granting the whims of headstrong children! Juvenile delinquency figures are on the increase; we have more youthful criminals and larger prisons, despite the fact that our schools are better equipped than ever. But the most wide-spread loss is sustained by the home itself, where untrained, undisciplined sons and daughters lose respect for their own parents and in time of stress even accuse them of neglect.

Through David's misplaced favoritism his son Absalom, of extraordinary appearance and physical endowment, fell into evil ways. He soon sank so low that he plotted to snatch the crown from his own father and seize the kingdom for himself. — American youth likewise is being enlisted for an uprising against the faith and the standards of the fathers, against the rule of truth and righteousness. The danger is so appalling that silence on my part would be cowardly. Some sections of our public education are deliberately promoting this rebellion. In certain tax-supported schools text-books are anti-American in spirit and statement. Subtly they attack the heroes of our early history; they belittle the Constitution, disparage our democratic form of government and guardedly praise collectivism. Much of our education has failed to sustain a patriotic love for the nation; and we must never overlook the peril by which the child without sound Christian training can easily become a tool for subversive, unAmerican movements.

More pronounced is the fact that students in some colleges and universities are being recruited for a revolt

against morality. Christian home-life with its ideal of
husband and wife joined together for better or for worse
till death parts them; Biblical teachings of childhood as
God's precious gift and parenthood one of His most marvelous blessings; Scriptural concepts of purity, premarital
chastity, virginity, basic for human happiness, are contemptuously tossed aside and ridiculed.

Even this, however, does not exhaust the extent of the
rebellion which modern youth, like Absalom, is encouraged
to lead. As he rose up against his father's God, so many
of your sons and daughters, Christian parents of America,
are being mobilized in schools, often by men whose salaries
your taxes help pay, for a wide-spread offensive against
the Gospel. Although a fundamental principle of American government clearly makes it illegal for a state official
or employee to use his office for attacking religion, many
public-school pupils, evening-school students, State-college
men and women, are told continually: "The Bible is full
of mistakes! Christianity must be discarded! Jesus Christ
is only one of a hundred saviors whom deluded men have
fashioned for themselves. There is no heaven — much less
a hell. The Ten Commandments have lost their force in
a modern world. The best of men are only refined and
exalted beasts. We ought to live our one life as instincts
dictate: We must throw off the shackles of the superstition and fear men call 'religion.' "

Now, if you have sent your children to a certain school
simply because it is well known or fashionable, and have
neglected to ask whether the instructors who help mold
their plastic minds are Christians or atheists; if your boys
or girls come home with text-books that would destroy
Biblical faith by discrediting divine creation or sub-
stituting the hoary hypothesis of chance origin or accidental
beginning; if their teachers, at public expense, try to coax

them from Bible truth — and you accept all this without protest; after the seed of doubt has brought forth its harvest of unbelief, perhaps you, too, will have to cry out in David's anguish, "Are my children really safe under the influence of men who deny the existence of a personal God?"

David could not know, when he voiced this question, that his son's corpse, stabbed through with cutting darts, lay beneath a pile of stones. Only a few hours earlier Absalom, riding through a forest in hasty flight, caught his long, flowing hair, of which he had been inordinately proud, on the branch of an oak-tree. His mount ran from under him, and there was David's vain, perfidious son, suspended helplessly. Despite royal orders that under no circumstances should harm befall Absalom, Joab, the general, thrust three darts through his beating heart. Since that did not kill him immediately, ten armor-bearers were dispatched to finish the ghastly work. When David finally heard the truth, a scene ensued which in some ways is unparalleled throughout Scripture. In an unforgettable passage we read that David sobbed in uncontrollable grief. Absalom had been conceited, treacherous, rebellious, murderous, but to David he was still his son; and during those seemingly endless hours of mourning the tortured father, Israel's sweet singer, author of many psalms filled with victorious faith, now had only one moaning lament. Here it is. It haunts us, this penetrating shriek of a father's love, cut to the quick, *"O my son Absalom, my son, my son Absalom! Would God I had died for thee! O Absalom, my son, my son!"*

Even Israel's king could not give his life for another. Throughout history only one could do that, our Savior, who died that we may live; and because David knew Jesus (the New Testament tells us that he was a prophet who saw the Lord Jesus), he could forgive his traitorous son. May you, too, realize by Christ's compassionate love how blessed it is to pardon particularly those of your own flesh and blood! Perhaps it is your special cross that your children cause you much heartache. They may bring disgrace to your family name and make you want to leave everything and start life over in a new locality to avoid reproach. They may even lose their faith, become sneering skeptics or brazen atheists. One truth cannot change, however: they are always your children. No matter what their mistakes have been, never banish your sons or daughters from your home! If our heavenly Father graciously forgives us for Jesus' sake; if Christ, in the agony of the cross, pleaded even for His enemies, how much more should you fathers and mothers open your hearts and homes to receive and restore your own children! David suffered untold grief because of seditious Absalom. The son who drove him from his throne weaned the hearts of the people from him, so that they threw stones at their king, reviled him with hate-filled names, and tried to hunt him down like a criminal. Yet David's love could forget all that to lament over his flesh and blood, *"O my son Absalom, my son, my son Absalom! Would God I had died for thee! O Absalom, my son, my son!"*

Though it was too late for David to help the arrogant rebel whose corpse was buried under a pile of heavy stones, there is still time for you to help your child. As you ask, "Is my son, my daughter, safe?" understand this clearly: Your children are not safe if they are in bad company and in sin, if they are living without Christ or against Him, if they are absent from church and opposed to its work. They are not safe if years ago you taught them to pray, but they neglect prayer now. They are not safe if they once were baptized and confirmed but today ignore Jesus in their lives.

Don't be satisfied if your children are physically strong, financially successful! What is their spiritual condition? We like to measure prosperity, peace, security, in outward forms; yet often we overlook the inner aspects and the soul itself. The United States has developed an admirable health program for the rising generation; but the spiritual health of three of every four American children is almost completely disregarded. The country is responding to a nation-wide infantile-paralysis campaign, a humanitarian effort which deserves generous support. Send your help now! Yet how little is said about the spiritual infantile paralysis which, leaving the body and its members untouched, unnerves the soul — I mean the rejection of the Lord Jesus Christ! Direct your prayers today to God Almighty, so that this more serious scourge may be checked!

When you inquire, "Are my children safe?" think of the awful alternative — heaven or hell, eternal blessing or endless punishment. As you parents beseech your heavenly Father to forgive what you have done wrong or have left undone, also ask Him, "What can I do to keep my children safe from sin, unbelief and crime, soul disaster and spiritual death?"

II

ALL OUR YOUTH CAN BE SAFE IN CHRIST!

How can we ever thank God enough that in the Lord Jesus He grants us complete safety for youth and old age, for time and eternity? When children cling to Christ in a personal, penitent, persevering faith parents need never cry, "Are my dear ones safe?" For here is our Savior's promise, *"Neither shall any man pluck them out of My hand."*

Picture to yourselves this blessed safety in Christ! He starts at the source of all dangers to our bodies, minds, and souls, sin, which destroys the tissues, fills our hearts with fear, and burdens our spirits with the doom of death.

Be sure that you understand this fundamental principle: There can be no security with your transgressions unremoved. These sins of youth, as Scripture calls them (and it means *"the lust of the flesh, the lust of the eyes, and the pride of life,"* disobedience to parents, selfish desires, the long list of sex sins, private or public, and indifference to God), must be paid for and divinely canceled if young people — and older folks, too — are to have the promise of peace for earth and heaven.

May none of you high-school pupils, college students, young workers, or men in the military service, be led into that most menacing of modern mistakes which satanically soothes questioning minds by insisting that sin does not matter; that "everybody does these things"; that a person cannot expect anything else with youth made as it is; that young people know how to avoid the consequences when they run out of bounds! While there are few real certainties in life and we are not sure what tomorrow will bring nor which course our country will take during the next months, one truth we do know: Every moral debt in your life must be paid; no wrong, secret or open, marked against you can escape punishment. Call that medieval, Puritanic, long worn-out and discarded, if you will, this does not make obsolete the divine injunction that no young person is safe with the stain of sin on his hands, words of wickedness on his lips, or the brand of evil on his mind. Two of every one hundred young men in the Selective Service Draft are rejected because their diseased bodies show sin's ravaging revenge. This proportion indicates, we are told, that at least two and one half million people, by the most conservative estimate, are living examples of the tragedy that there is no physical safety in sin. Add the many more millions, their minds distressed by restless confusion, their hearts filled with fear, their consciences lashed by terrifying remorse! Whatever else you young folks may take lightly, learn to regard sin with a deadly earnestness — but with the confidence that it has been completely conquered through Jesus Christ.

Ever-blessed Savior that He is, He atoned for every misstep and mistake in your life, including those serious offenses which still bring the blush of shame to your cheek. In His own holy body He suffered on the cross of torture — O matchless love! — the pain and penalty we should have endured, so that nothing remains of our guilt. Here is the promise of the greatest grace, the deepest devotion, and the highest hope we can ever have: *"While we were yet sinners, Christ died for us."*

With Jesus you are freed from the charge and guilt of breaking God's Law. If your conscience accuses you; if remorse haunts you and you wonder, "Am I really saved? Did Christ die for me, too, with all my wickedness?" "Is the pledge of the cross, the blood and the open grave, meant for me?" then remember: It is the glory of the Gospel promise that through faith your transgressions are laid on Jesus; and since He assumed them, they are yours no longer. Take God at His word and exult, *"There is now no condemnation for them that are in Christ Jesus!"*

From the moment He is acclaimed your Redeemer, you escape sin's punishment. When a man is made right with God through Jesus, he who was *"dead in trespasses and sins"* becomes alive with righteousness and grace; he who was born of the flesh is reborn of the Spirit; he who lived under divine wrath now has a blessed, God-directed life in which the Father's love, and not His anger, rules. Of course, shadows of sorrow may darken the pathway of

many Christian young people. Four of our ten million
still unemployed are young men and women. Hundreds
of thousands are sick, poor, lonely; but it is the blessed
promise of undeserved grace that whatever may seem cruel
and heartless comes to the Savior's followers as a means
of purifying, strengthening guidance. Last week more
than two thousand detectives and policemen guarded the
inaugural procession in Washington to protect our President from disaster; with Christ you have the higher assurance that an angel guard will watch over your soul and
permit only those afflictions to befall you which you can
bear and which come for inner growth, eternal welfare.
A hundred dangers may assail you from the left and another hundred from the right, but, looking to Christ, you
can say: *"Whoso putteth his trust in the Lord shall be
safe." "Hold Thou me up, and I shall be safe."*

With Jesus you will also be protected from the repeated
assaults of temptations. Don't think for a moment that
as Christ's you will escape the coaxing and tugging to do
what God has forbidden. The evils that besiege Christian
young men and women are many times more numerous
and insistent than those which confront a hardened sinner
who rejects the Lord. The forces of hell do not need to
exert themselves against any one who hates the Savior, but
they are ceaselessly approaching those who love the Savior.
You are being tempted by the same weaknesses and wicked-
nesses that appealed to Absalom. In a dozen ways you are
urged to regard your Church as out of date, your parents
as old-fashioned. Like David's proud son, American youth
is frequently told — to the neglect of the lasting truths —
that personal appearance, fine clothing, outward impressions, are the important things of life.

If you young folks had to find your own way through
this bewildering decade; if you had no better instruction

than some teachings and examples of your elders, you certainly would deserve pity. Praise God! you need not go through life alone. You can walk side by side with Christ and follow His holy example. Jesus is the most faithful Friend young people can ever have. He knows and loves youth, for He was young Himself. He understands your passions and problems, for the Bible tells us that He was *"tempted like as we are, yet without sin."* In His name I assure you today that He wants to aid you in resisting temptations and breaking away from each degrading influence. If you want pardon for your past sins, comforting assurance for every future difficulty; if you want the power to conquer wrong, by the grace of God accept Jesus fully as your Savior. Then youth at its best, youth in safety, is yours! Think how closely the two words "Savior" and "safety" are related and then ask the Spirit to push aside every opposition that may keep you from Christ.

Reject Him, however, and you send yourself to hell despite your mother's prayers, you damn yourself despite your father's pleas. God prevent that! Rather listen closely once more as Christ calls you, for whom He, the eternal God, shed His blood! Accept Him in the bloom, the power, the optimism, of youth! Bow before Him with sincere repentance! Approach Him with unswerving trust! Give Him your heroic faith!

You parents also must assist before it is too late and the tears of remorse will be useless. As you hear David's anguish break out anew, *"O my son Absalom, my son, my son Absalom! Would God I had died for thee! O Absalom, my son, my son!"* put everything else aside and act now! Your foremost ambition for your boys and girls should not ask that they lead their classes in school, learn the social graces, become expert musicians, athletes, singers, make an early, prominent mark in the financial world. As desirable as these achievements may be, keep first things first! Bring them to Christ!

This implies, of course, that you fathers and mothers accept Jesus yourselves. You cannot expect the children to show any interest in the Church if you yourselves do not. Few tragedies in life can be more terrifying to parents than the realization that their unbelief, worldliness, and rejection of Christ have not only excluded them from heaven's blessing, but have kept their family from the Savior. Fathers, put your own house in order! Mothers, give time to your children's souls.

If you want to dedicate your sons and daughters to Jesus, arrange now to have them receive the blessing of Baptism! This Sacrament, the washing of regeneration, not merely by the pouring of water, but by faith, brings your boys and girls to the Christ who said, *"Suffer the little children to come unto Me and forbid them not, for of such is the kingdom of heaven."* God has been so good to us that after every broadcast in which I have pleaded for Baptism some friends, won for Christ, have written to request its blessing. May He grant that today be no exception, that from the East and the West many will follow God's holy command, *"Be baptized for the remission of sins."*

The children of this nation must be kept safe by the Christian training they receive at home. Parents should never be so preoccupied that their sons and daughters grow up in spiritual ignorance or misunderstanding concerning life's greatest truth and joy: their Savior's sin-removing, Heaven-bestowing love. God has entrusted us with priceless treasures in the immortal souls of our little ones. Ninety-three years ago on Friday gold was discovered near Mariposa, California. A little girl, playing in the yard of her father's ranch after a heavy rain, was attracted by a number of new, shiny "stones," to which she called her father's attention. One proved to be a twenty-eight-ounce nugget of solid gold. The family had been seeking to make its fortune in various ways, but there concealed in its own yard was a source of undreamed wealth. You parents in the poorest cabins can be similarly rich, without going beyond the walls of your own dwelling, if, as that rain washed the soil from those gold nuggets, you will remove the indifference and neglect covering faith's golden treasures. No happiness on earth can be greater than the knowledge that your children are God's children.

The home alone, however, cannot fully perform the task of keeping our young people safe. It demands, in addition, a Christ-centered education. I am not repeating this offer too frequently when I tell you again that your children are individually invited to enroll in the Christian day-schools which my Church supports in hundreds of communities throughout the country. Many parents thank God with us because their boys and girls receive the benefits of these religious schools, where, besides the usual secular subjects, they are daily taught the Bible, our holy faith, and Christian hymns. Let us tell you about the school nearest you, open to your children without charge.

Training that can keep young people safe, make them thank God that they are Christ's, help them choose the clean, courageous, happy life, goes beyond these elementary schools. In the high-school years, the period of adolescence, and particularly during college years, your son or daughter needs the Savior's constant support and guidance. Contrary to some opinions, there are splendid Christian schools in this country. I know one well, our Valparaiso University in Indiana, and I guarantee you that no student enrolled there will hear a word raised officially against the

Bible or the Gospel-message of hope in the blood and the cross. This school starts where Christian training should begin, with the fear of God and the love of Christ.

When we are safe with Christ in this life — O blessed assurance! — we shall be safe with Him in the next. Time rolls on in its rapid course. For some the years will be many, for others this will be the last. Whether days are added or subtracted, whether this country faces peace or war, whether we are to be richer or poorer, our health better or worse, the love of *"Jesus Christ, the same yesterday and today and forever," never changes.* With that glorious prospect, let this comfort and conviction be our constant joy:

> Safe in the arms of Jesus,
>   Safe on His gentle breast,
> There by His love o'ershaded,
>   Sweetly my soul shall rest!
>
> Safe in the arms of Jesus,
>   Safe from corroding care,
> Safe from the world's temptations,
>   Sin cannot harm me there!

God give us all this eternal safety for Jesus' sake! Amen.

THE PRAYER
THAT MAKES MEN FREE

*"At midnight Paul and Silas prayed and sang praises
unto God; and the prisoners heard them. And
suddenly there was a great earthquake, so that the
foundations of the prison were shaken; and immediately all the doors were opened, and every one's
bands were loosed."* — Acts 16:25, 26

God, who Hearest the Prayers of Humble, Contrite Hearts:

*Teach us always and everywhere to take refuge in Thee, to lay our
fears at the cross and there find pardon for our transgressions by the
mercy of the Lord Jesus Christ! Fortify our faith with the confidence that through the Savior's grace, the heavier our burdens become, the more closely He walks beside us to share their weight!
Forgive us the lethargy and lukewarmness by which we have neglected the privilege of communing with Thee! When war clouds
gather and evil forces strengthen their rule over the world, let Thine
answers to our daily petitions guide us in building a constant and
courageous trust! If men break their promises and nations discard
their treaties, give us a steadily increasing conviction that our plea to
the throne of Thy mercy will be answered in Thy time, place, and
manner! Hear us now and bless our broadcasts through Jesus, in
whose name and by whose command we have raised our hearts to
Thee! Amen.*

THE most urgent of the many needs in human affairs
today is peace. With all that is good and uplifting
in our civilization at stake; with the growing menace of
intensified warfare so terrifying that among its consequences
this generation may number world revolution, uncontrolled
inflation, repudiation of debts, bankruptcy, a cry should
go up not only from the United States but from all war-
racked nations to the very ends of the earth, demanding,
"Give us peace!" Militarists, of course, who make slaughter
a science, destruction a technique; international traders and

bankers who know how to manipulate stocks, buy and sell munitions, despite legal limitations, for huge profits; evolutionists, who claim that conflicts are necessary to purify the race, remove weaklings, and permit only the fittest to survive (although every struggle first cuts down those selected for their youth and physical stamina!); men with such theories or motives may urge the continuance and extension of every war — but not the common people, who have the most to sacrifice, yet the least to say! They know despite flag-waving and band playing that war, unavoidable though it sometimes may be, is, as Martin Luther repeatedly outlined, incomparably the worst of all afflictions, since it assaults, injures, even destroys bodies, minds, and souls. Therefore they want peace — not any kind of truce, of course, but a just and humane settlement, as lasting as it can be in a world that cannot remain permanently warless; not simply a breathing spell or a twenty-year interim, during which the babies of the first World War can become the soldiers of the second, but a peace, under God, that will stop aggression and give us and the next generations — for it will take that long — an opportunity to rebuild the ruins.

The question of surpassing importance, therefore, is: "How can an honorable, international concord be achieved?" Statesmen have two answers. First: "Crush the enemy into submission" — peace by force, and, second: "Try to establish an understanding between embattled nations" — peace by negotiation. Personally, I do not see how Christians can scream, "Crush them! Destroy the last man of them! Grind them to pieces!" when they have Christ's unrestricted command, *"Love your enemies! . . . Do good to them that hate you, and pray for them which despitefully use you and persecute you, that ye may be the children of your Father which is in heaven!"* But whichever way statesmanship may choose, the Savior's followers have a divine energy at their disposal, which, if it be God's will, can establish and strengthen the bonds of harmony. That, my fellow-countrymen and fellow-redeemed, is the power of prayer in Jesus' name. If every disciple of Christ throughout the world today — and let us never overlook the truth that we have brothers and sisters in the faith on both sides of this suicidal slaughter — would humbly, penitently, ask God to check all tyranny, stop this bloodshed; if every Christian home throughout the world, in daily fervent supplication would beseech the Almighty to tie up the wounds of war; if every church would become a house of prayer and preachers — instead of clamoring to put this country into the struggle — would petition equitable agreement in the name of the Prince of Peace, we should have a mighty force to help liberate mankind from the terrors of the present hostilities.

Under divine guidance prayer can do all this and more. It can help deliver us from our fears, doubts, sorrows, afflictions, weaknesses; it can — and this is its basic blessing — strengthen the assurance that we are free from our sins, rescued from death itself.

This benediction can be yours if you learn to know

THE PRAYER THAT MAKES MEN FREE

To this end we shall study the promises in the instructive story of the apostle's deliverance, Acts, chapter sixteen, verses twenty-five and twenty-six: *"At midnight Paul and Silas prayed and sang praises unto God; and the prisoners heard them. And suddenly there was a great earthquake, so that the foundations of the prison were shaken; and immediately all the doors were opened, and every one's bands were loosed."*

I

SUCH PRAYER COMES FROM A TRUSTING FAITH LIKE PAUL'S AND SILAS'S

The scene of this miraculous rescue is Philippi, a city in Northeastern Greece, and the time, the beginning of Saint Paul's European missionary work. This valiant messenger for Christ had hardly crossed from Asia to Europe, answering the appeal of the vision, *"Come over into Macedonia, and help us!"* when in consequence of his brave Gospel testimony he and his assistant Silas began to suffer disgrace and punishment. They were falsely accused, found guilty, beaten with the lictors' rods, and then cast into the public prison. By His unsearchable ways, so completely higher than our understanding that we must remain baffled before His wisdom, God often permits His children to experience severe blows, even when they are engaged in His service, testifying to His grace and walking in His footsteps. Then, oh, for a faith like Paul's and Silas's, which can praise our heavenly Father, knowing that whatever happens to us as Christ's is for God's glory and our own ultimate benefit! If the apostles had not been thrown into the dungeon, humanly speaking, they might never have met the jailer, the very man who a few moments later would fall on his knees before them to cry, *"What must I do to be saved?"* who, together with his entire household, would soon be brought to Christ after hearing this most treasured of all assurances: *"Believe on the Lord Jesus Christ, and thou shalt be saved, and thy house!"* By the same mercy God may use you, your courage in affliction, your faith in adversity, for such hallowed purposes that heaven's angels rejoice.

It was midnight, then, when those two beaten witnesses of the Savior, their hands and feet bound by heavy bonds, languished behind the bolted doors of the Philippian prison.

As far as men could see, Paul's hope of converting Macedonia to Christ was shattered. The end of his career, so others may have concluded, had come. Yet in that dark hour and in the dank, damp cell, their hands and feet shackled, their backs twitching in pain, when deliverance seemed impossible, Paul and Silas turned in confident prayer to God, the never-failing Source of strength.

Is it midnight in your life, too? Are you shackled by fears and phobias? Does sorrow's darkness and the night of heavy adversity enshroud you? If you are cut off from your family and friends by a weary siege of sickness, by the loneliness of other cruel separations, including imprisonment (how we thank God here in these broadcast headquarters that many penitentiary wardens with the same faith the jailer at Philippi confessed, have this program tuned in every Sunday!), or if you have resigned yourself to the thought that there is no chance for you to find freedom for your soul, take heart as you recall the faith of these two missionaries and learn "what a privilege it is to carry everything to God in prayer!"

Don't think that Paul and Silas had the false but popular idea prayers should be reserved for emergencies and used as a last resort when other means fail. It is quite understandable, of course, that, when people see human hope dwindle a short time before they face their Maker, they eagerly grasp at prayer and push all else aside. When President Grant lay dying of cancer, his old Civil War friend General Howard praised his leadership in the war and extolled his prominent part in preserving the Union. But Grant slowly shook his head, raised his hands in protest, and earnestly pleaded, "Howard, tell me something more about prayer!" The outpouring of the heart to God can offer untold comfort in those last lingering moments; and if God ever gives you the responsibility of watching beside death-beds, don't trouble harassed souls soon to wing their way into eternity with questions about a will, hidden money, past secrets, or remarriage! Pray with them to Christ for forgiveness, life and salvation.

Yet to Paul communion with the heavenly Father was the language of the living no less than the refuge of the dying. Listen to him when he asks for Christians *"praying always with all prayer and supplication"* or when he tells the Colossians, *"Continue in prayer!"* and resolve that at work, at play, at your studies, day and night, in prosperity as in adversity, you will daily, regularly, perseveringly, come before your God through Christ!

Nor did Paul recognize any exclusive place for his prayer. There were no churches then in which he could kneel. However, whether on board ship or traversing the mainland, while employed in tent-making or locked in prison, while addressing philosophers or dealing with slaves, wherever he was, he could pray and meet his own standard, *"I will, therefore, that men pray everywhere."* — Keep this contact with heaven! On the same day that Napoleon captured the city of Ulm with its forty thousand defenders, his navy was destroyed in the battle of Trafalgar. By way of explanation Napoleon said, "I cannot be present everywhere at once." But God can be with every one of His children on all their ways. Keep Him at your side! Say to Christ, "Take Thou my hand and lead me o'er life's rough way," and He will answer, *"I will never leave thee nor forsake thee."*

Note also that the apostles' prayer here, as we see from his other recorded intercessions, was not simply a series of self-centered requests, a string of "Give me this, O Lord," and "Give me that!" "Make me this!" or "Make me that!" These two men of God (their wrists, no doubt, heavily

chained, their strength completely exhausted after the cruel
lashing of the whole painful day) could hardly raise their
hands; yet they lifted their voices in thanks. The text
says that they *"prayed and sang praises unto God; and
the prisoners heard them."* The love of the Lord Jesus
Christ, which they constantly experienced, the outpouring
of His mercy, by which they had been reborn in spirit, the
grace that as a divine magnet drew them to the Cross —
this compassion was so utterly undeserved, so much greater
than the worst they had ever suffered, that even in their
bonds they could not keep silent.

I have often wondered what those hymns were which
broke the midnight silence. Probably some of David's
ancient, yet ageless psalms, perhaps the second, with its
challenge, *"Why do the heathen rage?"* the one hundred
and thirtieth, *"Out of the depths have I cried unto Thee,
O Lord,"* or the forty-sixth, which, set to music in Luther's
"A Mighty Fortress Is Our God," has been the first hymn
on each of our broadcasts for eight seasons. As our Savior
during the agony of the cross raised His final plea in the
language of the Old Testament, *"Father, into Thy hands
I commend My spirit,"* you, too, can bring down Heaven's
blessing if, as you commune with your Father, you speak
in Scripture's dynamic words. — These disciples were not
satisfied with limiting their petitions to what some one else
had said. They also spoke their prayers from their own
fervent souls; and we, too, should learn to come to God in
language of our implicit confidence, in terms of our own
heart, with praise for our personal benefits. It is not the
number of the petitions we direct to the Throne nor their
length, their beautiful language, their intensity, which
sends them heavenward. It is rather our own childlike
trust which, taking our Father at His word, makes our
prayers acceptable to Him.

When Paul and Silas prayed in their Philippian prison, it was not with bitterness toward the men who had falsely accused them, the rabble which had jeered, nor the magistrates who had cruelly sentenced them to be beaten with rods. If some of you were compelled to witness a flogging, you would faint at the sight of that revolting spectacle. These two missionaries, however, reflected so much of the Savior's surpassing love that they could not hate even the heartless mob, the corrupt judges, the lying witnesses. Thus did Saint Paul practice what he preached, *"Bless them which persecute you; bless, and curse not! . . . Therefore, if thine enemy hunger, feed him. If he thirst, give him drink."* One of the happy signs in this dreadful war is the prayer of humble British Christians for their foes across the channel and the intercession of faithful German followers of our Lord for their English enemies. Sometimes you are not heard because you approach God for pardon while you yourselves are not willing to forgive those who have offended you. If in your heart you nurture hatred of race, color, creed, class, hatred even of your family, recall the mightiest Christians beseeching God for their enemies. See our Lord Jesus in the unspeakable grief of Golgotha pleading, *"Father, forgive them, for they know not what they do!"* Then remember that if in the Lord's Prayer you request, *"Forgive us our trespasses, as we forgive those who trespass against us,"* yet are not ready to forgive but want to keep on hating, you are not following the Savior. Every time you pray with such falsehood in your heart, you insult God.

Particularly do these imprisoned apostles teach us — and this principle separates the Christian's intercession from all others — that every prayer, to be heard, must be directed not to some vague, indefinite, higher being, not to the great Unknown and Unknowable, not to some hazy, distant divine Spirit, but to the Father, the Savior, and the Holy Spirit — blessed Trinity and glorious Unity! — the true and only God! He alone can hear the outpouring of our hearts. No matter how loud and long, how earnest and eloquent, your petitions may be, if they are not addressed to the Deity revealed in the Bible, they have no promise of answer. Call that narrow and bigoted if you will; the unbreakable truth of the divine Word remains: *"I am the Lord and there is none else; there is no God beside Me."*

But our Father is so holy in His absolute, heavenly perfection that you and I, our hearts, hands, lips, and bodies marked by repeated transgressions of His will, cannot even approach Him. We are barred from His presence by our multiplied iniquities. If we think that our sins mean nothing in His sight, that in our wickedness we can expect an answer to our prayer, then listen to God's startling rejection of rebellious Israel, *"When ye spread forth your hands, I will hide Mine eyes from you; yea, when ye make many prayers, I will not hear."*

Here again Jesus Christ — all hail His blessed name! — comes to us with His unconditional, limitless grace to remove the barrier of separating sin. The approach to God was not easily granted. It required the toil and agony, the sweat and tears, the groaning and crying, the wounding and bleeding, the suffering and dying, of God's own Son for us. There was no other way, even for the all-wise and all-powerful God, by which we could be brought back to a loving Father, saved from our doom, delivered from death, and given the privilege of acceptable intercession — no other way except that hard, blood-marked death when Jesus, nailed to the cross, paid the whole penalty for every transgression, secured the release for every sinner, and so completely became our Savior, our Substitute, that when

God beholds us we now have no sin, no guilt, no condemnation.   What a glorious, blessed Savior Christ is!
What magnificent mercy, this invitation to return to God
for full pardon without cost, without condition, contribu-
tion, cooperation, on our part, simply by the free mercy of
God's Son as our Substitute, through faith alone.

With our sins removed, we have access to the Father.
May our prayers therefore always be humble, never dic-
tatorial, as though we had right or reason to demand anything from God!   To the contrary, in the spirit of the great
apostle who called himself "chief of sinners" and with
the penitence of the publican who dared not lift up his eyes
but could only strike his breast and repeat, *"God be merciful to me, a sinner!"* may we turn to God with repentant
prayers!   Not every kind of pleading will be heard; rather,
only those petitions which follow Christ's instruction
"Whatsoever ye shall ask the Father in My name, *He
will give it you."*   Whatever else you may learn about
prayer today or at any other time, let this be the corner-
stone on which you build every request: "I ask this in my
Savior's name, by His merits and His promise."   Your
name or mine, no matter how men may acclaim it, how
many university degrees adorn it, or how often it appears
in print, means nothing except that it always designates
a sinner.   But Christ's name, no matter how frequently
blasphemous men may desecrate it in cursing and profanity
or atheism seek to besmirch it, is still the name above all
names.   Many modern promises must be followed by
ominous question marks; yet this truth should be inscribed
in every living soul with letters that can never be changed:
God will answer all humble, contrite, trusting, faith-founded
prayers spoken in Christ's name though the earth itself
be moved.

II

SUCH PRAYER GRANTS BLESSED FREEDOM LIKE PAUL'S AND SILAS'S

In a very real sense the ground was shaken in answer to the apostles' prayer. When human help collapsed, God sent a mighty earthquake, which rocked the jail. An accident, you say? A coincidence? That is what enemies of the Bible have always claimed and many modern preachers continue to say, as they tell their congregations: "Miracles never happen." But ordinary tremors could never loosen the bonds from all the prisoners and open the cell-doors, as this earthquake did.

The divine power which broke the prison, snapped handcuffs, and released fettered feet still works under the love of the same almighty God. Has He not promised, *"Call upon Me in the day of trouble; I will deliver thee"*? Has Jesus not pledged, *"Ask, and it shall be given you; seek, and ye shall find; knock, and it shall be opened unto you"*? Dozens of passages in the errorless Bible state in language a child understands that God hears prayer; and before one of these pledges is proved exaggerated, misleading, or false, heaven and earth must pass away. Today, too, if God chooses, He will suspend the iron-clad laws of nature and send His unseen angels to carry out His purpose. History shows that our Father keeps His word, and thousands in this radio audience can testify from their own experience that the Almighty has answered their pleading. Each year many of you send me evidence of victorious prayer from your own lives. Annually also I ask unbelievers and skeptics in this audience — as I now formally do — to show that God refuses to answer *true* prayer. But in these eight years of broadcasting no enemy of the Christian faith could produce such proof.

We must insist, of course, on true prayers. You can

not ask the Lord for a sixteen-cylinder automobile, a mink coat, a four-carat diamond ring, a winter home in Miami Beach or California, and a town house in the *élite* section of your city — wait for a few days — and then expect to receive all this. Were prayer to do that, it would become a most destructive force. The human heart is so greedy and covetous that, if these selfish petitions were granted, you would soon be ruined. You would start to pray that you be given more than your nearest rivals. Hate would fill your heart, and before long you would find some way of injuring your successful competitors. Conflict, bloodshed, disaster, would ensue. And because the same frenzy would grip every one else as blinded people used prayer to secure articles that injure bodies, stultify minds, and send souls to hell, the whole world would be a chaos such as the human mind can hardly picture. Even Saint Paul, that outstanding hero of faith, admits, *"We know not what we should pray for as we ought."* God loves us so much that He wants to save us from bringing destruction on our own heads; therefore our heavenly Father demands that every prayer be made according to His will, and that means, for our soul's welfare, our spiritual advancement, our progress toward heaven. For this reason Jesus taught us to pray, *"Thy will be done in earth as it is in heaven."* In this spirit Christ resigned Himself to His Father in the never-to-be-fathomed anguish of Gethsemane, *"Not My will, but Thine be done."* Saint Paul directs us to prove *"what is that good and acceptable and perfect will of God."* If we were to analyze the reason many prayers by members of this radio audience have not been answered, it would become evident that you have not only prayed without trusting, humble faith, but have also made some selfish request, which, were it granted, might lead you into sin and strengthen your proud self-sufficiency.

Some of you, of course, object that you prayed for
health and it certainly would have been for your good to
be spared the wasting disease which now attacks you; you
besought God to save your business, but it was taken away,
and you cannot see how such loss was for your good. You
pleaded with God to let your righteous cause prevail;
instead, unrighteousness and corruption have triumphed;
you are accused, maligned, and the bitterness of your
heart wells up to protest, "What good has there been for
me in this suffering?" Some of you widows write that for
days, almost without interruption, you stayed at the side
of your husband's sick-bed and implored God with all the
strength you could marshal to save your beloved; yet, even
while you prayed, his soul was taken. If I now say that
the Lord did not spare your husband because this was not
according to His purpose, you may be tempted to scream
out charges of cruelty against our heavenly Father. But
stop! We have never said that we can understand God's
will and with our human vision discern His purposes.
His ways, often completely hidden from His children, are
always good and perfect. Only the smallness of our faith,
the limits of our earth-bound vision, prevent us from
realizing the comfort we shall know fully in heaven.

Perhaps God has refused to grant the trusting prayers
of His faithful in order to give them far better answers
than they asked. Thus His love may have withheld bodily
strength because first He wants you to have spiritual health.
He may not have helped you keep your business because
at some future time in His own way He has higher, greater
things in store for you. He may have left the plea for
your husband's life unanswered to give him something incomparably greater. Now, if you have asked for pebbles
and God gives you priceless jewels; if you plead for tinsel
that can tarnish and He enriches you with pure gold, should

you complain? Rather cultivate the spirit of Job, *"Though He slay me, yet will I trust in Him,"* and believe that, if God does not fulfil our desires as we request, it is only because His gracious will has planned to grant us far more than we ask.

Build your faith, then, on the Scripture promise, *"This is the confidence that we have in Him, that, if we ask anything according to His will, He heareth us."* He may not answer at once, of course. Carey and his fellow missionaries labored seven years in India before one Hindu convert was baptized. In the throbbing heart of Africa's jungles Robert and Mary Moffat toiled for ten years without winning a single soul for Christ. The first missionaries to Greenland struggled for seventeen years before gathering the first-fruits in the Savior's harvest of souls. Yet their prayers were finally answered. Your petitions, too, will be heard in God's time, always the best time. His help may come swiftly, even before you ask it, or it may take long, weary, grinding years. *"Though it tarry, wait for it; because it will surely come."*

As these apostles were freed from prison, so your trusting, Christ-directed prayers can help to liberate you from the tyranny of your sins, from the slavery of your fears, and give you the courageous outlook on life we need particularly in these disturbed days. Prayer can free you from the burden of afflictions. It can break the bonds of misunderstanding and empty loneliness. It can liberate you even from the terror of death and let you breathe your last with a released smile of joy.

This is not theological theory and wishful thinking. A Cincinnati woman, embittered by the staggering blows of an unhappy life, writes: "You say Jesus Christ is the solution for everything. Have you ever been in arrears with your rent? Let's say that Mr. Smith, the landlord, knocks at your door and you greet him something like this: 'Good afternoon, Mr. Smith. I don't have your rent, but the Lord will take care of you.' Why, the landlord would have you put out of the house on the ground of insanity."

I tell that mistaken woman and every one else who shares her resentment that, if you are a child of God (not in a try-Christianity-and-see-what-happens spirit, but in unshaken faith) and behind in your rent; if you have nothing to eat in your house and don't know how you will ever get the money to pay your other debts, take these needs to the Lord in prayer, and just as surely as I am speaking to you, He will answer and send some one or something to help you pay the rent, buy the groceries, meet your bills, or grant you far better blessings.

You doubt that? Here is proof. A few days ago an unnamed friend sent me the last annual report of George Muller's orphanage in Bristol, England. That great institution was conceived in prayer and then dedicated to the demonstration of its power. In his life-story George Muller wrote: "Sometimes it would happen that at nine o'clock in the morning there were no provisions in the orphan houses, neither was there money on hand to purchase the food needed for the dinner; then, in answer to the earnest cries of those who were engaged in the work, money was received in time to secure supplies and get the meal ready by the dinner hour at one o'clock; but often afterward there was nothing left for supper. Another united prayer meeting was held, therefore, in order that they might beseech the Lord to appear mercifully on their behalf; and this He invariably did." Now, after 104 years of service to the orphans, that Christian foundation, a living proof of prayer, has not only continued its God-blessed ministry, but was permitted to enter the last calendar year despite the burden of war with a surplus of more than $30,000.

There is nothing theoretical about that orphanage in Bristol, England. By the same definite dynamics God will prove His love in answering our prayers. Ask Him to forgive us our sins for Jesus' sake, to look down mercifully on those whom we regard as our enemies, bless them with a knowledge of Christ's saving, purifying love, shorten the days of bloodshed, check the tyranny of aggression, and grant this generation, twice visited by the bloodiest wars of history, peace and international understanding, according to His will. It cannot be permanent peace, of course, for men's overreaching desires will not long remain restricted; but as the hands on God's clock move toward midnight (it was pointedly said that it is now five minutes to twelve according to the divine schedule, and that was previous to the declaration of hostilities), may God grant, before the stroke of doom sounds on a war-torn world, an age of rest in which men can devote thought to their souls and consider the alternatives of eternity! As our hearts, imprisoned in sin, strife, greed, look to Christ and the mercy of His marvelous love, God's power will loosen our bonds and — O glorious liberty! — make us free from sin and its penalty, free from despair and its anguish, free from hell and its condemnation, free from death and its terrors, free for time and eternity, through Christ and for Christ, to whom with the Father and the Spirit be the glory and honor of our prayers! Amen.

THE KEY TO THE KINGDOM —
REBIRTH IN CHRIST

*"Verily, verily, I say unto thee, Except a man
be born again, he cannot see the kingdom of
God." —* Saint John 3:3

Renewing Spirit of God:

*Bring us all to a Christ-centered faith and keep us with Jesus, that,
twice-born by Thy power, we may be brought from death to life
and as new creatures walk in the light of grace, truth, and righteousness! We know that unless Thou dost touch our hearts and
purify our spirits, the best outward efforts can cleanse only the
surface. Therefore we pray, "Create in me a clean heart, O God,
and renew a right spirit within me!" How can we ever thank
Thee, Lord of Love, for calling us from sin to the Savior's blood-
bought salvation! Teach us, however, that, once we have the light,
we must daily follow its radiance to show forth the praises of Him
who hath called us out of the darkness! Bless our message today!
Make it Thy means of summoning sinners to repentance, strengthening the weak, comforting the hopeless, cheering the lonely,
lightening the burdened — all through Jesus Christ, our only
Ransom from sin! Give our stubborn, blind, suffering world more
of His peace and blessing! Let the kingdom of God come mightily
as men all over the earth are turned from fear to faith through the
Savior, in whose name and by whose mercy we pray! Amen.*

WHAT do you suppose is the most remarkable discovery in our age? Ask American scientists, and
many will agree that "one of the greatest, if not *the*
greatest, discovery in modern" times is U-235, a chemical
twin to uranium. Enthusiastic investigators claim that
one pound of this new substance will develop energy equal
to that in 5,000,000 pounds of coal or 3,000,000 gallons of
gasoline. If methods for extracting sufficient amounts can
be perfected, the results anticipated will be startling beyond
imagination. All the present sources for energy, we are
told, will become mere children's toys by comparison.

Therefore scientists on both shores of the Atlantic are feverishly at work behind closed laboratory doors in the attempt to secure large quantities of U-235 — an achievement which, it is freely predicted, could bring victory in the present war to whichever side first completes the process.

Christians, however, know an immeasurably more dynamic power than U-235. When Sir James Simpson, noted anesthetist and scientific authority, was asked which of his discoveries was the most important, he answered with the simple Christian faith that, I trust, will be reechoed in millions of hearts throughout America this afternoon, "My greatest discovery was the realization that Jesus Christ is my personal Redeemer." Other intellectual leaders who have found no conflict between reason and religion have likewise acclaimed the redeeming Savior their greatest discovery. I hope that you agree; for with Christ, in whom the power of heaven itself is brought down to us on earth, we have a source of divine energy far more dynamic than U-235 ever can be, even if it meets the most optimistic predictions. We have the Holy Spirit, who can do what U-235 can never do — change the human heart, give sinners the rebirth of grace, and make them new creatures with purified souls.

Our suffering world clamors for a renewing, regenerating force that will change human lives and mold men's inner impulses for good. Unless there is some force that can restrain evil, check the horrors of this war, call a halt to its destruction of life, liberty, homes, churches, cities, nations, we may indeed face dark ages with unspeakable misery for millions. In spite of the ridicule showered on every plea for peace, recall the very words of David, "*I am for peace; but when I speak, they are for war,*" the Gospel of Jesus Christ is the only agency that can bring about this rebirth, deliver the world from its own bestial cruelty, especially rescue you, every one of you, from sin, despair, eternal death. For faith in the Lord Jesus Christ, through the blessing of God's Spirit, which the Savior pledges, so completely changes us that we who were *"children of wrath"* become *"children of God"* and can enter the kingdom of His grace and glory.

May the holy Comforter grant these words power to show every one of you with deep personal conviction

THE KEY TO THE KINGDOM — REBIRTH IN CHRIST

As a guarantee for this grace I give you not human opinion, not scientific theory, but the words of the Lord Jesus Christ Himself, introduced with a double oath to offer double assurance, the statement of John's gospel, chapter three, verse three, *"Verily, verily, I say unto thee, Except a man be born again, he cannot see the kingdom of God."*

I

WHAT IS THIS REBIRTH?

It was during the hush of a Palestinian night that Jesus spoke these momentous words, when Nicodemus, an influential member of the Sanhedrin, the Jewish governing body, came to Him for guidance. He was a secret disciple, hesitating to confess Christ openly; yet our Lord welcomed him, just as He will gladly receive every one in this audience, the rich and the ragged, no matter how weak or wavering your faith may be. As they sat face to face in some unnamed house at Jerusalem, this eager, inquiring Jewish teacher and the patient, gracious Savior, Nicodemus started by acknowledging our Lord's preeminent position. *"Rabbi,"* he began, *"we know that Thou art a Teacher come from God; for no man can do these miracles that Thou doest except God be with him."*

The Savior's response was startling. He seemed to

ignore everything Nicodemus had said, to overlook entirely
the fact that this Jewish leader had just called Him
a divine Teacher and acclaimed His many wonders; for
there is something vastly more important than miracles,
more essential than the fact that Christ is merely *"a Teacher
come from God"*: Nicodemus must acclaim Jesus the Son
of God, the Savior of the world.   Therefore, in the climax
to that nightly discussion Jesus declared — and how blessed
Nicodemus was to hear from Christ's own lips this Gospel
summary, which has brought indescribable joy into millions
of lives, as, God grant, it may also fortify every one of
you now! — *"God so loved the world that He gave His
only-begotten Son, that whosoever believeth in Him should
not perish but have everlasting life."*   But as Jesus led up
to this promise of grace, He answered Nicodemus, —
although it hardly seems to be an answer, — *"Verily, verily,
I say unto thee, Except a man be born again, he cannot
see the kingdom of God."*   It was as though Jesus would
say, "I am glad that you, Nicodemus, a man of influence
and wealth, come to Me and acknowledge the power of
My miracles and My teaching; but that is not enough.
The greatest thing in your life is your entrance into the
kingdom of God; and for this you *'must be born again.'* "

Nineteen centuries have not dimmed the Savior's *"Ye
must be born again."*   More than any other age ours speaks
and writes about Christ, discusses and debates His words
and works.   Only atheists, sensualists, materialists, will
deny that Jesus was a great Man or refuse to admit that
His statements and deeds prove Him to be a Heaven-sent
Teacher; but this is not enough.   The question of surpassing importance to every one of you is not: "Am I to
be conscripted?   Am I to succeed in business?   Am I to be
married?   Am I to enjoy health and happiness?" — but,
"What is Christ to me?"   You must ask yourself, "Am
I born again?"

To answer, drop everything else which may distract your thoughts! Think of this broadcast, not as a huge system with 275 stations in sixteen countries, but as a message directed personally, individually, especially, to you, as though you and I were alone before our God seeking assurance for this pivotal question, "Am I born again?"

Now, if even Nicodemus with all his Old Testament knowledge could not understand this rebirth but asked Christ, *"How can a man be born when he is old?"* is it strange that many today inquire, "What is this second birth?" Because the Savior's plain words have been twisted to give many contradictory explanations, let me tell you first of all what the new birth is not. Rebirth in Christ is not simply a hazy, happy religious response, an emotional upswing. You do not build your business or sustain your daily work on sentiment; even less can you establish your faith on feelings and passing impressions. Your religion must be rock-grounded; you must be able to say with Saint Paul, *"I know whom I have believed."*

This rebirth is not simply sorrow over your sins. All men are sorry for their transgressions when they have to pay the penalty. Judas was seized by remorse for betraying Christ. Yet, as he hanged himself in despair, he was far from this new birth. About 20,000 people in the United States also commit suicide every year. Think of it, a group of our countrymen about as large as the entire population of Reno, Nevada, each twelve months destroys itself and is cut off forever from the hope of a blessed eternity! Grief over their mistakes and missteps has brought them only terrifying anguish.

The rebirth which the Savior means is much more than the resolution to lead a better life, far more than self-improvement; it is quite the opposite of the popular notion that human society is constantly being reborn and elevated from the animal stage in its pilgrimage toward perfection. That delusion is taught to many of your children in American schools today. A few days ago a teacher wrote me: "Even in the first or second grades the teachers have to read stories about the little five-toed horse, the cave man, the way prehistoric men learned to use fire, tools, weapons, and other evolutionary theories. The text-books in the higher grades are charged with evolutionary ideas. In biology it is hard to get a volume without much evolutionary material in it. Indeed, I have been surprised to find such teachings and text-books where you would least expect them." This is not rebirth; it is retreat! I shudder to think what will happen to this country and its youth if day by day our boys and girls are taught as truths, theories which contradict the Bible, eliminate God, leave no necessity for Christ and His atonement. At a time when, with all our boasting culture, we have better and longer educational training for the masses, we also have the bloodiest, ghastliest, costliest destruction by war known to history. We ought to be honest enough to face the facts and admit that in this generation the world has moved backward and that, unless God Almighty intervenes, the worst we have yet known may be soft and easy compared with the revolutions and upheavals before us. Only one large European nation has kept out of war, atheistic Russia. With its Christless Communism the Red *régime* is planning the overthrow of all democratic governments which will be weakened by the excessive drains of war and by the readiness of their impoverished peoples to clutch at anything that seems to offer hope.

No, this rebirth of which Jesus spoke to Nicodemus is something far above improvement. It is not the patching, mending, repairing, of the old; rebirth means just what the term itself implies, a second birth, which produces an entirely new creature and a totally new existence. We live our old sin-marked lives until by God's grace we are brought to Christ, and then our old love for sin and hatred of righteousness stops. Our heart with its rebellion against God and its rejection of His mercies is changed; our mind with its love of lust is remade. While our bodies retain the same form and features, nevertheless our souls and our entire spiritual careers in Christ are absolutely new.

"How can these things be?" you demand with Nicodemus. To understand the marvel of this twice-born life, you must know the three *R's* of Christian faith: man's ruination, Christ's redemption, and the Spirit's regeneration. You must see at the very outset, without compromise or reserve, that the entire race needs rebirth; that mankind in its exceptionless totality, and above all others, you and I individually, are of ourselves hopeless and helpless in our sins. We must admit — and this is the hardest confession to wring from the lips of our smug, self-satisfied fellowmen today — that without Christ we are God's enemies, enemies of our own souls, servants of sin, living only for ourselves, the gratification of animal desires, and the heaping of money and power as the means of satisfying our lusts and ambitions. *"Without Me,"* Jesus says, *"ye can do nothing";* and there is no exaggeration in this sweeping statement. See Rome, for example, before Christ's Gospel reached that city of seven hills but seven thousand horrible vices. See France, without Christ during the Revolution, when wholesale murder and other equally terrifying perversions so firmly gripped the nation which had declared itself atheistic that the French assembly had to meet and acknowledge God's existence. Picture this world today rising up against its Maker, Redeemer, and Sanctifier and then realize that in the same way, if you are not for Christ (and remember His words, *"He that is not with Me is*

against Me"), you are spiritually dead. Just as little as a corpse in a casket can raise its cold, death-gripped arms, so little can you do anything good and God-pleasing. It is hard to say this, but you can never have the rebirth unless you know that without it you are "*dead in trespasses and sins.*" Just as you are perpetually grateful to the physician who discovers a hidden sickness, no matter how well you may feel, and prescribes the cure, so some day, please God, many of you will be thankful, if not here on earth, then in the better country above, for this warning, "Without Christ you are spiritually dead, eternally lost."

But oh, the marvelous mercies of Christ, by which we turn from man's ruination to Heaven's redemption! That glorious grace by which many of you join me to exclaim,

> Oh, the height of Jesus' love,
> Higher than the heavens above,
> Deeper than the depths of sea,
> Lasting as eternity!
> Love that found me, wondrous thought,
> Found me when I sought Him not!

No other devotion is comparable to the Savior's. We exalt, and rightly so, the patriotism of our American youth in these days of defense preparation. How indescribably greater is Christ's love for us! Hundreds of thousands of our young men, were the decision left to them, would not engage in military service. They are drafted. But there was nothing compulsory about Christ's yearning for our souls' salvation. The defenders of America are honored and paid, even if inadequately, for their patriotic services; Congressional medals and citations for bravery are their outstanding rewards. But Jesus was hated, persecuted, tortured, when He came to free us, and the only tribute He received was the cruel mockery that placed a crown of thorns on His bruised head, clothed Him with mock purple, and sarcastically forced a reed scepter into His hands. Men have laid down their lives for their country, but Jesus gave His own holy life for His enemies. He died for every one of us, died so that — our sins forgiven, our souls washed in the blood of His cross, the handwriting against us blotted out, the demands of God's Law fulfilled by His perfect obedience, the penalty for our wicked emotions, thoughts, and actions paid, every item of it, by the ransom of His love — we might live eternally.

Friend, do you know this second chapter, Christ's Redemption, in the greatest story ever told, this assurance that Jesus, while He is the Deliverer of the entire race, is particularly your personal Savior; that as He hung on the cross, He readily forgave those whose treachery and hatred had nailed Him there, but that He was also thinking mercifully of you and your place in heaven? Will you not let me know whether there is anything I can do to help bring you His redeeming love, anything at all which any one of the thousands of Christian pastors associated with us can offer to remove any doubts that may keep you from rejoicing in your salvation, to assist you in coming, humble and penitent, to this divine Deliverer from sin, the grave, and hell?

The assurance of that redemption brings rebirth in Christ. As soon as we say, "Jesus is mine, and I am His," and kneel in spirit before our Savior with the marks of the cross still impressed on His hands and His feet and the wound of the spear-thrust visible in His side, to declare, O Jesus, I am less than nothing, but Thou art more than everything to me! I am born in sin, filled with sin, surrounded by sin; but Thou, God's holy Son, didst become sin for me that I might be made righteous by the agony of the cross and Thy death at Calvary," in that very moment and by that faith we are reborn. We can join Saint Paul's exalting confidence: *"If any man be in Christ, he is a new creature; old things are passed away; behold, all things are become new."* We were *"dead in trespasses and sins,"* but now, in Christ, we are alive in grace and truth. We were *"children of wrath,"* but now, through our Savior, we become *"the sons of God."* Ours is a new mind; for while we loved evil, now we hate it and come to that higher plane in which we can seek *"whatsoever things are true, whatsoever things are honest, whatsoever things are just, whatsoever things are pure, whatsoever things are lovely, whatsoever things are of good report."* Ours is a new heart; for while cruel fears and weighted worries seek to burden us, we hear Jesus say, *"Let not your heart be troubled,"* and taking Him at His word, we have new hope, new courage, to face whatever His wisdom may send. Reborn in Christ, we have a new sense of victory. Temptations can be rejected, sins conquered, doubts dispersed. We can — and what a blessed assurance this is for the trouble-burdened days that may lie ahead! — meet famine, nakedness, peril, sword, and yet triumph: *"Nay, in all these things we are more than conquerors through Him that loved us. For I am persuaded that neither death, nor life, nor angels, nor principalities, nor powers, nor things present, nor things to come, nor height, nor depth, nor any other creature shall be able to separate us from the love of God, which is in Christ Jesus, our Lord."*

That rebirth, although it is inward, spiritual, must be shown by our daily conduct, in our homes, business, or school, during social or recreational activities. *"As ye have received the light, so walk ye in it"* is the universal rule for all Christians. You cannot truly be Christ's without radiating His love. You must be ready to *"show forth the praises of Him who hath called you out of dark-*

ness into His marvelous light." Let me say an earnest word
to church-members who are not light-bearers for Christ.
If you think that all the Lord wants of you is a more or
less regular weekly attendance at services, and if you believe
that for the other six days of the week you can live as the
Christless world does; if despite your Christian profession
you lie and deceive in your business, cheat in your marital
relations, fill your words and actions with hate; if people
see you in church on Sunday, taking up the collection or
ushering, and on Monday night they find you in a raw
night-club or watch you walking home unsteadily after
long hours in a tavern; if some of you women in church
societies spread scandal and enlarge on false rumors, belittle your own sisters in the faith; if your homes are dirty,
your children neglected; if your selfish nagging and bickering helps make your household a perpetual center of strife;
if some of you young people can speak enthusiastically
about Christ in your youth groups and then straightway
refuse to follow Him by supporting your parents, keeping
your minds and your bodies free from sensual sins, you
ought to ask yourselves, "Am I really born again? Is my
Christianity only a matter of habit instead of heart-deep
conviction?" It is tragic enough when unbelievers live in
open revolt against God, but it is twice as fatal if those
who call themselves Christians have their faith only in
name, and through godless living even become agents of
hell by helping to keep others from the faith.

This matter of the second birth, this becoming a new
creature in Christ, is not just a figure of speech or a
vague platitude. Think of the intense significance Jesus
attaches to this new life when He says, *"Verily, verily,
I say unto thee, Except a man be born again, he cannot
see the kingdom of God."* Here, then, repentant, redeemed, regenerated believers are offered the keys to the

kingdom. Without this rebirth you will never be enrolled as a citizen in your heavenly Father's kingdom.

If you would face your God to receive His mercy and forgiveness, it is not enough that you say: "I have always tried to think right, speak right, and do right. My life is an open book." (How about the uncut pages and the suppressed chapters that you are really ashamed to have any one read?)   To enter the kingdom, you need much more than that self-satisfied claim so often expressed in your letters to me, "I don't smoke, drink, or play cards." If you have nothing more to offer God, you will never see heaven.

You do not have the key to the kingdom when you declare, "I don't swear, I don't beat my wife, I don't gamble." You young folk should not regard yourselves as Christians simply because you are outwardly better than the fast crowd or because you have kept yourselves cleaner than many others.   Self-respecting heathen and atheists can say the same thing, and you are as far from heaven as they are, if you seek entrance to the Kingdom only on the record of personal performances like these.   Do not be satisfied with mere outward membership in a church; for, first of all — and how hard it is to say this! — there are churches today, as always, which are leading men's souls from Christ, questioning His truth when they ought to affirm it, denying His deity, belittling the blood of the cross and preaching salvation by character, good conduct, self-discipline, by anything except His atoning death; and in the second place, even if you belong to a true Church, outward affiliation is never enough.   Recall Christ's warning, *"Not every one that saith unto Me, Lord, Lord, shall enter into the kingdom of heaven, but he that doeth the will of My Father which is in heaven."*

Do not rely only on your baptism or your early Chris-

tian training at home! If your religion is in the past
tense, it can have no present blessing and future promise.
You cannot enter heaven by proxy, through the faith of
a God-fearing husband, wife, parents, or children. You
cannot earn your way into heaven by singing in choirs,
purchase entrance through large contributions, demand admission because you are a congregational officer or a young
people's society official. I thank God with you today for
everything that is good, noble, uplifting, in your life; but
the best we can offer is not enough in God's sight. Here
is the statement of the Lord Jesus Christ Himself, introduced with double assurance for twofold force: *"Verily,
verily I say unto thee, Except a man be born again, he
cannot see the kingdom of God."* Jesus does not say that
modern architecture, imposing organizations, powerful religious combines, heavy financial reserves, social-register
membership, ostentatious ritual, or political influence is
required to bring men into His kingdom and keep them
there as subjects of His glorious grace, but He does say,
"Ye must be born again!"

II

HOW CAN WE BE REBORN IN CHRIST?

What question, then, could be more vital than this
personal searching inquiry, which, I pray God, has been
forming itself in your hearts during these moments: "How
can I be reborn in Christ to receive these blessings? What
must I do to become a new creature and live this new life
of joy, hope, blessing?"

Now, men can change much by ingenuity, power,
science, scheming; but they cannot change themselves.
Prominent Americans, from New York to Hollywood, alter
their names, and it is commonly stated that an unofficial
yet drastic anti-Semitic policy at certain large universities
causes prospective Jewish students to petition the court for

new names; but this cannot mean new lives, new ideals, new power. Nikolai Ulynov may call himself Nikolai Lenin, Leiba Bronstein may parade as Leon Trotsky, but in the sight of God this change of names brings them no advantage whatever.

Again, people can change their appearance. For a while plastic surgery helped Dillinger, America's public enemy No. 1, escape the police; but face-lifting, hair-dyeing, feature-molding, never deceive the all-knowing God, never change the soul.

Medical science can perform startling alterations, for example, transplant the cornea from one person's eye to another and thus, in a sense, give new eyes for old. Drug treatments can help restore certain types of mentally deranged people to clear thinking; but all that surgery and medicine combined ever can do will not be able to remove human sin or grant inner rebirth by answering David's prayer, *"Create in me a clean heart, O God; and renew a right spirit within me."*

The anniversary of Abraham Lincoln's birth this week reminds us that the Emancipation Proclamation could free an entire race in this country from its slavery; but no merely human hero who has ever trod this earth can of himself liberate a single soul from sin.

Men can alter their religion. English history recounts the chameleonlike changes made by the Vicar of Bray who was a Catholic before the time of Henry VIII, a Protestant in his reign, a Roman Catholic again under Bloody Mary, and a Protestant once more under Elizabeth. The newspaper last week told us that Pastor Niemoeller, languishing in a Nazi prison, had left the Lutheran Church and become converted to Catholicism. This was a malicious falsehood, of course, and was soon denied; but it takes much more than a change of church-membership to get right with God.

Men can change their nationality, as did Benedict Arnold, who after his traitorous disloyalty fled to England; they can change their family — and how frequently this occurs when men or women are divorced, five, six, seven, or more times, contrary to God's laws and the simplest requirements of decency; they can change their minds — witness preachers who a few years ago proclaimed that they would never endorse a second war, now clamoring the loudest to send our young men across the seas for another European struggle; they can change the whole tone, trend, and tenor of a nation, as France revised its motto from "Liberty, Equality, Fraternity" to "Labor, Family, and the Fatherland"; men can redirect the course of rivers, blast high hills away, redraw the maps after military campaigns or treaties, yet, fellow-sinners and fellow-redeemed, listen closely, one change there is that ingenuity and power can never produce: this regeneration of the human soul.

For that we need the Holy Spirit. As God the Father created man without human cooperation; as God the Son redeemed us without any help on our part, so God the Holy Spirit Himself changes our lives by His almighty power. God could have made our conversion and regeneration a hard, complicated, lengthy process; but He loved us too much for that. So His wisdom and love combined to offer this method for your rebirth: Whenever or wherever you read or hear God's Word and learn to say, "Christ died for me"; however, in a Bible sermon, by a Christ-centered radio message, a Gospel tract, the contemplation of a picture showing Christ's suffering in your stead, — you know that Jesus is your Savior and Substitute, — the Holy Spirit is at work through that Word to call you out of the darkness into the light, from the first birth to the second, from death to life.

When Jesus continues to tell Nicodemus, *"Except a*

man be born of WATER *and of the Spirit, he cannot enter into the kingdom of God,"* He also shows us that through faith in Baptism's promise we are likewise washed of our sins. Frequently those who accept our radio mission's invitation to Christian instruction and Baptism send me pictures after their baptism and admission into the Church, and among our highest spiritual joys are these evidences that through water and the Spirit many are being reborn, whom we shall perhaps never meet here on this earth, but who on the Great Day will stand beside us, face to face with Jesus. May God likewise bless this appeal and show to many of you who have misunderstood or neglected Christ's plain teaching the heavenly blessing that can come through faith, by the washing of regeneration!

Therefore hear the Word of God: Be baptized! Let the Spirit work for your new life! Since the only barrier that can ever keep men from this rebirth is their own unbelief, the call of this hour is to preach and believe the pure, undiluted message of Christ's love and the cleansing power of His Cross to establish Bible-reading in our homes and increased Bible-reading in our churches.

First of all, you need Christ and His Word. Wherever your radios are and however you receive this message, — in the quiet of your home or in a hotel far from your loved ones; in a speeding automobile or a public institution; a crowded restaurant or the seclusion of your room; on a stream-lined train or in a hut far beyond the fringes of the railroad, — now I am speaking to you individually: God has led me in this moment, heavy with the possibilities of unspeakable blessing, to ask you, "Have you been born again? Have you accepted Jesus Christ as your own Savior? Have you come before God to confess your repeated sins and unrighteousness, to find, as you behold the cross, the life-giving assurance that all your guilt is removed by Jesus' blood as far as the East is from the West?" In His name I can promise you — and thousands in this audience will support what I say by the yea and amen of their own experience — that in our blessed Lord there is the joy, peace, power, and victory that make life despite all its sorrows a hundred times worth the living, and death in Christ, even with all its pain and parting, ten thousand times worth dying.

Mark this day on your calendar as the day that Jesus has called you to come to Him, to be reborn in Him, to live forever with Him! Pray, as I have prayed for you, that as the Savior's arms are now stretched wide in the appeal of His limitless grace which says, *"Come unto Me, all ye that labor and are heavy laden, and I will give you rest"* — rest through redemption, rest through rebirth, rest for soul and mind, rest during war and peace — the Holy Spirit may find an unobstructed way into your heart and help you say, "O Christ,

> " 'Just as I am, without one plea
> But that Thy blood was shed for me
> And that Thou bid'st me come to Thee,
> O Lamb of God, I come, I come.' "

Amen

BACK TO THE EARLY CHRISTIAN CHURCH!

"A whole year they assembled themselves with the church and taught much people. And the disciples were called Christians first in Antioch." — Acts 11:26

Triune God:

Accept our heartfelt thanks for the preaching of Thy saving Word, Christ's promise of pardon for every evil in our lives and the pledge of Heaven's blessings through faith in His merciful atonement! For His sake forgive us our slowness and sleepiness in spreading the message of hope and happiness pledged by the Cross! Make us zealous to enlarge the boundaries of Thy Church by leading lost souls to Jesus! Holy Spirit, use our broadcast as the means of converting sinners to their Savior, recalling the unfaithful, comforting the bereaved and afflicted! Bless true Christian congregations with increasing loyalty to Thy Word! Grant them a greater degree of outward unity in doctrine and practice! May those who love Thee as their only Redeemer and therefore are members of Thy Church Universal also be united before men, even as Thou, our Triune God, art one! Rebuke every one who would split the churches by doctrines opposed to Thy Word, confusing many minds and promoting dangerous heresy! As the clouds of war darken, show us the gleam of hope radiated by a loving faith and make us light-bearers in an age of gloom! In Jesus' name we ask this and whatever we need for soul and body. Hear us by His promise! Amen.

OVER in war-torn Europe, the newspapers state, churches must be kept open day and night. What reassurance we could find in this report if the new regulation had been made to accommodate vast throngs, reverently, repentantly crowding God's house from early morning until midnight! Instead, the opening of these buildings is simply designed to prevent loss of time in breaking through locked doors when fighting fires caused by incendiary bombs!

In our own country we sorely need fire from heaven to

stir Christian zeal into flame and direct many of our churches to keep their doors unbarred, so that, day or night, those without Christ — and Jesus Himself has told us that means without eternal hope — can hear and study God's plan for their redemption. We should have churches that bring Christ to the people on street corners and in public meetings, in gold-coast apartments and slum tenements, on the right and the wrong sides of the railroad tracks; churches which will deflate the boast of the Communists that they alone are interested in all groups and races; churches preaching the full Christ to all classes and masses, colors and conditions, ranks and races.

No one can carefully study world trends today without quickly coming to the conclusion that millions of our fellow-men, perhaps we ourselves, may meet privation, suffering, horror, on a far wider scale than ever before. The war is spreading. Its shadows have already overcast the Balkans. The thunder of approaching battle may soon begin to rumble over the Near East, and on our own shores statesmen predict a definite date for America's entrance into the war.

How crucial the task of Christ's Church in such times! Where, in the midst of soul sorrows, individual anguish, a hundred kinds of grief and trouble, can we find courage, guidance, unfailing hope, if not in our Savior's sin-canceling, burden-sharing love and in the Church that proclaims His grace? Other agencies are trying to prepare the American people for difficult days. The millers and bakers have announced a new kind of bread, with minerals and vitamins that will help the nation "withstand the stresses and strains of war." But *"man shall not live by bread alone,"* especially not in heart-trying periods like these. The churches must give spiritually famished men the Christ who says, *"I am the* LIVING *Bread."*

Politicians cannot solve our perplexities, especially not when they admit that preelection pledges are nothing more than "campaign oratory." Our vast defense program, as necessary as it is, alone can offer no assurance of personal protection. The supreme need of every age, but the emphasized superneed in this crisis, is the Lord Jesus Christ; and the divinely appointed institution for bringing us this Savior is the Church.

God grant that in this hour of dark urgency, while the souls of men are dying, American churches will not fritter away their time by preaching self-improvement, self-righteousness, self-deliverance (and that is essentially the sum and substance of Modernism), but point sinners to the cross!

If we are to be blessed by loyal churches that can save the world from itself and speak peace, pardon, comfort, strength, hope, to men's hearts, we must disavow every modern denial, every twentieth-century question-mark, every present-day compromise between truth and error. We must return to the fundamental principles that lived in the first-century Church.

With the cry, then,

BACK TO THE EARLY CHRISTIAN CHURCH!

let us through God's Spirit learn vital lessons for today from His Word in Acts, chapter eleven, verse twenty-six: "*A whole year they assembled themselves with the Church and taught much people. And the disciples were called Christians first in Antioch.*"

I

IT WAS A TRULY *CHRISTIAN* CHURCH

Saint Paul, mightiest missionary of Jesus Christ, together with Barnabas, his assistant, founded the first Christian church in Antioch. This city, the third largest of the

Empire — sometimes called "the second Rome" — promoted everything that the apostle's message sternly forbade. In that imposing metropolis of long, broad, colonnaded avenues paganism had built a temple to Apollo, perhaps the most magnificent edifice of its day; and by contrast, Christ's first followers were probably far too poor to have even a small, one-room church; instead, they turned their homes into churches. The central object in that jewel-studded, lavishly adorned temple was a huge marble statue, glorifying Apollo, chief of many conflicting gods and goddesses; and the ceremonial pomp with which he was worshiped was most spectacular. In contrast, Saint Paul could offer only a blood-stained cross with the crucified Savior, whose atoning death for sinners was irreconcilably opposed to everything which the heathen temples in Antioch taught or the masses believed and practiced. Outside the city were the notorious groves of Daphne; and there, in the name of religion, commercialized vice, unbridled sensuality, hideous perversions, flourished for the profit of pagan priests. Into that stronghold of sin, superstition, and savage lust Paul and Barnabas, alone, were it not for the Savior's presence, unarmed except by God's Word, came to issue the warning that this degrading idolatry, these practices too abhorrent even to mention, were helping to send masses in Antioch to hell; that the pretentious temples would fall and the glittering idols crumble; that the proud image-worshipers, boastful of their Greek culture, relying on the wealth and commerce of their city, must turn in repentance to Jesus Christ and acclaim Him who in despised Judea had died as a convicted criminal, their living Savior and true God.

It took courage to speak with such unsparing denunciation of sin; and God give us preachers today who will not be moved by thoughts of personal gain or loss nor by

fear or favor of their membership, but who as true watch-
men over souls will issue clear-cut warnings against the
inescapable destruction that follows all godlessness! More
than courage, however, was required when Paul and Barnabas, according to our text, stayed in Antioch for a whole
year and during the first part of their joint ministry *"assembled themselves with the church and taught much
people."* They had God with them, and neither the influence nor the money in that stronghold of satanic vice
could defeat their efforts.

Note that they *"taught"* the people of Antioch. We
pay far too little attention to solid teaching and sound
indoctrination. I will venture to say that today there are
dozens of churches in any large American city which receive
as members people who have no previous religious training
and who may not even be Christians at heart. Membership thus easily gained is frequently broken with cor-
responding ease. How different the insistent teaching of
Paul and Barnabas, this week-after-week building the
groundwork on which an unshaken faith could be reared!
No wonder those Antioch Christians could defy ridicule
and torture!

If twentieth-century congregations are to regain the
power too many have lost and prepare their members to
withstand the perils of a threatening future, the cry
must be: Back to the early Christian churches for their
earnest, painstaking, thorough teaching of God's truth!
Christian pastors, back to the apostles' patient, persevering
instruction in the saving Word! Give us sermons with
texts from the Scriptures rather than subjects from magazines or motion-pictures, Bible classes in churches rather
than dramatic-arts classes, daily Christian soul- or heart-
training for our children in preference to any modern
theories of mind-training, catechisms with the Christian

doctrine explained in questions and answers, a thousand times rather than some of the Sunday-school books with stories about bluebirds and pussy-willows, yet not a syllable about Christ! Let the church-workers go from house to house, introducing family prayers, family hymns, family Scripture-reading; and by this sound instruction we shall be able to recapture the unconquerable courage of those first Christians.

What was it, do you suppose, the apostles taught those first worshipers in Antioch? If you know Saint Paul, that question answers itself. Wherever he went, to whomever he spoke, he could say, *"I determined not to know anything among you save Jesus Christ, and Him crucified."* His soul, heart, and mind were moved by a single purpose. You can sum it all up in one word: Christ. He believed Christ, trusted Christ, preached Christ, practiced Christ, defended Christ, exalted Christ — Christ always and Christ alone! Listen to him as he condemns every rival creed and tells the Galatians, *"Though we or an angel from heaven preach any other gospel unto you than that which we have preached unto you, let him be accursed!"*

On this international radio system that your interest and prayers, under God, have helped build to astonishing proportions, we likewise have only one message: Christ's eternal Gospel of grace. All else in life is so trivial, temporal, and worthless in comparison with this privilege of repeating for you Jesus' first sermon, *"Repent ye and believe the Gospel,"* that every broadcast finds its basic appeal in the Cross, the promise of salvation through Christ's atoning death.

Once more, then, we cry out across America: Behold the Lord Jesus Christ, the truest Friend you can ever have, the only Guide to eternity, the one unfailing Counselor in all affliction, the divine Companion on life's hardest, dreariest ways, the heavenly Helper for each need of soul and body — but first of all your Savior from sin, your Redeemer from ruin, your Deliverer from death! Behold Christ in His unbounded love for each of you, sinful, disobedient as all men are! See Him in His eternally finished atonement as your Substitute, suffering the terrors of your sins, so that nothing remains for you to earn, fulfil, or complete! Consider Christ in His astonishing mercy, by which every one of you, overshadowed by dark sins of the past, distrustful of your own ability to defeat evil, fearful of what the future may bring, can make Christ your own, without price or payment, condition or credential, introduction or recommendation, simply by believing His blood-bought promises! Lift up your eyes to the cross in this faith — and Christ will not only grant you *"the power of God unto salvation,"* forgiveness for your own soul, courage and strength for your own heart; He also gives to twentieth-century churches their one message, their supreme purpose, their only right to existence.

But Christ — and I mean the Biblical Savior, the true, eternal, and all-powerful God, and not merely an exalted human figure; Christ, the bleeding, dying, resurrected Redeemer, not simply the Example and Leader — is being systematically pushed out of many pulpits, barred from numerous churches, passed over silently in large religious periodicals, repeatedly attacked in divinity schools. Recently a theological professor at one of the oldest universities in our country wrote a new book on Christian revelation. That man, employed to train students for the ministry, unhesitatingly declares that the Scriptures are not inspired and inerrant, that Jesus Christ is not literally the Son of God, that the Virgin Birth is unnecessary and other miracles impossible. He denies, as Modernists regularly do, the sinfulness of all mankind, and hence he has no room for the vicarious atonement, no place for the cross, the blood, and the open grave as the evidence of our personal redemption. Jesus, according to his book, is not the only Way, Christianity not the only creed. The Bible is by no means the final revelation; instead we witness a constant development and growth by which the race with increasing clarity can understand the divine will.

Because such denial of every fundamental Christian truth is shared and supported by a constantly growing number of clergymen, congregations, theological seminaries, we need not wonder why the richly blessed United States has experienced, side by side with this apostasy, deep-rooted national, industrial, and social perplexities that neither statesmanship nor the expenditure of increasing billions has solved. If in His all-wise providence God sees fit, despite our prayers, to have our nation hurled into active conflict, do not say that we have not deserved the terrifying ordeals which even victory must bring! As empty pews, closed houses of worship, and waning religious influence remind us that many churches are slipping fast, let the cry that sweeps across this land demand: Back to the early Christian Church for its loyalty to Christ! Back to Gospel-preaching, Bible-teaching, Scripture-searching! Back to the Cross!

If this be a summons asking you of the clergy for a more definite, unhesitating acknowledgment of Jesus Christ in your sermons and in your testimony against apostasy in your own denomination; if this cry, Back to the preaching and teaching of Paul! Back to the simple Gospel! mean that in churches where the crowded calendar of socials, card parties, dramatics, dances, and other non-spiritual activities leaves little time for personal missionary activities, you strive to see that the Lord is accorded the first place; if this cry, Back to the early Church! lead

you of the laity to protest against the assault on the Lord
Jesus Christ from the very pulpits of buildings you have
helped erect and, when such protest is unheeded, to with-
draw entirely from any church that sells out to Modernism — I still say, Back to the Christ-centered loyalty of
the early Church!

It was faithfulness to Christ which helped give the
believers in Antioch and us the name "Christian." For
a dozen years the name of Jesus Christ seemed to have been
ignored entirely by the world at large. To all human ap-
pearances the crucifixion was the end. Jesus had failed
completely. Those who followed Him called themselves
"brethren," "children of God," "believers," "disciples."
And when in Antioch, almost thirteen years after Christ's
death, the term "Christian" appears for the first time,
it seems to have been introduced as a title of ridicule. In
only two other passages is the term "Christian" found:
once when Agrippa, having heard Paul's impassioned plea
to accept Christ, turned to the apostle and objected,
"Almost thou persuadest me to become a Christian," as if
Agrippa would say, "You have nearly succeeded in making
me, with all my wealth, power, and dignity, one of those
low, outcast followers of Christ." In the other passage
Saint Peter speaks of suffering *"as a Christian";* he implies,
we may suppose, that the word "Christian" called forth
the picture of a persecuted, martyred believer following in
the footsteps of his Savior's suffering.

The sophisticated Greeks and Jews in Antioch did not
name the first believers after Paul, Barnabas, or any noted
disciple of Christ. The mighty apostle and his assistant
so effaced themselves that the only impression heathen
visitors at these early Christian services ever received was
the continued exaltation of the Lord Jesus. One name
constantly stood out in the sermons, the hymns, the

prayers: the Name above every name. Christ's Word was their guide, Christ's cross their glory, Christ's death their life. If a doctrinal difficulty arose, they inquired, "What does Christ say?" If they were confronted by a question of daily conduct, they asked, "What is the verdict of Christ's instruction?" If thoughts of increasing sorrow burdened them, they said, "What comfort does Christ give?" No wonder, then, that with their faith completely pervaded by Christ, they were called *Christians!*

How about us? If the world today were to give American churches names derived from their teachings, what would we be called? Not always "Christian," I answer; for I have copies of sermons by reputed leaders in which the mention of Jesus is so incidental or directly opposed to the true Christ that, if some one who knew nothing about Christianity were to pronounce judgment, he could easily call these preachers "reformers," "socialists," "politicians," "moral uplifters," "war fomenters," but would never think of them as "Christians," because they offer Christ scant attention. There would be much more honesty and mutual understanding, much less hypocrisy and misleading of trusting souls, if those who have rejected Christ as the Savior, our one and only Redeemer, would also discard His name and say openly, "We no longer lay claim to the title 'Christian.'"

Another fact must also have been responsible for this title: the Christ-directed life of those early worshipers. In heathen Antioch one could see that they were a separated people by their language, the absence of profanity, licentious talk, slander. Their homes were different. They kept their distance from the groves of sensual Daphne. As an early writer concedes: "Christians marry and have children like every one else, but they do not expose their children. They have meals in common but not wives.

They are in the flesh, but they do not live after the flesh."
Another Greek writer exclaims, "What women these Christians have!" So it was, then, that Antioch in its blunted paganism, unable to understand the strange people in its own midst, called them after Him in whose footsteps these believers tried to walk.

We note, however, that the word "Christian," when spoken by a customary but slight change of pronunciation in the Greek, could mean "good," "virtuous," "gentle," and it is more than likely that this was an additional element of sarcasm. The Christians, so worldly-minded Antioch concluded, thought themselves better than the rest. They were the virtuous people, the "goody-goodies" who were not to be found in the pleasure palaces, the drinking-dens, gambling-places, or before the depraved spectacles at the arena. They lived Christ and hence were called "Christians."

We have reason for pause here. Once again we may well ask, "If our names described our conduct, would we still be called 'Christians'?" Thank God, the renewing power of rebirth in Jesus, today as always, under the Spirit's blessing produces *"new creatures."* It can be shown in a hundred ways that true faith helps to keep Christians from lawbreaking and crime; that of all classes in the United States the followers of Jesus Christ as a group are the most law-abiding in the nation and its leading moral force. But it is similarly true that often the requirements for congregational membership become lax. If I mention the term "church discipline," more than half of you will not understand me. But among the early believers this rule prevailed: Whenever any one who belonged to the Church became guilty of a public, scandalous sin, he had to repent publicly; and if he then stubbornly refused, he was excommunicated. In how many churches is this rule still maintained? Is it not true today that in some congregations which bear the Savior's name men and women are tolerated as members or even function as officials who are engaged in an enterprise that wilfully destroys morality, who transact shady business deals, oppress the poor, connive with unrighteousness, profiteer through others' losses? Is it not a practice that churches craving the limelight of publicity open their pulpits to atheists, multi-divorced actresses, unconverted millionaires? Is it not common knowledge that some religious societies — you can see the pictures in your newspapers — put on entertainments that differ only in degree from the *risqué* theatricals of the world? If you want one of the reasons the churches have not grown as they should, you can find it in the tragedy that the line of separation between believer and unbeliever is being systematically erased, that the requirements for church admission are too frequently dependent upon the size of contributions rather than the extent of a consecrated life. Correspondingly, if you want a source of new blessing and convincing publicity for the Savior's cause, more direct than any advertising which men control, have Christians live their faith! Let every follower of Jesus put His teachings into practice for a year or two, and this nation will be shaken by the greatest upheaval for good it has ever experienced. Let Christians throughout the world live Christ, without compromise or concession, and as hard as it may be in those areas where the conflict between Christ and Caesar means persecution, confiscation, imprisonment, it will not be long before the marvelous dynamics of God's Holy Spirit are working stupendous changes over the entire earth. What else, then, must the cry be if not: Back to the early Church for its insistence on a Christ-centered life!?

If you young folks know that by accepting Christ as your Savior you cannot go with the fast crowds which reject Him; that you must deny yourselves and follow the instruction of His Word: *"Flee youthful lusts!"* *"Keep thyself pure!"* ask God for strength when worldly companions sneeringly call you a "Christian," to resist these tempting assaults! Resolve that, God helping you, the name of Christ which you bear will not be blasphemed by refusing to keep yourself clean and pure for your marriage.

Realize, every one of you, that the title "Christian" is the highest and holiest of all names any one can ever bear. A few of you can say, "I am a millionaire." Thank God that you are! But your millions will never solve your earthly problems or purchase your entrance into heaven. Others can say, "I am a Harvard graduate, a Phi Beta Kappa, too," and I will answer: "My hat is off to you for your achievement. But what help can a Cambridge diploma and a fraternity key bring when the doctor whispers, 'Only a few minutes more!'?" Some of you say, "I am a Daughter of the American Revolution," "I belong to the United Daughters of the Confederacy!" — and I would be the last to belittle the benefits that are yours through illustrious ancestors. But you yourself are fighting on one side or the other in a battle far more decisive than the Revolution or the Civil War. The supreme question for you is not, "What title does my money, my learning, my social position, my ancestry, bring me?" but: "Am I a Christian?" "Am I Christ's in my faith and life?" Everything else will pass away. Prizes, university degrees, public acclaim, will be hushed by the silence of the grave; but when on that great Day we stand before the throne and can say, "I am Christ's, and He is mine," we shall recognize that this title "Christian," "Christ's," once used in sarcasm, has become the seal of a triumphant faith which brought us to glory.

II

IT WAS A TRULY CHRISTIAN *CHURCH*

If you are blessed by this trust, then no matter what the color of your skin is, whatever race or creed may be yours, you are a member of the holy Christian Church. If you reject Jesus as God's Son and your Savior, then, lest there be any fatal misunderstanding, I repeat God's truth: you do not belong to His Church, though you may be a fully enrolled member, a deacon, an organist, even a pastor of a congregation.

So much misunderstanding lurks behind the term "church" that I want to explain it to you, as Saint Paul showed its meaning to the early believers. In the first place, there are churches which you and I can see, local groups or congregations, like that which our text describes when it says of Paul and Barnabas that *"for a whole year they assembled themselves with the church."* In such bodies there may be hypocrites and unbelievers, and it is a serious mistake for any one to believe that if he is a member of a local congregation, he has the keys to the Kingdom. Equally wrong is the attitude which refuses affiliation with a true congregation where the Word is preached and God's ordinances are obeyed.

At the Apostle's time such groups of Christians were found in Judea, Samaria, Syria, in various sections of Asia Minor, and they were glorious congregations, despite their weaknesses. They had one blessing which men have removed from us, entire agreement in faith. At Jerusalem, Caesarea, Damascus, Cyprus, here in Antioch, all Christians confessed the same creed. There were no denominational differences then, no Protestants or Catholics, no Lutherans or Reformed, no liberal or conservative churches. These primitive Christians lacked much that we enjoy. Many groups had no church-building or pastor of their own. Theological seminaries did not exist. Despite these difficulties, however, they had what we, with all our wealth and advantages, have never been able to achieve: complete unity.

Today in the United States alone there are over two hundred different forms of Christianity. In place of co-operation we have competition, and not always fair, clean competition. Instead of churches standing together against their common enemies, atheism and Modernism, we read in religious papers, for example, savage attacks like these on the Church I represent: "With the exception of the fall of man the human race has suffered no disaster comparable to that of the Protestant revolt. . . . Adam's disobedience separated men from the friendship of God and cast them out of Paradise; Luther's rebellion separated men from the friendship of Christ and cast them out of the Church." Instead of worshiping together, Christians are kept apart; for no true follower of the Lord Jesus will knowingly make any concession to wilful error. Within some denominations (you write me this yourselves) there are two distinct trends, one clearly modernist and Christ-denying, the other loyal and Christ-exalting. You would not tolerate a fundamental difference of that kind in business; yet it flourishes almost unchallenged, it seems, in the King's great business.

Often the claim is raised that denominationalism is good because it strengthens the spirit of competition. If there were blessings in such rivalry, it certainly would show itself today, when we have more Christian creeds than ever before; but, as the Government census reveals, one large denomination after the other has lost in membership during the last decennial census. Whichever way you look at it, with all the good God has permitted to be accomplished by denominationalism, the fact that there are so many different creeds in conflict, the one denying what the other affirms, is ultimately due to sin, some one's refusal to take God's Word as the supreme authority, some leader's insistence that reason, perhaps even pride or personal acclaim, must be placed above divine revelation.

If you stop for a moment to realize what a completely harmonious Church would mean, with Christians unanimous in their acceptance of every Scriptural, revealed truth; if you could see church-members throughout the world united in the same faith, their hostility buried forever (and there is no hatred more cruel and deep than the antagonism which has burned thousands at the stake, cut off their heads, dropped them into seething oil, choked them before a crucifix), does not this prayer form in your heart, "O God, bring us back to the first Church with its unity of faith!"?

Can such outward oneness be reestablished? God is great and all-powerful. Who among us would dare to say that this is impossible under His blessing? I feel equally sure, however, that if outward Christianity does not pray and work and strive in efforts far greater than in the past, unity will not come, since God will not force it upon us. Therefore pray for true unity, a 100-per-cent acceptance of God's Word — no outward agreement reached by behind-the-scenes concessions or double-meaning phraseology, but by absolute inner oneness.

Work for a return of unity! In my own Church we are eager to unite the Lutheran bodies, and I ask those within my group to pray to our heavenly Father that these efforts may be blessed, in His time, by a true, God-pleasing agreement. But why should such efforts be restricted to the Lutheran Church? The great Reformer protested until the last against the use of his name to designate those who followed him. He did not want the churches separated.

We are ready to go as far as God's Word goes on these questions. When we are asked to go beyond the divine Word, however, no matter what the cost of refusal may be, we, too, put our hand on the Bible and say with Luther: "Here we stand. We cannot do otherwise. God help us! Amen."

If only every Christian who subscribes to these two statements, "We believe the Bible to be the inspired and inerrant Word of God; and we believe that through faith in Jesus Christ, God and man, our only Savior, we are redeemed for time and eternity" (the two truths uppermost in the hearts of many of you Baptists, Methodists, Congregationalists, Presbyterians, Roman Catholics, Greek Catholics, and other Christian groups) would systematically study the differences that separate us, with the resolution: "I will not be moved by tradition, association, or human authority. I will not consider loss or gain. I will not put my denomination above Christ nor any man-made creed above His Word. I am willing to come out and be separated from any form of denial," we could feel confident that God would give us far greater outward unity.

With all existing differences, however, we should not forget that the term "church" is also used in the Scriptures, and was so explained by Paul and Barnabas to the people of Antioch, as a designation for an invisible group that you cannot count, the congregation of "all believers," whoever they may be and wherever they are, the Church Universal. "The communion of saints" has no foundations of brick or granite, no dated corner-stone laid by man's hand. It is built rather *"upon the foundation of the apostles and prophets, Jesus Christ Himself being the chief Corner-stone."* What surpassing comfort in the truth that the kingdom of God, as Jesus promises, is *"within you"!* This great Christian Church is not an earthly but a spiritual realm. Although we are separated into various denominations, in this one holy Christian Church, which extends from continent to continent, all who love the Lord Jesus are bound together by ties that will be fully expressed only in the perfect oneness of heaven! In that invisible, glorious Church there are members of every Protestant or Catholic division, people of every color and clime, land and language! For, however else they may differ, they are one in their complete acceptance of Jesus Christ and of Him alone as their Savior, no matter what their Church may teach in contradiction.

My fellow-redeemed, if you are a church-member, what appeal could be more direct than the apostle's plea, *"Examine yourselves whether ye be in the faith; prove your own selves!"* If you are outside the Church and want to have the assurance of forgiveness, God's guidance for all troubles, Christ's help in every need, the Spirit's blessing in resisting temptation, ask God with your whole heart to make you — not wealthy, learned, influential, but — a Christian, redeemed by Christ, washed in His blood, blessed by membership in a true Church! God give you that surpassing grace for our Savior's sake! Amen!

SON OF GOD, GIVE US THY GLORY!

"The glory which Thou gavest Me I have given them that they may be one, even as We are one: I in them and Thou in Me."— Saint John 17:22, 23

Precious Savior:

As we prepare once more to witness Thy suffering in our stead, Thy crucifixion on our behalf, Thy death for our life, give us a humble spirit that banishes all self-righteousness; a contrite heart clinging penitently to Thy mercy; a trusting soul which, freed from doubt, confidently builds its hope only on Thy blood-bought atonement! O Jesus, our God, our Sovereign, our Redeemer, bless us during the coming Lenten season, above all else, with this glorious faith! By the Spirit's indwelling remove every sinful distraction which would prevent us from centering our love on Thy suffering and dying for our redemption! Help us gladly to hear the Passion-tide message and apply its truths to ourselves! In Thy love stifle every doubt that would keep us from confessing our transgressions and finding pardon and peace in Thee! Give us both the desire and the power to walk in the light and show forth Thy praise before men! Preserve us in this truth until Thou shalt come to call us home to Thy glory! O Christ of endless compassion, hear us, as Thou hast promised! Amen.

IF you are burdened by cares and worries; if you suffer pain of body, mind, or soul; if you are dissatisfied with yourself, distrustful of others, disturbed by fears for your salvation; if, above all, you want certainty of faith, here is Heaven's promise, the seventeenth chapter of Saint John's gospel. When our broadcast is over, do Christ the honor of taking the three or four minutes required to read this glorious chapter thoughtfully for yourself, aloud for your family. When you have finished, you, too, should say: "What a hallowed glimpse of the Savior's love has been ours! What holy self-giving, heavenly strength, divine comfort, lives in these twenty-six verses!"

Many Christians acclaim this intercession the greatest

[250]

of all prayers preserved in the Scriptures; yet no one knows the exact place nor the precise hour of the night it was spoken. Perhaps the Holy Spirit would center our entire attention on each word overflowing with sustaining truth and remind us that through Christ, particularly before ordeals and trials such as many of us face, we, too, can approach God anywhere, at any time.

We do know, however, that the outstanding mark of this monumental prayer was Christ's personal pleading for His disciples. As in Old Testament days the high priest interceded for the people before God, so Christ, both the eternal New Testament High Priest and the everlasting Sacrifice for the world's sins, implores His Father in this unparalleled chapter for those who are His. Before twenty-four hours have elapsed the Lord Jesus will have been betrayed, taken captive, beaten, buffeted, bespat, crowned with thorns, condemned to death, crucified, killed, and laid in the quiet of Joseph's new grave; yet with the rest of His earthly life measured only in hours, the Savior in this prayer primarily thinks not of Himself, the anguish in the Garden, the agony at the hands of His own country-men, the soul-crushing guilt of all human sin that would nail Him to the cross; with less than a day separating Him from torture such as mankind has never known, Jesus, in His boundless love, intercedes for you and for me. Clearly He says, *"Neither pray I for these* [the disciples] *alone but for them also which shall believe on Me through their word,"* that is, for every one who since that Thursday night has accepted Christ as the only but all-bestowing Savior. Hold fast to this promise of Jesus praying for you, your own High Priest, not adorned with sacred ephod and robe nor with breastplate of precious stones and triple crown of gold but dressed in the ordinary clothing of His day, a true man among other men, yet the Son of God on

His knees in earnest intercession as His petition wings its
way heavenward for your redemption!

Only a divine Christ could pray that way. Only the
unquenchable love of God's own Son could speak these
entreaties for you and me a few hours before the horrors
of hell would break loose upon Him. What better can we
do, then, my fellow-redeemed, as we prepare for the Lenten
pilgrimage to Calvary, than direct our attention to the
Savior as He appeals for us in the words of this high-
priestly prayer (Saint John, chapter seventeen, verses
twenty-two and twenty-three), *"The glory which Thou
gavest Me I have given them that they may be one, even
as We are one; I in them and Thou in Me,"* and to send
an echo of Christ's words back to Him in heaven as
we pray,

SON OF GOD, GIVE US THY GLORY!

the glory of sonship, of spiritual unity, and of Thy constant
indwelling in us.

I

GIVE US THE GLORY OF DIVINE SONSHIP!

What is this glory that Jesus gives all believers? Bible
students have offered various answers; but if we approach
God's Word without bowing to contradictory reason, tradition, or expediency and take His statements at full value,
we find Christ's greatest glory in this, that He is the
eternal Son of God. Blunted, bigoted enemies may speak
of Him in a dozen other ways and diabolically seek to
destroy this central truth. Yet Jesus remains God's Son.
That is the glory He had with the Father before the beginning of the world; and now, as His earthly life draws to
its close, Jesus, ever-blessed Savior that He is, in this
high-priestly prayer says that He shares the glory of His
Sonship by making us the sons of God!

If the Scriptures had not given us this assurance, we would think it blasphemy to presume that we in our sins can ever become sons of God in His holiness. But His Word, which can never be broken though the earth beneath us give way, though the mountains move, the seas dry up, and the heavens fall, His inerrant, inspired truth, pledges, *"Behold what manner of love the Father hath bestowed upon us that we should be called the sons of God!"* Here is the additional surety, *"As many as received Him, to them gave He power to become the sons of God."* Here is repeated certainty, *"As many as are led by the Spirit of God, they are the sons of God."*

Despite this multiplied grace our too human heart exclaims, "We the sons of God?" This is such astonishing mercy that in an age of treachery, cruelty, degeneracy, we hurry to ask, "Oh, where can we find the promise of becoming God's sons to share Jesus' glory?" At the cross, we answer, where Christ's blood cleansed us from our sins! At Calvary, where He cried in the agony of black lone-liness as our guilt brought its punishment upon Him! At Golgotha, where He died to reconcile us with His Father and make us children of grace instead of wrath! You become God's sons through faith, by knowing, believing, trusting Jesus, by approaching Him in contrite sorrow over your sins, yet in the confidence of their complete removal. You become God's sons through that new and second birth in which all who are born of the flesh are reborn in the Spirit.

With that limitless grace, why do Christians ever say that they are poor when they are heirs and joint heirs with Christ of everything God possesses; when despite earthly poverty their heavenly Father can give them, if necessary, the riches of the universe? Why do Christ's disciples often feel that they are helpless when angel legions can be summoned to assist God's sons? Why do we who love the Lord Jesus think at times that we have been defeated when life's sorrows crowd in on us? We ought to believe that God Almighty, who knows our needs better than we ourselves, will turn every trial into triumph, each bodily affliction to our spiritual advantage. We ought to have the confidence that, since our Father cherished every one of us with a devotion that sent His Son to a death of shame and horror for us, He loved us too much to have life's cruelties overwhelm us.

If you are Christ's, then hold your head high as you direct it to the cross; for you are God's child and share the Savior's glory. If men revile or condemn you, do not lose courage! In this high-priestly prayer Jesus declares that He *has* given you this glory, not that He *will* give it. His indescribable blessing starts here on earth when you are brought back to God through faith. You can be God's son now. The glory that Christ wants to bestow on us begins in this life, in the peace of soul and mind we have with God as our Father, in the calm confidence for every earthly anguish that *"the sufferings of this present time are not worthy to be compared with the glory which shall be revealed in us."*

It was of this heavenly radiance, too, that Jesus spoke in our text. Because we are God's sons through His suffering in our stead and our behalf, we partake of His glorious eternity. Our bodies may be wasted in disease, broken by accident, worn out through old age; the time may come — it is closer to some of you than you realize — when the lungs stop breathing, the heart stops beating, the warmth and color of life turn to death's cold pallor; but if we have Christ, who says, *"I am the Resurrection and the Life; he that believeth in Me, though he were dead, yet shall he live,"* we know that the grave is not our destiny.

Because our Savior proved His everlasting Sonship by removing the shrouds of death and bursting the rock-sealed tomb, no question nor uncertainty, can linger regarding our own resurrection. As God's sons we *must* live again. Because Jesus pleaded in this divine intercession, *"Father, I will that they also whom Thou hast given Me be with Me where I am; that they may behold My glory which Thou hast given Me,"* and because Jesus is now enthroned in heaven's power and radiance, we shall share that glory with Him.

The Scriptures promise — oh, how we fail to grasp fully the merciful riches of His endless grace! — that there with the ten thousand times ten thousand *"we shall be like Him, for we shall see Him as He is."* What surpassing grace! Hear it again, *"We shall be like Him"*! Who can begin to describe the fulness of that splendor? There, through faith, when earth's toils and labors, its sorrows and agonies, are over, we shall have His glorious resurrection body, with the marks of sin and sickness removed, the limitations of time and space conquered. *"We shall be like Him"* because we shall be endowed with His joy in that better land, which has no more suffering and pain, no more fear or fright, no more discontent and disappointment, no more aching hearts or anguish of mind, no more trials and tears, no more decay and death — nothing but indescribable rejoicing!

To live forever in heaven with Jesus; to behold Him face to face before whom the angels sing their *"Holy, Holy, Holy"*; as sons of God to partake of the rapture of His presence — all this is likewise the glory that Jesus mentions in His high-priestly intercession, *"The glory which Thou gavest Me I have given them."* This promise should so completely sweep aside everything else in life that now in millions of hearts the resolution is formed, "I want to

become God's son, too!" If the Spirit has awakened in
you only a flicker of that desire, my fellow-redeemed, do
not waste a moment! Pray now with all your soul, "O Son
of God, give me the glory of Thy sonship!" Do not let
anything bar you from approaching the merciful Savior
with that petition! Your own unworthiness, your repeated
transgressions, need not keep you from Christ; He asks
you to come just as you are, despite your own unworthiness
and your multiplied sins. Your weak faith must not
deprive you of these full blessings, since He tells you,
"My strength is made perfect in weakness," and the
humbler we are, the mightier is the demonstration of His
divine power. Your past antagonism to the Cross, your
previous hatred of the Savior's precious name, even your
recent blasphemies, are no insurmountable barrier on the
way from earth to heaven; for as Christ, a few hours
after this prayer, mercifully beheld Peter, who had denied
his Lord and cursed as he denied, so He is ready to wipe
out the handwriting against you and give you the strength
to start life anew. For the sake of Christ, so that the
cleansing power of His blood and restoring grace of His
cross may not be rejected by your unbelief; for the sake of
all who today would thank God on bended knees if some
of you stubborn, self-satisfied sinners would give yourselves wholly to God (I am thinking of a devout father
or mother to whom your unbelief has brought more agony
than you yourself can ever atone, a Christian helpmate
whose life you have made heavy through rebellion against
your Redeemer, children who may coast down the highway
to hell by your example of indifference or hatred of Christ) ;
for the salvation of your own soul I ask you now in Jesus'
name: As in spirit you see the Christ, the High Priest of
all the world, interceding particularly in your behalf,
kneel beside Him to pray, "O Son of God, give me Thy

promised glory! Bring me to the Father!" and even as this prayer is spoken in your heart, a new sense of joyous deliverance will dawn on you. Returning to God through Jesus with this plea of the penitent, "*I am not worthy that I should be called thy son,*" His Father's heart of overflowing mercies will answer, "Thou art My son through Christ and the glory of the grace that He has given you."

II
GIVE US THE GLORY OF UNITY

This seventeenth chapter could also be called the Christian Unity Chapter, for five times Jesus repeats in substance the prayer "*that they* [the believers] *may be one.*" What striking lessons we should learn from this fivefold petition for the complete union of all Christ's followers! A single plea would have been ample evidence of our Lord's holy desire; but four additional appeals should show us that Jesus seems to have forgotten the impending agony of the crucifixion in His concern over the sacred oneness of all who would call Him their Savior. Do not lose sight of the fact, either, that this was Christ's last night of earthly life and that His words therefore should have an intensified meaning for us. How we treasure the final utterances of great leaders! How rigidly even the cold statutes of the law safeguard the last will and testaments of men! Should we not pay redoubled attention to our Lord's petition "*that they may be one,*" when we know that it was part of His farewell prayer, His final instruction to the Church! God grant us the love to echo Christ's prayer, "O Jesus, give us the glory of true unity!"

Now, there is a magnificent oneness in the Church Universal. Look wherever you will throughout the world, and at every place where sinners have penitently turned to Christ as their only Redeemer, you will find Christians bound together by a sacred bond, hidden from man's eyes, yet blessed beyond expression. Even though believers, reborn in Christ and sanctified by His Spirit, look different, follow contradictory customs, speak conflicting languages; though they live in democracies or monarchies, under totalitarian or even Communist control; though they be forced to fight against each other on opposite sides during this disastrous war, though they represent the extremes of culture or ignorance, riches or rags, they are united in Christ just as marvelously and divinely as He and the Father are one. The Savior Himself said He is a Vine and they are the branches. He is the Head and they the members in the one spiritual body. No earthly conflicts can break this unity. True followers of Christ, in whatever denomination they may be, however many the errors in that group, are blessed by the fellowship of the faith. You can see therefore how presumptuous and anti-Scriptural it is to insist that there is no salvation outside a particular, exclusive Church or that the way to heaven is found in obedience to the teachings of only one denomination. Enemies have charged my Church with making this claim, and I take this opportunity publicly to deny that charge and to repeat Scripture's promise that *"whosoever,"* in whatever denomination he may be found, *"shall call upon the name of the Lord,"* and with all his heart acclaim Christ his divine Redeemer, *"shall be saved"* and by his faith be made a member of the international, world-wide, ageless communion of saints. There are, however, churches which officially teach that the only pathway to Paradise is marked by their man-made creeds, the only vessel on which you can safely reach the celestial shore is the ship of their Church. Few claims, it seems to me, are more arrogant and cruel than this flat rejection of our Savior's own word and the prayer that all who sincerely believe the Lord Jesus Christ have in that faith and without any human additions the assurance of spiritual union here on earth and in heaven.

No unity that men can ever effect is as glorious as this oneness of faith. Over in Europe the Nazi philosophy cries, "Unity!" but it strives for racial union, which systematically excludes the Jew, while the Church of Christ welcomes Hebrew Christians just as it embraces all disciples of Christ, regardless of color, country, or continent. I ask you to thank God with me that a powerful 50,000-watt short-wave station in San Francisco is now sending our Gospel appeal to the entire Orient, that the equally strong short-wave station in Schenectady will soon direct our Spanish messages to South America, supplementing the almost fifty weekly broadcasts we already have in Latin America. Pray God with us that the 50,000-watt short-wave station in Boston, which reaches Europe, may soon be added, so that at last we can invade the Old World with the promise of newness in Jesus. Radio, you see, is one of God's particularly powerful means for helping people to understand the strengthening, soul-building doctrine of the one holy Christian Church spread over the earth.

In our own country the cry that reechoes in this disturbed hour asks for national unity; but can we be a truly united people when, as the Tuskegee Insitute report on 1940 lynchings shows a Southern Negro was murdered simply because he tried to vote? By contrast I say to you colored Americans that you can have an uncontested citizenry in Christ's commonwealth, shoulder to shoulder with me; that in the sight of the Lord Jesus your dark skin and my light make no difference whatever; that despite unfair human discrimination the Lord loves you as He loves me; that on the day after speaking this prayer for Christian unity He gave Himself into the death on the cross for your sake.

We have organizations which seek to emphasize the brotherhood of men and which for this reason are called "fraternities." But how frequently are applicants for membership blackballed and barred! God be praised, there is no blackballing in the brotherhood of Christ's true believers! Jesus promises, *"Him that cometh unto Me I will in no wise cast out."* By this pledge of God's sinless Son I appeal particularly to you who have lived your lives without the Savior and ask you to remember that here, in Christ's Church, is a world-wide group to which every one of you can belong though you may have been excluded from other organizations. Here, by the freest grace that God Almighty Himself could offer, by the merits of the Savior's bleeding and dying on the cross for you, by the power of faith that can conquer sin, the world, death, and hell itself, you have the invitation of Jesus: *"Come unto Me"* and His heavenly assurance *"Neither shall any pluck them out of My hand."*

When our Savior, in the sacred solemnity of that last hour, prayed for His followers and for us *"that they may be one,"* even as He and the Father are one, He asked that this inner unity be zealously guarded. A hundred forces are mobilized to tear Christians from their faith and its fellowship. Temptations increase, moral standards give way; betrayal of Jesus steadily becomes easier as sin is popularized, and unbelief constantly attempts to pull us from Christ's altar. We must not delude ourselves into believing that we can maintain our unity by our own strength and through our own resources. We need Christ not only every hour but every moment. There is no strike among the forces of hell engaged in this unholy task of undermining your trust. The agencies of destruction are working on twenty-four-hour day-and-night shifts, seven days every week, to make you deny the Savior who pur-

chased you with the price of His own blood. If Jesus found it necessary to pray that we may be kept in the unity of faith, how much more should every one of us who wants to lead a clean, consecrated life defy the lusts of the flesh, destroy grasping selfishness, choke off hatred, conquer doubt and distrust, kneel before Jesus, and pray, "O Son of God preserve me in this fellowship of faith!"

Jesus also wants us to express our unity. Twice our interceding High Priest asks His Father in this prayer that by our oneness *"the world may know"* Christ's truth as it is demonstrated in outward unity. How dismally we have failed in this respect! During long, dark centuries men sought to kill each other in the name of religion. The most devastating war in Europe's history was a church conflict that lasted for thirty years of unspeakable horror. Today, too, in the face of modern progress, we have not established external unity. The world cannot know that God has sent Christ nor recognize the glory of the Gospel by the divisions, subdivisions, and sub-subdivisions in outward Christianity. On the contrary, skepticism and unbelief point to the opposing creeds that claim to be Christian and sneer, "Is that how you have followed Christ's instruction?"

We must try to remove that reproach. Many cries for unity resound throughout our world today with an emphasis we have never before known. Some have proposed that this country be combined with Great Britain. Others have advocated the Old World form a United States of Europe, even that all countries be merged into a great international federation. But with this striving for agreement, little is done systematically to promote the union of Christ's churches on the basis of a true, inner, and complete oneness. Only entire accord, Scripturally grounded and Christ-exalting, can have any hope of blessing. All church unions by force, through the government, all compromises dictated by church politics, are worse than worthless. Pray Christ, "O Son of God, give us the glory of greater outward unanimity!" Though men may deny this possibility, divine mercy and omnipotence can give us a far greater and more truly united front before the world than many of us are ready to concede.

However imperfect this outward spiritual harmony may be on earth, it will be one of heaven's highest glories. There before the glorified Savior — and how the last book of the Bible emphasizes this thought! — those who are Christ's will be gathered with members of every *"nation and kindred and tongue and people,"* the ransomed, white-robed redeemed before Christ's throne in unbreakable, eternal, heavenly unity. O Christ, give us that glory!

III
GIVE US THE GLORY OF THY INDWELLING!

This seventeenth chapter of Saint John may also be called the Indwelling Chapter, for repeatedly Jesus speaks here of His being in the Father, to prove His divine Sonship, and of His being in us, to strengthen our souls with the promise of His constant companionship. *"I in them and Thou in Me"* — these words of our eternal Intercessor contain the assurance we need for dangerous days like these. It seems that with each recent Sunday on which I have spoken to you, world conditions have become more terrifying and confused, with wars and threats of new hostilities increasing from week to week. If we look ahead and ask, "What of the future and the new social order that most competent authorities agree must follow after the wake of this war?" little doubt will remain that America must face the most serious problems in its existence and that the post-war order can bring sharper

suffering and more complicated perplexities than we have yet known. Atheism made serious inroads into every European country which participated in the first World War, and new indications point to wider conquest by anti-Biblical forces over the earth when the present conflict ends.

Millions in this country must therefore learn to adjust themselves to new levels and find spiritual contentment in a discontented day. That is a hard lesson, and it is acquired not by psychology courses, high-souled resolutions, the practice of self-denial, but through acceptance of this truth, "God in Christ and Christ in us," through trusting the heavenly guidance which enabled Saint Paul to face hatred, persecution, suffering, greater than you and I will ever know and still say, *"I have learned in whatsoever state I am therewith to be content. I know both how to be abased and I know how to abound; everywhere and in all things I am instructed both to be full and to be hungry, both to abound and to suffer need. I can do all things through Christ, which strengtheneth me."*

Take these words, "God in Christ and Christ in us," as the motto for a victorious life! Let the worst that a cruel world may be able to inflict seek to destroy your happiness and peace of mind! Face it calmly because you are not alone; Christ, your Savior, is in you! We are told that the late Dr. Wilfred Grenfell, who left a life of luxury in London to become a medical missionary among the isolated fishermen of the forbidding Labrador coast, was once summoned on an emergency call which necessitated his crossing a frozen bay. Suddenly, however the ice broke with a thunderous roar, and Dr. Grenfell found himself carried on a large floe out to sea. After a few moments of reflection he killed one of the dogs and made a distress flag from its bones and skin. His next action was surprising; he lay down to sleep partly to save his strength and partly because he knew that Christ was with him. Drifting toward the open ocean, he slept as quietly as at home. And his confidence was not unrewarded. Some hours later the Eskimos began a search for him, discovered his perilous plight, and rescued him. Such confidence does not come automatically. It is born of the sustained realization that through faith Christ is in us; that earth and hell together are not powerful enough to defeat His gracious purposes.

"God in Christ and Christ in us," despite our weakness and wilful wrong, that is the victory cry by which we can overcome evil, defeat temptation, rejoice in adversity, endure pain, conquer fear, triumph over death itself. "God in Christ and Christ in us" — can there be for earth and heaven a more blessed, soul-strengthening conviction than this pledge of the Savior's presence in our reborn, revitalized lives? "God in Christ and Christ in us" — the promise of power and blessing these words convey to you by faith is so magnificent that you ought to be ready to give up everything which seeks to keep you from Christ. May God's Holy Spirit today touch your heart, so that as you prepare to follow the Savior along the pathway of His suffering, you may begin with this prayer, "Son of God, come to me, strengthen me, abide with me, dwell triumphantly in me through life and death until, saved by grace, I behold Thee face to face in heavenly glory!" Amen.

AWAKE! WATCH! PRAY!

*"He cometh unto the disciples and findeth them asleep
and saith unto Peter, What, could ye not watch
with Me one hour? Watch and pray that ye enter
not into temptation."* — Saint Matthew 26:40, 41

Christ, who didst Suffer Agony in the Garden for Us:

*Give us the penitent faith which recognizes that, when the weight
of human sin crushed Thy soul almost into death at Gethsemane,
Thou didst endure such anguish for us! Abide in us, O strengthening Savior, to reenforce the faith by which we may overcome the
slumber of carnal security and, watching prayerfully, resist evil
forces which would keep us from Thee! Contritely do we confess
that the sleep of sin has often overtaken us when, instead of arous-
ing ourselves to faithful vigilance, we rested unconcerned, while
enemies of Thy grace sought to restrain the Kingdom's course.
Pardon us for every refusal to follow the appeal of Thy love with
unwavering devotion! Continue to look down mercifully on a
world that has forgotten and betrayed Thee! If it be Thy will,
restrict the horrors of further war! Grant us, although we have
not deserved it, a beneficial, building peace! O Jesus, without Thee
we can do nothing. Bless us, then, and enrich our souls by the
grace of Thy Cross and the cleansing power of Thy blood!
Amen.*

CRUCIAL days have dawned for America. Perhaps
even before I speak to you again momentous decisions
will have been reached by Congress. Whether we realize it
or not, the nation's destiny is being shaped not only for
this crisis year but for decades to come.

Little doubt remains that we are close to war. Every
day on the Senate floor the assertion is emphatically repeated that the United States must take an active part in
European military operations. Confidential reports released
by financial experts regard our part in the struggle as practically inevitable. After the first World War we said,

"It must not happen again!" Now we fear, "It will happen again." Only a miracle can save this country from war.

Even if the miracle should occur and we be spared actual participation in bloodshed; if, despite its unworthiness, the world be granted an honorable, constructive peace, for which I still ask you to work and pray in this eleventh hour, we nevertheless stare into a problem-filled future. We shall experience financial hardship; for even though we hardly glance a second time at head-lines reporting multibillion-dollar appropriations, these staggering expenditures *must* finally be paid by the people. War or peace, active belligerency or passive, long-drawn hostilities or quick armistice, we should prepare to counteract the immoralities which flourish in days of easy money and lavish spending like these. The most alarming upswing in American crime began after the last war. Have we any reason to suppose that with the far greater proportion of our present-day difficulties the revolt against God's Law and man's will decrease during the years before us?

Dwarfing these social and moral perplexities, however, is the increase of opposition to Christ which the churches will soon meet. In this national emergency every American Christian should understand clearly and personally that our faith will be tried as never before. Recent reports from Britain tell us that through constant war strain the Church of England has been paralyzed. What reason have we to suppose that the Savior's cause in the United States will not suffer appalling setbacks? If the late war put Karl Marx and his atheism over Jesus Christ and His Gospel in Russia, placed the State over the Church in Germany and Italy, helped to enthrone reason more solidly over revelation in Britain, France, and our own country, let us put on our spiritual armor to defend ourselves, before it is too late, against a large-scale assault on Jesus within our borders.

Although circumstances which have brought about this crisis are now out of our control, we have a command by Christ, our Savior, that marks our path of duty and promises peace, courage, confidence, to all who love Him and follow His instructions. I thank God that in this first Lenten message I can give you as the crisis cry for inward and outward struggle, the battle-call for the Church in its conflicts, this motto of militant Christianity:

AWAKE! WATCH! PRAY!

a plea which takes us back to the beginning of our Savior's Passion in these words of Saint Matthew (chapter twenty-six, verses forty and forty-one), *"He cometh unto the disciples and findeth them asleep and saith unto Peter, What, could ye not watch with Me one hour? Watch and pray, that ye enter not into temptation."*

I
AWAKE!

This command by Jesus broke the nocturnal stillness in the Garden of Gethsemane, one of the few Palestinian localities, hallowed by our Savior's suffering, that can be identified with some certainty. If it was of the same size as the present site, this enclosure, which Saint John alone calls the "garden," was a small plot, only about fifty yards square; but the whole world would not be large enough to contain adequate descriptions of the agony which Christ experienced there. Only eight gnarled olive-trees today mark the place, but the most magnificent and costly monument that wealth and art could erect would never begin to commemorate worthily the convulsive agony which there almost crushed Jesus into death.

Gethsemane was only half a mile from the Jerusalem city walls; and the pathway which crossed that distance could have been traversed leisurely in fifteen minutes. Yet what startling difference a half mile and a quarter hour produced in our Lord! Before that last walk we hear Him in His high-priestly prayer, confident, joy-filled, triumphant, concerned chiefly about the preservation and deliverance of His disciples; but now, after this short span of space and time, rejoicing has given way to relentless anguish. His thoughts are riveted on the impending ordeal. Until this hour the disciples depended on the Master, but in Gethsemane, Jesus needs His followers with the deepest urgency. He selects three, perhaps those of whom sympathy and perseverance may best be expected: Peter, James, John; and taking them with Him to a secluded spot, He engages in the most penetrating prayer earth and heaven have ever heard. As the Passover moon sends its beams on Christ, we can witness terror and soul-searing pain, such as human eye will never otherwise see. The Scriptures themselves can hardly find adequate words to picture that agony. They state that Jesus was *"sorrowful," "sore amazed," "very heavy," "full of sorrows."* Neither these four terms nor four hundred more can plumb the abyss of His grief. Jesus falls on His knees to plead with His Father, only to find that the torment of His soul casts Him prostrate on the damp ground. Had it not been for the preordained plan of our redemption, Christ would have died then and there. And He almost did, for He moaned, *"My soul is exceeding sorrowful, even unto death."* No human agency could save Him. An angel had to come from heaven to revive Him for the climax on the cross.

The voice which the three selected disciples had heard defeat the grave when Jesus, gripping the cold hand of a lifeless corpse, cried, *"Maid, arise!"* now pleads for help. Thrice that never-to-be-forgotten cry rings out through the night, *"O My Father, if it be possible, let this cup pass from Me!"* The countenance which these favored followers had seen glorified on the Mount of Transfiguration, where the Savior's face shone as the sun, is now pale and covered with bloody sweat!

As you ask God ever to keep this glimpse of the Savior's unparalleled agony before your mind's eye, stop to learn why Jesus was stretched out on Gethsemane's soil! It was not merely fear that almost took His life, a cringing before His crucifixion, a dread of death, as modern enemies of the Cross declare. Our Lord knew how to overcome such terror. See Him a few hours after this ordeal in the Garden, when, calm and composed, He endures one cruelty after the other by His Jewish countrymen and the Roman authorities. Behold Him on the way to Calvary stopping to preach to the women who fringed that road! Picture Him on the cross as He promises a penitent thief the immediate glories of Paradise. Confidently He cries, *"It is finished!"* and commends Himself into His Father's hands. You need not be a Christian to know that there is nothing fearful and cowardly in the Christ of Gethsemane.

The only true explanation of this mystery in the Garden is that there the Savior's suffering for all human transgressions begins. We sometimes limit Christ's agony to the physical pain He endured throughout the various hours of torture that culminated in His death on the cross; but we should not exclude Gethsemane's soul-grief which Jesus sustained (not for His own sins, since He had none; and even His enemies' perjury could invent no true charge against Him) for my iniquities and yours. Here, by God's eternal plan for our redemption, the Guiltless languished for the guilty, the Faultless for the fault-filled, the Lawgiver for the law-breaker, the eternal God for His death-marked creatures!

What a terrifying curse Jesus assumes as He prepares to die by man, yet for man! A single sin in your life can open the flood-gates of unspeakable misery for the rest of your days. The one misstep that some of you young folks take can torment you as long as you live. An isolated transgression can visit its disastrous consequences on the third and fourth generation. How immeasurable, then, must be the penalty for the wrong committed! But how horrifying the retribution which God's outraged justice must demand for the total of all sins committed by mankind throughout every century of mankind's sordid history! Yet nothing less than that appalling aggregate was laid upon Christ in the Garden. There His soul was afflicted for social outcasts, prostitutes, degenerates, murderers, war-profiteers, white-slavers, debauchers of youth, as well as for you, the self-righteous and self-satisfied. You brought Him to Gethsemane. You made Him cry, *"Let this cup pass from Me!"* You, no matter how good you think you are or try to show yourself, regardless of the esteem in which you are publicly held; you, whoever, wherever, whatever, you are, made Him fall to the ground and require the strengthening angel. Admit that now! Declare before your God that Jesus bears the brunt of this indescribable pain for you!

Then you will not wonder why Christ in that last conflict craved the companionship of His own followers. He was so truly human that even their presence would have brought Him assurance in His anguish. So He asks His three trusted disciples, the inner circle, we may say, of the Twelve, *"Tarry ye here and watch with Me!"* What a modest request that was! We gladly keep long night-vigils at the bedside of our beloved ones. A true Christian pastor will gladly forego sleep to pray with any one in his charge who is besieged by heavy sorrows. Even the Government grants a convicted murderer the sustaining counsel of a spiritual adviser in the final hours before the electric chair. Yet small as was this last service which Peter, James, and John were asked to render the Lord, it was too great. What depth of human weakness we see in these words, *"He cometh unto the disciples and findeth them asleep."* Their cruel slumber seems too much even for the gentle Christ; and beholding Peter, who only a few minutes before had loudly boasted that he would readily die for Him, now relaxed in heavy slumber, the agonized Savior cries, *"What, could ye not watch with Me one hour?"*

We seek an explanation for this heartless sleep, and the Scriptures give two reasons: the disciples were weary, and they were heavy with sorrow. Yet, before we pour out our scorn on these men who could not stay awake for a single hour during the one crisis for which Jesus asked their companionship, let us be honest enough to admit that the best among us fall asleep when Christ's cause suffers attack and we should be awake to the danger. Jesus has just as little help from many a professing Christian today as He had from that slumbering trio. If Saint Paul had to tell first-century believers, *"Now it is high time to awake out of sleep,"* the cry that should shake twentieth-century church-members from their lethargy asks, "Christians of America, awake! Our faith is being assaulted! Wake up to the truth that the Savior is being assailed by indifference, compromise, and denial within the churches! Wake up to the peril that modernist unbelief is often capturing your pulpits, divinity schools, church-papers! Wake up to the realization that many churches are spiritually dead, without the living Christ in their sermons, without missionary zeal in their members' lives! Wake up to the dangers of this hour, when atheism, materialism, sensualism, are arrayed against the Church in the strongest force ever mobilized in this country! Wake up, churches of America, to the conviction that in this crisis only Christ can solve our difficulties!"

The Savior's appeal for wakeful followers, however, is an individual plea to every one of you. May it reach some who are slumbering securely in the carnal sleep of sin! Too many of you are in a constant coma of spiritual carelessness, as unconcerned about your soul as a sleeping man is about his body. You think your life without Jesus is satisfying. You don't want Christ because you claim that you do not need Him! Or do you? Before long the sins you serve will find you out. Before long you will face eternity, when death, which this week summoned king and commoner, comes to you. How terrifying, then, this spiritual encephalitis, the sleeping-sickness of the soul! Before it is too late, wake up! See Christ convulsed in the Garden and say, "O Jesus, all this agony was for me! Forgive me! Make me Yours! Keep me awake!" And that plea will be answered.

II

WATCH!

Christ demanded more than mere wakefulness. "*Watch,*" He told the disciples, "*that ye enter not into temptation!*" Encircled, as He was, by sorrows without number, He is now concerned with His followers' welfare. Satan, He knows, will assault them with redoubled force; temptations will multiply. In His betrayal, capture, and arrest their human weakness will need support. So He pleads, "'*Watch!*' Be on your guard! Be prepared!"

The same trials which tested these disciples surround us day and night. The enemies of the Cross have increased, and it is still true even of the most loyal among

Jesus' followers that *"the spirit indeed is willing, but the flesh is weak."* Ten thousand forces of evil, each one a crafty, superhuman power of hell, line up against us; and daily do we need the Savior's warning *"Watch . . . that ye enter not into temptation!"*

"'Watch,' Christian youth of America," His Word commands; "guard against the evil which appeals to your baser nature, asks you to reject the sacred statutes of purity and to run along with the world!" *"'Watch,'* Christian parents of America! Resist the dark forces which seek to destroy Christian home-life, belittle parenthood, childhood, and the sacred marriage vow!"

"Christian citizens of America," Christ would say, *"'Watch!'* Take steps to guard the religious liberties, the separation of Church and State, the right of assembly, the freedom of worship that is constitutionally ours!" War emergencies may seek to restrict or destroy this heritage. Last week the people of Germany were told that they were not primarily Protestants or Catholics. First of all, their *Fuehrer* commanded, they were to be Germans. Let us hope that in our own country, as the times become more critical, no false nationalism will demand that we give Christ a second place. No conflict ever need arise between our Christian creed and our love for country; but if the time should ever come (and in view of present tendencies, who will say that it cannot?) when we are told, "You are Americans first and Christians second," may the Holy Spirit strengthen us to declare, *"We ought to obey God rather than men,"* and give Jesus uncontested supremacy in our hearts!

"'Watch,' Christian churches of America," the Savior cries to us from the Garden. Prepare for the darker day! Get ready now for the new conditions that will follow the war, by bringing the Gospel to the masses! Let American

people know that this Christ in Gethsemane is the Savior of the common people, too! When Millais' picture of Jesus in the carpenter shop was exhibited throughout England, great throngs of working-men flocked to inspect the canvas, because, they said, "This is our Comrade." American labor should repeat their acclaim of our Lord. You men in the factories, as welcome letters assure me, are passing the word from one worker to the other that this broadcast is for the masses and not reserved for a few, just as Christ is the universal, not the restricted Savior. The churches should *"watch"* by fortifying our children against the temptations of these coming years, giving the rising generation daily Christian instruction in church-supported schools. With the mandate from God Himself *"Comfort ye, comfort ye, My people, saith your God!"* ringing in our ears, we who are Christ's must *"watch,"* so that churches do not waste their efforts in political or cultural discussions which leave souls untouched. Instead, they must bring the pure message of Christ's saving, sustaining Gospel to the distressed multitudes. The poor, the dispossessed, the unemployed, may be won for any future revolutionary upheaval unless churches show a more concerted desire to help the destitute and avoid slanting their favoritism toward the rich. Remember what happened in Russia, Spain, and Mexico! Let us preach Christ's Gospel with greater force and frequency, pointing overburdened souls to the grief-gripped Christ in Gethsemane, with this message, "He suffered for you so that you might be spared eternal agony"; directing the forsaken to that solitary Sufferer with the assurance, "He was abandoned, deserted, so that you need never be alone in life or death."

Despite that pleading, warning, repeated *"Watch!"* the disciples failed. Sleep continued to weight their eyes. Yet Christ mercifully forgave them! And He can pardon us!

We are moved by the story which tells how Abraham Lincoln extended clemency to a soldier sentenced to death for having fallen asleep at his post. Today, in this glimpse of sacred Gethsemane, Christ offers you complete acquittal for every failure to keep awake and watch, for each instance in which Christ's enemies have triumphed because you have fallen asleep on duty. As Lincoln's commutation of sentence called forth inexpressible gratitude in the sentry saved from the firing-squad, so may the Savior's pardoning love make both us and the angels of God above rejoice when we, unfaithful soldiers of Christ, are restored and saved!

III

PRAY!

The Savior's command to the drowsy disciples also asked them to *"pray,"* to implore God for strength that they might resist the temptations to disloyalty which would soon confront them. Jesus Himself knew and practiced the power of such petition. This was doubtless not the first time He knelt in the Garden. The Gospels tell us that He customarily retreated to its shade and protection. Our Christian life would be stronger and the number of soul-tragedies reduced, were prayer a holy habit with us! If Christ, the sinless Son of God, found refuge and strength in prayer, how eagerly should we follow the appeal *"Ask, and it shall be given you"*!

Have you ever recognized that His pleading in the Garden, as a sort of final but unspoken instruction, summarizes everything we need to know about prayer? Jesus, kneeling in Gethsemane, shows us to whom our petitions must be addressed as He cries, *"O My Father!"* the only recorded instance He uses the word *"My"* in addressing His Father; and it is only when we address the Triune God, whom Jesus clearly revealed, only when we, too, call

God "our Father" through Christ, that we can have assurance of answer.

Jesus, pleading in Gethsemane, also teaches us how to approach the holy God despite the unholiness in our sinful lives. Pointing to Christ, we say, "Father, that Savior whose soul was *'exceeding sorrowful, even unto death'* has made me Thy child." Jesus Himself promises, *"If ye shall ask the Father anything in My name, He will give it you."* What a clear-cut rejection of all Christless prayers! What a sacred promise for Christ-grounded petitions!

We must likewise be impressed by our Lord's earnestness. Can we read the story of Gethsemane without being moved by the truth that this prayer, far from being mere routine, was the outpouring of the Savior's innermost soul? Blessed are we, too, if we speak our petitions with the fervor of faith! Jesus falls on His knees; if God's Son could thus humble Himself, who are we to forget that posture of lowliness?

The suffering Savior prayed alone, in solitude with His Father; and while we need prayer in the churches, prayer in the family, we must also cultivate the private, personal pleading, which brings its rich reward in stronger faith and intensified courage. Select some spot in your home or, as the Savior did, in the realm of nature and learn what a privilege it is to speak confidently with your God, without any distraction whatever!

Note that Jesus pleaded three times, *"Let this cup pass from Me!"* The last night of His early life reminds us how necessary protracted prayer often is. Do not expect the Almighty to hear you immediately when Jesus had to repeat His petition! Our omniscient Father sometimes delays in answering because postponement makes us realize more keenly how completely we depend on Him. Wood used in carving must be seasoned to prevent warping; and if God wants to fashion your life into a masterpiece of His mercy that will not lose its symmetry, do not complain when the process takes time! Keep on praying, and you continue to store strength!

Particularly, however, let us learn of Jesus how to plead submissively, in accordance with God's gracious will. In His soul torture, bearing the total of human transgressions, suffering as our Substitute, Jesus begs that the cup of sorrows might be taken from Him; yet He adds, *"if it be possible,"* and *"Nevertheless, not as I will, but as Thou wilt."* How contrarily our requests specify their answer! We even dictate to God the time, place, manner, of His response, and we are so short-sighted that, if He were to follow our petulant demands and give us everything we ask, we should ruin ourselves. For your spiritual advancement and for the glorious triumph of faith learn to follow Jesus when you implore God in the Third Petition, *"Thy will be done in earth as it is in heaven"!* With the Spirit's help, overcome stubborn self-will and acquire the calm composure of a life completely surrendered to God!

The cup did not pass from our Lord. He had to drink it to its bitter dregs. Yet His crucifixion was not the end, death not the final chapter. After Calvary came the resurrection; after the cross, the crown of heaven. Similarly in our lives it often may seem that God is deaf to our entreaties; yet all the while His loving heart has planned to give us something far better than we have requested. If He keeps us poor on earth that we may be unspeakably rich in heaven; if He checks our ambitions and we remain unnoticed during this life that during the next we may experience how blessed is the fulfilment of His promise, *"The last shall be first,"* why should we dare to think unworthy thoughts of our Father when He gives us gold instead of glitter?

May the Holy Spirit touch you so that this sincere wish will form itself in your contrite heart, "I want to pray as Jesus did"!

Do not be discouraged by the tragedy that we have so little Christ-centered prayer today! During difficult times, men think that they themselves can build defense against the approach of every evil, individual and national; but you cannot build a life, a home, a church, a community, a country without God and expect that it will prosper. As I look into the future, I fail to see a single ray of purely human hope which can guarantee peace and blessing. Yet come war, with its wounds and death; come inflation, repudiation, bankruptcy; come the restriction of our religious liberty, persecution for the churches; come a totalitarian America — if we behold the Christ of Gethsemane, hear Him plead, "Awake! Watch! Pray!" and ask God, "O Father, keep me wakeful, watchful, prayerful, with my Savior!"; if at the cry: "On your knees, America!" "Prayer in the homes!" "Prayer in true churches!" we humble ourselves penitently before the Almighty, then just as Gethsemane gave way to the resurrection glory, so we, too, shall meet our nation-wide perplexities and emerge from our personal afflictions stronger and better than ever before. May God thus graciously show every one of us that the Savior's grief in the Garden becomes our sacred pledge of spiritual peace on earth, our assurance of redemption in heaven! May we learn, if necessary in heart-trying experience, that the pathway to Christian power is marked by obedience to our Redeemer's repeated request, "Awake! Watch! Pray!" We ask this in Jesus' name! Amen.

PUT UP YOUR SWORDS!

"Then said Jesus unto him, Put up again thy sword into his place; for all they that take the sword shall perish with the sword." — Saint Matthew 26:52

Blessed Lord Jesus:

Forgive us our hatred, envy, strife, and by the power of Thy bleeding and dying for us, merciful Son of God, enable us to walk meekly and humbly in Thy footsteps as we search for reconciliation with God and our fellow-men! Help us to pray for our enemies, even as Thou didst intercede for those who crucified Thee! Destroy all selfish prejudices against men of other races, colors, creeds, and classes! In an hour of great national crisis we implore Thee, if it be Thy will, to prevent the spread of bloodshed, stop the horrors of these hostilities, and bestow true, equitable peace. Bring to naught the treacherous counsels of those who seek war for war's sake, who grow rich by the blood spilled on fields of battle, or who spread hate-breeding falsehood! O Jesus, without Thy love complete darkness would encircle us! Give Thyself to us by the Holy Spirit for our comfort, guidance, light, strength, and salvation! Bless this message in many hearts! Let it bring multitudes to the cross and help those who know Thee to persevere in the faith! We ask this by the promise of Thy mercy. Amen.

NATION-WIDE interest was aroused last week by the unusual proposal of a Louisiana sheriff. He held in his custody four men, convicted murderers, sentenced to die in the electric chair. Believing that a warning from their lips might help to keep others from breaking the law and suffering a similar end, the sheriff arranged to have a microphone placed in the death-cells; and shortly before they entered the execution chamber the four doomed prisoners were to tell the world by radio that crime does not pay. State authorities objected, however, and the broadcast was rightly canceled. Much more than last-hour expressions of regret is required to stop murder and felony. Many different confession magazines, so-called "true-story" publications, are issued today; but if all these crime accounts, gangster motion-pictures, and underworld broadcasts were a real influence for good, our penitentiaries would not be overcrowded with the largest penal population the country has ever known.

In these days of widening war, when every week extends hostilities, an appalling age of brute force, with falsehood enthroned and truth sentenced to the scaffold — we need a *divine* arraignment of all aggression, tyranny, mass murder, a *divine* power, to check savage blood lust and ruthless destruction. No merely human agency can outlaw the glorifying of bloodshed and the exalting of savage strength which sinister forces support. What more revealing evidence of men's sinfulness could be required than the demonstration that despite our culture, scientific progress, and social advance neither legislation, education, diplomacy, nor international conflict has been able to teach this generation that violence does not pay. Have you ever stopped to realize how much of man's time, effort, and money is devoted to malice and destruction at this crest of human achievement? We have paid far more in men and dollars for the turmoil of crime and losses through war than any previous quarter century. Yet war hysteria continues. Therefore, we must have a heavenly voice to resound above the shriek of bombs and the explosion of torpedoes, a power from God which will enable us to overcome the hateful, violent tendencies of the human heart. That command and that power — thank God! — are granted us by the Lord Jesus Himself. Beholding this world of weak and wicked men, each one inflamed by the passions of hatred, He, the Son of God and the Savior of the world, cries out:

"PUT UP YOUR SWORDS!"

How else can we interpret these words of the Lenten story (Saint Matthew, chapter twenty-six, verse fifty-two) in which Jesus tells fiery, impetuous Peter and those of like mind in our age, *"Put up again thy sword into his place; for all they that take the sword shall perish with the sword"*?

I

HOW NECESSARY THIS WARNING!

When Jesus rose from that intense wrestling with human sin in the Garden, the Roman soldiers, accompanied by the priests' henchmen, broke into Gethsemane's stillness. Their torches and lanterns soon revealed Christ, who, because of His holy, heavenly love for us, made no attempt to escape (how different the Europan monarch whose further flight was recorded last week!), but resolutely assured His captors that He was Jesus of Nazareth whom they sought. The Savior had hardly declared, *"I am He!"* when, as if in final demonstration of His majestic greatness, the entire hostile throng, bearing spears and staves, retreated before His commanding presence and fell helpless to the ground. Once more our Lord asked, *"Whom seek ye?"* and when they replied, *"Jesus of Nazareth!"* He showed His deep concern for the welfare of the disciples — the same devotion He extends to you — and declared, *"If . . . ye seek Me, let these go their way!"* How completely in accord with our Lord's substitutionary atonement! He, the Innocent, is captured; yet He pleads that we, the sin-stained, may be freed!

The scene was now set for the most dastardly deed in history. By connivance with the Savior's enemies, so no possible slip-up could mar their plans, Judas, in the arch-treachery of the ages, approached Christ for the betrayal. If in that moment lightning had flashed from heaven to strike down the perfidious disciple, or if the ground had opened to swallow him, our human sympathies would almost breathe a sigh of thankful relief. But the Savior's mar-

velous mercy calls Judas *"friend,"* an intimate, appealing
term, which in the original means "comrade." He asks,
"Wherefore art thou come?" pleading with that disloyal
disciple to reconsider the terrifying consequences of his
crime — just as Christ often warns you who are planning
evil, betraying your trust in God, breaking promises to
fellow-men, perhaps even to your own husband or wife.
But Judas had sold out to Satan. Nothing that Christ
said stopped him. Smirkingly he kissed the Savior, whom
he had betrayed for thirty pieces of silver. Paltry
pieces of blood money, we say — yet an amount larger
than the sum many of you have received in payment for
your denial of Christ. That traitor's kiss was the pre-
arranged sign, and the soldiers, who otherwise might have
been unable to identify their Victim with certainty, now
quickly laid their hands on the Savior. That capture served
as a signal to the disciples, who, awakened by the tumult,
stood about bewildered, helpless, while Pilate's legionaries
bound Christ. Suddenly it seems to have flashed across
their conscience how inexcusable their sleep was when Jesus
had asked them to watch and pray. Peter especially must
have recalled his boastful promise of loyalty made hardly
an hour earlier when, as the disciples' spokesman, he had
declared, *"Though I should die with Thee, yet will I not
deny Thee!"* Dismayed and desperate because Jesus was
captured by His enemies, while he and his companions had
done nothing to save Him, Peter, with a feeling we can well
understand, cried, *"Lord, shall we smite with the sword?"* —
Two of the disciples, it appears, were armed. Perhaps they
believed in being prepared, or perhaps their weapon was
the large swordlike knife used shortly before in connection
with the sacrifice of the Passover lamb. Without pausing
for an answer or stopping to consider how futile it would
be to fight with only two blades against a company of fully

trained soldiers, Peter draws his sword, begins to slash about in a holy war and cuts an ear off the high priest's slave. Then, in the rebuke which rings out clear and decisive through the centuries, Jesus, spurning every thought of self-defense and of recourse to arms, tells Peter, *"Put up again thy sword into his place!"*

If only all who have followed the Savior since that day would have heeded His command! Throughout church history misguided men have used violence against their opponents or in spreading their doctrines. Under the threat of pain and punishment thousands of pagans in ancient France and Germany were forcefully made nominal Christians, baptized at mass ceremonies, while regiments stood by, ready to use their swords, should any prove unwilling to submit. No one has ever been able to compute the toll in millions of lives and the unspeakable suffering sustained through the seven crusades when European Christians sought to tear the Holy Land from Mohammedan control. Zealous bigots were so blinded that they even encouraged children to undertake a special crusade, believing that perhaps by some miracle boys and girls could capture the places made sacred through the Savior's life. About 95,000 children under twelve took part, but only 10,000 returned. The rest were killed, sold into slavery, or died of disease and starvation. The darkest chapter we find in the records of the Inquisition, the torture practiced by churches against those who would not submit to their teachings. Nothing has brought greater reproach to the Christian cause than the fact that in Jesus' name the most excruciating cruelties and devilish devices were employed to murder women and children, whose only "crime" was the insistence with which they followed the dictates of their conscience in worshiping Christ. Church medals have been struck to commemorate massacres in which many thousands of Christians were killed. Long defenses have been composed to justify these persecutions, but they still shriek in protest to the highest heaven. If you want proof of the depths to which men can sink, survey the instances when, under the emblem of the cross, they massacred their fellow-men, worshipers of the same Savior. Get from your public libraries the old classic that deserves restudy, particularly in dangerous days like these, Fox's *Book of Martyrs,* and you will read records of hanging, beheading, drowning, burning, racking, stoning, starving — instigated by both friends and foes of Christ! Go over to Europe's museums, and you will see the Iron Maiden which the victims of the Inquisition had to embrace, a cruel machine in the shape of a beautiful virgin, so designed that when its victim was locked in its arms, sharp daggers stabbed him to death. You will see cages too small for a prisoner to stand, too uncomfortable for him to lie down. You will see ropes with which Christians were hanged to the ceiling by their thumbs, and heavy weights with which at the same time they were pulled to the ground. You will discover the most hideous apparatus that vicious inventors could devise — all used in the name of the church and its Lord.

How fervently we pray God that this may remain a part of the past! But who, in view of the present debacle, would dare to say that streams of martyr blood will never flow in this country? Even today many groups forget that Christ's realm is not of this world and therefore cannot be extended by earthly force. During the last decades we have seen repeated instances of governmental intrusion into the Church's work. Most of the Protestant congregations in Germany have been brought into a Nazi-directed union, and on our own shores voices are asking for one national American Church, where, of course, faithfulness to the Lord Jesus Christ and loyalty to His teaching will be secondary or ignored altogether. Throughout Abyssinia and Albania Protestant mission-work is stopped; and on this side of the Atlantic infuriated mobs destroy the churches of a small sect (whose teachings I can in no way endorse) only because its adherents refuse to salute the American flag. Loyal otherwise, they simply have the mistaken notion that this is a gesture of disobedience to God which violates the First Commandment. Throughout Europe, we are told, the freedom of worship is restricted, as, for example, in Norway, where soldiers of the occupation attend services to report on the sermons; and in the United States superorganizations are at work, attempting to direct and control Protestantism, dictate who may have the privileges of radio broadcasting and punish those who disagree with their policies. Old World churchmen have repeatedly petitioned civil authorities to enact laws for the support of their particular denomination or religious group; and in the State of Delaware Christians who do not understand that the Old Testament dispensation is past and that there is no New Testament Sabbath keep Sunday blue-laws, which require the fine or imprisonment of those who refuse to respect this error! While we thank God that despite the prevalence of tyranny throughout the earth our divinely blessed nation still enjoys the liberty of conscience, worship, and expression, let us be on our guard during these problem-weighted years before us lest our freedom be undermined. When Jesus calls to His disciple, *"Put up thy sword!"* may His command help to check every use of force, physical, legal, or financial, by any religious group! Though we can never compromise with error or refuse to indict attacks on Christ and the doctrines of His faith, even such protest can be made in charity and without personal reference or animosity. Besides, we can pray the Holy Spirit to give all who love the message of salvation as the only hope for a perishing world a greater degree of true unity, real agreement on every Scriptural teaching.

The Savior's cry "Put up your swords!" also reminds us that each unjustified use of force must likewise be denounced. Those who deny that fundamental truth without which one cannot understand why Christ shed His blood, the Biblical doctrine that every man by birth and nature is sinful, vile, and wicked, should survey the horrifying record of wars fought from the beginnings of time. Because this is an age of aggression, we ought to restudy and restate the Bible's pronouncements concerning war. Avoiding the extremes of the pacifists, we must clearly understand that there may be just conflicts, particularly those fought against invaders or in national defense. As you protect your home, property, and dear ones against burglary, fire, and other similar calamities, so you must be prepared to guard with your lives, if necessary, these homes, and the country that gives you its blessings. Avoiding the extremes of militarism, which seeks to glorify all bloodshed, we must understand that there may be unjust wars, those which are purely acts of organized thuggery, in which an empire without cause falls on a smaller, helpless land. The annals of humanity have been filled with such unrighteousness — and it should be clear that, regardless of consequences to themselves, we cannot support conflicts of this kind. If it is wrong for you and me to attack a man, destroy his property, and take his life, it is wrong for Christians to help their government in any aggressive act that seeks to despoil another people. Now, it may often be difficult to decide whether a war is defensive or aggressive, right or wrong; and in such uncertainty Christians should obey the government, which must bear the responsibility for its actions. Those who are honest conscientious objectors should be treated with consideration.

Let it be recognized that, whether a conflict is justified or not, it comes as a scourge from God, with its destruction of life and property, its multiplied hardships, its moral degradation and hostility to the Christian Church. Therefore, Christian citizens urge the Government to weigh carefully now, before it is too late, the consequences of war's terror. After a declaration is made, that action is beyond recall. We must understand, too, that God's Word lays it on the conscience of His children to work for peace, to pray earnestly for the avoidance of bloodshed. I pause in this crisis moment to ask American Christians whether they individually have met this obligation, by interceding for the preservation of tranquillity. How we wish that the cry of the captured Savior, reechoing down through all the changes in human affairs, "Put up your swords!" would be heeded by those who promote international strife, who selfishly profit by every life lost and every day the battle is extended!

This disavowal of force should be followed also in the prolonged conflict between employer and employee, in the savage struggle between classes and races, but notably in the third divine institution besides the Church and the State, the home. Here, where a man and a woman are united by the most enduring bonds, protected by the closest ties and the deepest blessings that God Almighty has given us for this earth, we certainly are entitled to expect the absence of constraint and, instead, the reign of love. Yet one of the most frequent problems with which we have to cope — a difficulty which each year brings thousands of letters asking advice and constantly leads a stream of people to my office — is the tragedy that hatred has usurped the place of love in many families, that physical force or legal power breaks an increasing number of American homes. This week a Missouri legislator introduced a bill to make our State a mecca for divorce-seekers. He pointed out that millionaires and motion-picture actors spend many thousands of dollars in dissolving their marriages, and he sees no reason why Nevada, Arkansas, and several other States should receive practically all this lucrative revenue. He wants Missouri to have its share — the same twisted logic which the bartender employs when he concludes that the half-drunken wretch before him will spend his money in some tavern anyway, that he may as well be the one who profits — as though there ever could be any benefit in money gained through disregard of the divine Law! Besides these organized onslaughts from without, the home suffers internally under the rule of resentment, selfishness, cruelty. Fathers and mothers tyrannize their children; sons and daughters, when their parents are too weak and worn for productive work, insist on sending them to the old folks' home. With husband arrayed against wife, parents against children, with distrust and suspicion often accompanied by unfaithfulness, our Lord's cry rings with double appeal throughout every unhappy home: "Stop this strife here at the hearthside, where, more than at any other spot, love and peace should reign! Put up your swords!"

Let us not pass lightly over this injunction, "Put up your swords in the churches, in the State, in the home!" When Jesus specifically warned, *"All they that take the sword shall perish with the sword,"* He did not exaggerate. Look at history! Many a European church, for example, in Spain, that a few centuries ago promoted inquisition has been partially or wholly destroyed, and before our generation ends, perhaps other religious groups that favored violence will similarly be wiped out. Countries which eagerly grasped the sword for conquest have been laid waste. Where are the great military nations of the past: Babylonia, Assyria, Egypt, Persia, Rome? Though they gathered the wealth and brains of the world, they were not rich and wise enough to escape the punishment that Christ here predicts, *"All they that take the sword shall perish with the sword."* Families ruled or broken by compulsion can never enjoy Christ's blessings of harmony and happiness. Brutal criminals, war lords, who promote strife, individuals who hate — these, by the punishment they suffer on earth and, if unforgiven, in hell, prove the inescapable truth of the Savior's verdict: Force leads to force! Taking the sword in violence brings back the sword in destruction!

II

HOW BLESSED THE SAVIOR'S SUBSTITUTION OF LOVE FOR FORCE!

By this command and His immediate healing of the slave with the severed ear, Jesus showed us that He had come to extend love, help, hope; that the weapons of His kingdom were not carnal but spiritual. — A severe testing-time may face Christians throughout the world as they try to follow Christ in this emphasis on love. We need a new understanding of His compassion, a new commentary on His Sermon on the Mount, with a practical, 1941 application of its inspired, divine program for peace and against violence. Every one who acclaims Jesus his Savior should in all seriousness seek to convince himself that Christ meant exactly what He said when He declared: *"Blessed are the meek, for they shall inherit the earth. . . . Blessed are the peacemakers; for they shall be called the children of God."* It is His clear instruction: *"Resist not evil; but whosoever shall smite thee on thy right cheek, turn to him the other also."* Deliberately does He command, *"I say unto you, Love your enemies, bless them that curse you, do good to them that hate you, and pray for them which despitefully use you and persecute you, that ye may be the children of your Father which is in heaven."* We have no justification whatever for taking these words in any other sense than that which we must find in their clear reading. Yet how far we are from that complete spirit of love! During a hearing at Washington the president of our oldest university, who urged that, if necessary, we send our youth to Europe's battle-fields, was asked in cross-examination whether, obedient to the Scriptures which he quoted, he had prayed for those whom he regarded as this country's enemies; he admitted that he had not. Most of you would have to make that same confession. Yet here is Christ's Word, teaching meekness, prayer, and intercession for enemies, love and forbearance! As the churches put these sacred requirements into operation, they will, by divine grace, receive new and heavenly strength; for it is still true in our day as 2500 years ago in Zechariah's time that the Kingdom is built *"not by might nor by power but by My Spirit."* And that holy, sanctifying Spirit comes with hearing, believing, practicing, the *whole* Word of God.

Jesus not only taught that love; He lived it. A hundred times His own countrymen so maliciously opposed Him that with our sinful emotions of anger and hatred we would have turned away in deep-souled resentment. Again and again their blasphemy was so vile that they even associated their Messiah, the sinless Son of God, with Satan. Had we been among Christ's followers then, we, too, would have joined John in asking the Savior to invoke destruction from heaven upon those who rejected Him. The Christ of endless compassion would not stoop to that. Nailed on the cross, He pleaded with His Father to forgive every one who had a part in making Him endure the agony and shame of the crucifixion.

Jesus, however, not only taught that all-enduring love and lived it; He shed His own life-blood and gave Himself into atoning death to prove it. We were God's enemies, estranged from Him by our wickedness. We had no claim for any consideration by Christ. If we had been made to bear the punishment of our innumerable and repeated sins, pay the full penalty, suffer the accumulated guilt of every transgression recorded day by day against us, we could have no complaint, no reason to charge our God with injustice. By that inexpressible devotion with which He loved us, frail, false, full of pride as we all are, Jesus, God's own Son, removed these iniquities, not simply by forgetting them or crossing them off; not merely by some mechanical transfer, but by assuming Himself in His own sinless body the retribution for every unholy impulse, every impure utterance, every selfish action with which we have served sin and rebelled against God's holiness.

Pray the Father ceaselessly that you may accept your Savior and, having confessed Him, to abide in His love, loyal unto the end! Nothing else in life counts in comparison with that Christ-directed faith. It is the one priceless possession for time and eternity; and this assurance of salvation through Him can be fully yours, so that conscience's protests, hell's furies, death's terror cannot move the rock of trust. The Savior's love can be yours freely; for if you have learned to say, "Jesus shed His blood for me," you know this keystone truth of the Christian creed: we are *"justified by faith, without the deeds of the Law."* You can have His love unconditionally despite the heavy transgressions which make you wonder whether there can be grace even for you. As you behold the Lord in Gethsemane disavowing the use of the sword and going unflinchingly to His death on the cross, now hardly twelve hours distant, believe that He treads this path of suffering for you; that He permits the nails of death to rivet Him to the cross for your sake; that He endures the God-forsakenness, the thirst, the ridicule, the anguish of body, and the incomparably worse agony of soul, so that you can be saved for a blessed eternity. As I beseech you in the name of the bleeding, moaning, dying Savior: "Give yourself to Christ now! Accept His mercy today!" may God's Spirit, without which my words would be only empty phrases, find His victorious way into sin-darkened, hope-robbed hearts and bring this answer to your lips: "O God, my Father, heartily do I repent of the wrong with which I have offended Thee. Contritely do I confess myself to be unworthy of all Thy mercies; but steadfastly do I cling to the cross of the Lord Jesus Christ, my Savior. His blood is the only cleansing for my sins, His death the one promise of my life, His truth the sole guarantee for heaven's glories!"

With such faith you will be able to practice the compassion which turns from violence and the sword. Just as *"there is none other name under heaven given among men whereby we must be saved"* but the precious name of Jesus Christ, so there is no antidote to the poison of hatred besides the pure Gospel of the Savior slain for the world's sins. A few days ago a scrubwoman, who each week-day evening cleans a Chicago office-building, was given a four-hour beauty treatment; her cotton house dress was exchanged for a fashionable frock; and a transformation was effected which, the newspaper said, turned a charwoman into a Cinderella. No human process can plant love in a heart of hate nor create that spiritual beauty which is reflected on the peaceful, happy countenance. Only the Holy Spirit can produce that regeneration. We must have the rebirth which makes us new creatures in Jesus!

The history of Christ's Church, from the time that

Stephen sought God's pardon for those who were stoning him to death, down to the present moment, bears witness to the renewing power of the Holy Comforter. Tamatoe, converted South Sea island ruler, discovered a plot contrived by those of his people who had remained heathen. They planned to seize him, together with native believers, and burn all Christians to death. Tamatoe captured the conspirators unawares, but to their astonishment, instead of killing them, he set a feast before them. This mercy was so unexpected that the sagaves deserted their idols and were converted to Christ. When Jesus reigns in our hearts, we, too, can have peace instead of poisonous envy. By His grace I promise those of you whose family happiness has been destroyed by rankling hatred that, if you make Jesus the Head of your home; if He abides with you in faithful family prayers and Scripture-reading; if you invite Him to every meal and ask His blessing at the beginning and close of each day; if with the Spirit's power you try to lead Christlike lives, you can master bitterness, selfishness, and disappointment. You can start over in your home (your letters prove that this is not theory but God's truth) with a fresh, happy beginning and the hope of better things to come. If in your individual lives envy, jealousy, malicious, covetous thoughts, rule where consideration and devotion to others should reign supreme, give Jesus full sway, and you will find that He truly can create a clean heart and renew a right spirit within you.

As the Lenten scene once more portrays Christ rebuking His disciples with the command, *"Put up thy sword!"* may we be given the grace to understand that God will take care of us, our country, our churches, our homes — as long as we are Christ's. If necessary, those twelve angel legions which Jesus could have called may be summoned for defense in danger and protection against enemies. What a blessed thought in the midst of temptation, sorrow, and trial to know that the same Father who directed His Son's destiny from Gethsemane through Golgotha and the grave to His glorious resurrection will lead us without hatred and fears, without the sword, from earth's trial to heaven's triumph! Unto Him, the all-merciful, ever-glorious, never-ending Christ, the Cleansing for our iniquities, the Savior of our souls, the Peace for our troubled hearts, Jesus, the only Hope in a sin-cancered world, the only Light during our sin-darkened days, the only Promise of inner peace throughout a war-racked world — unto Him be the loyalty of our contrite hearts, the praise of our Spirit-filled lives, the adoration of our ransomed souls, both now and forever! Amen.

MORE THAN REMORSE —
REAL REPENTANCE!

*"Judas, which had betrayed Him, when he saw that
He was condemned, repented himself and brought
again the thirty pieces of silver to the chief priests
and elders, saying, I have sinned in that I have
betrayed the innocent blood. And they said, What
is that to us? See thou to that. And he cast down
the pieces of silver in the Temple and departed and
went and hanged himself."* — Saint Matthew 27:3-5

Beloved Lord Jesus:

*Keep Thy Spirit uppermost in our souls and help us realize in
humble, personal faith that Thou didst suffer for us! Our transgressions nailed Thee to the cross of shame, and Thou didst taste
death as our Substitute when Thy life was offered as the one ever-
valid sacrifice for all humanity's sins! We confess, precious Savior,
that we have often denied, even betrayed Thee by impure ambitions,
unholy living. This weakness and wickedness rests heavily on our
conscience, and today, without reservation or excuse, we come before
Thee to express heartfelt sorrow for our disloyalties. We promise
wherever possible to make amends for our shortcomings. Penitently,
yet confident of Thy mercy, we look only to Thine atoning mercy
for pardon and peace. Deepen our appreciation of Thy truth and
show us that we must come to Thee with more than sorrow over
our iniquities, with real repentance and immovable faith in Thy sin-
removing love! Plant the certainty of salvation into our souls,
O Jesus, and draw us ever closer to Thee — if necessary, by affliction! Hear us, for we have no other hope in life or death!
Amen.*

SORROW for our sins, remorse over our failures, can
become life's most terrifying scourge. Every day your
letters testify to the fury of an aroused conscience. A Kentucky young woman writes that since she violated her
chastity, only to be jilted, she can hardly find forgetfulness
even in sleep. An Indiana couple, each previously divorced
and now married to each other against the Scriptures, is
tortured by the realization that for years both have openly

lived in adultery. A county official in a Western State
who stole public money and lost it in speculation is almost
paralyzed by fear over the State auditor's impending visit.
A Michigan girl, because of previous transgressions, is
haunted by the terror of having committed the unpardon-
able sin. A Kansas listener laments that she has been
robbed of peace because she opposed her parents, neglected
them in their needs, and, now they are dead, can never
make amends. Although forty years have elapsed since
the crime, an Ohio mother is relentlessly pursued by remorse for having destroyed her unborn child.

Life is not secure under the torment of self-condem-
nation. The appalling suicide toll in the United States
takes many who mistakenly felt themselves driven to self-
destruction under the lash of an outraged conscience. We
are, of course, accustomed to read of suicides after naval
disasters when a captain (by a code of the sea which all
civilized nations should revoke) deliberately goes down with
his ship. For years self-murder has been an accepted social
escape in Japan. There military officers who fail are expected to destroy themselves by the prescribed rites of
hara-kiri. Annually hundreds of Nipponese young people,
frustrated in love, join hands, leap into the crater of a
favorite volcano, and are burned to cinders by molten lava.
How shocking to hear that the number of suicides in the
United States is practically as large as in pagan Japan!

The most intense sorrow over missteps and mistakes is
not enough. A lifetime of regrets is not sufficient. Suicide
only brings eternal horror and suffering. We must learn
the lesson millions in America have forgotten, the truth
which can change our existence from years of extended
fears to a career of sustained peace in Christ, the conviction that for the removal of our sins we must, beholding
Jesus, have

MORE THAN REMORSE — REAL REPENTANCE!

To this end may God's Holy Spirit guide us in our study of the warning and, by contrast, the comfort offered by Saint Matthew, chapter twenty-seven, verses three to five: *"Judas, which had betrayed Him, when he saw that He was condemned, repented himself and brought again the thirty pieces of silver to the chief priests and elders, saying, I have sinned in that I have betrayed the innocent blood. And they said, What is that to us? See thou to that. And he cast down the pieces of silver in the Temple and departed and went and hanged himself."*

I

REMORSE IS NOT ENOUGH

We often think of Judas as a hideous monster, an ugly, misshapen, beastlike creature, a veritable Frankenstein, while in truth he was an ordinary man, doubtless with many amiable qualities. When as a boy he played in the streets and fields of Kerioth, a little village in the South, often, doubtless, his parents, smiling at their happy child, dreamed of the day when their Judas would be a respected, successful citizen, an elder in the community council, even as you fathers and mothers like to envision your sons as making their mark in the world. After he grew to manhood, he cannot have been destitute of ideals, for a day of destiny came when a Stranger, mysterious, yet compelling, a Galilean Teacher called Jesus of Nazareth, preached a heart-searching message and confronted Judas with the invitation, *"Follow Me!"* Although he knew that obedience to the Lord meant bearing the cross of affliction, Judas gave up everything to accept the Savior's leadership. Among the Twelve he, the only disciple from Judea, gained a certain distinction; for before long he was entrusted with the treasury, meager though it was. We search in vain throughout the early gospel records for evidence of his disloyalty; there is none. Like his eleven comrades he, too, acclaimed Christ, who, he thought would liberate Israel and establish a magnificent kingdom. When, after a hard sermon by Jesus, many of His followers forsook Him, Judas did not leave. I am trying to impress on you the truth that Judas was one of us. If in a surge of self-righteousness some of you protest, "Well, I certainly would never do what he did!" you don't know Judas, and you don't know yourself! The only people who cannot commit his sin are the heathen who have never heard of Jesus; those are the closest to repeating his betrayal who, as he, are nearest Christ. *"Let him that thinketh he standeth take heed lest he fall,"* the eternal Word warns; and not until we see in that thankless disciple the same guilty, evil impulses which occupy our own hearts are we honestly concerned with our immortal souls' welfare.

The trouble started with Judas where it often begins in our lives: with money. Other explanations, of course, have been advanced. A favorite theory claims that Judas wanted to bring Christ's cause to a climax; so he betrayed his Lord only to create a situation by which Jesus would be obliged to demonstrate His power. But the Scriptures know nothing of this. The gospels tell us that Judas loved gold; and gradually, it seems, he became disappointed in Christ. His materialistic imagination had pictured the Savior with a resplendent crown on His head; but these hopes were soon replaced by resentment when our Lord spoke of submission to His enemies, of martyrdom and a death of shame. It may well be that Judas argued within himself: "I will still get something from following Christ! The Temple authorities want to put Him out of the way! They can use me, and I will make them pay."

Whatever his reasoning was, he went to the priests, perhaps soothing his conscience with the alibi that these men were supposed to be representatives of the Most High, that they would welcome his betrayal as a pious, God-pleasing act. People use the same tactics today. Sin loses its stigma if the Church can be made to approve it. The unjustly divorced often want a preacher to solemnize their second matrimonial venture. The bereaved relatives of a foul-mouthed infidel who died without a thought of Jesus are eager for a Christian burial, since it would remove the disgrace. Gamblers like to have roulette wheels, dice, cards, games of chance, in congregational buildings for the sanction and prestige that religion offers. War-promoters— and we shall constantly hear more of them — piously call the present hostilities a battle for God, a crusade for Christianity, a struggle for the faith, so that the churches' influence may be enlisted to throw our youth into the vortex of Europe's war. But we need much more than outward religious sanction to justify our actions. It must be said to the shame of certain church groups that frequently they have become part and party to proposals which utterly repudiate Christ. In the blessed name of Him who is Peace and Love clerics have preached hatred and destruction. They have sanctioned murder, theft, false witness, divorce, adultery, unjust, aggressive wars of conquest.

Masking his hypocrisy in mock piety, Judas approached the religious leaders with the age-old question of grasping greed, *"What will ye give me?"* And those Temple officials, the men required to show God's holiness, bargained with a traitor! "Abhorrent!" you exclaim, but not so depraved, I answer, that a similar desire to get rid of Jesus does not animate some churchmen today. They exhibit the same outward zeal of Annas, Caiaphas, the scribes, and the Pharisees, but they also have the same hatred for the Biblical Christ. *"Away with Him!"* their cry reechoes, repeating the malicious verdict of the first Good Friday. "Away with Jesus as God's Son and the world's Savior, the virgin-born, crucified, resurrected, ascended Redeemer! Away with Him as the only Hope of a perishing world!" This rejection has become so wide-spread and influential that it can keep Gospel broadcasts off the country's largest stations. Voices regarded as authoritatively Protestant often reject the basic, Biblical truths. — If you love Christ, work and pray that this discarding of His deathless Word be stopped in many churches now!

"What will ye give me?" — this barter of greed is quite modern. *"The love of money"* is still *"the root of all"* (kinds of) *"evil."* Stripped of its disguises, most war is promoted by avarice. Commercial supremacy, domination of the seas, more territory, fertile farmlands, productive oil-fields, rich mineral deposits, economic ascendancy — these are the objectives for which world meddlers have laid unsuspecting, high-idealed youth on gory altars before the idol of war in a human sacrifice far more despicable than the Canaanite child-offerings in Hinnom's valley. *"What will ye give me?"* — this selfish inquiry motivates the struggle in our American industrial circles, where, instead of cooperative harmony, we witness growing antagonism. *"What will ye give me?"* — this personal profit-seeking urges Christians to stretch out their hands for unholy gain in a hundred different forms of theft, which some of you have been able to conceal, not, however, from your conscience and Almighty God.

Judas's sin was heightened because he was ready to sell a life for blood-money. It has been questioned whether he actually believed the Savior's enemies would go to the extent of crucifixion. But how could any one accompany Jesus for three years and doubt that the priestly venom would be satisfied with anything less than death? Many today share the same guilt. This generation particularly should read carefully the scandals of past wars with their hideous profiteering. During the first world conflict British soldiers in the Dardanelles were mowed down by British guns in enemy hands. Austrians on the Galician front were killed by rifles originally made or repaired by Austrians. Two French firms were able to import, on their own account, German steel through Switzerland. We, too, have tragic records of spoiled meat, inferior equipment, defective weapons deliberately sold to American armies; and even now a Congressional committee has been appointed to investigate evidences of profiteering in our defense program. Not many forms of depravity are lower than this clutching desire to march on to wealth over bodies sacrificed to greed. Few figures are more despicable than international munitions-manufacturers who, though decorated and knighted by a dozen governments, as some were, grew rich and powerful through unscrupulous arms traffic.

Many of you, however, who would shrink from harming your neighbor in his body may for the sake of profit cause his soul to suffer. With the drop in morality that war brings already unmistakable (London reports an increase of 40 per cent in juvenile crime) ; with taxi dance-halls springing up around our half-finished military camps (and I pause to ask you Christian young men in the service for loyalty, not only to your country, but also to your Christ) ; with a growing army of Americans making their livelihood directly or indirectly from the sale of suggestive books and sex magazines, pictures or plays that glorify sin, drugs or drink that injure the body and serve lust, there can be only one course for those who serve Christ, and that is specified by the command *"Come out from among them, and be ye separate!"* I do not stand before this

microphone to utter a blanket condemnation; for the
Savior's word is clear, *"Judge not, and ye shall not be
judged!"* I do pray, however, that the Spirit may fortify
these words: If you work as owner or employee in an
office, factory, store, or business where the enterprise deliberately seeks to take people away from Jesus, attacks
the Bible, assaults Christian morality, destroys the ideals
of truth, purity, and honesty; if young people can point
their finger at you, charging, *"You* helped lead me on the
road to sin," then remember Judas! Ask our Lord's forgiveness and the strength to stop the heinous wrong, give
up that destructive employment forever! This will take
courage. Immediately you will hear whispered objections:
"Where can I get another job? This position pays a good
salary. If I don't make or sell this, some one else will.
I give a large check to the Church every week." But that
comes from the same satanic Tempter who brought Judas
to fall. Steadfastly look to Jesus, and as you exalt Him,
you will find His promise fulfilled, *"If any man serve Me,
him will My Father honor."*

Lured by avarice, Judas not only deserted Christ, con-
nived with His enemies, bargained for blood-money; as
history's most damnable Fifth Columnist he sold the Savior,
not for 30,000,000 pieces of silver nor even 30,000. We
could understand how a depraved wretch might have been
tempted by such fortunes. But thirty paltry pieces!
Hardly enough to buy food and clothing for a few
months! Barely sufficient for the priests to purchase an
unwanted, out-of-the-way piece of land as a potter's field,
the burial-place of the unclaimed or criminally dead!
Christ sold for thirty pieces of silver, $18 in our money!
"How incredible!" we exclaim. Satan does not always
have to bid that high. Some of you have sold Christ
for less. A wild night's entertainment which cost your

companion, say, $15; a $9.98 set of antichristian scientific volumes which an unbeliever *gave* you; a *free* visit to a spiritist medium, who usually charges a dollar; a fifty-cent blasphemous book or a five-cent blue paper-covered infidel pamphlet that some atheist sent you without charge — these may be the only inducements the devil had to offer in turning you against Christ. For trivial honors and the smallest sensual satisfaction people are sometimes ready to adopt Judas's tactics and beneath smirking hypocrisy array themselves against Christ.

The Gospel narratives do not tell us how Judas spent the time after he placed the kiss of betrayal on the Savior's cheek. If it is true, as a few scholars claim, that he followed Christ at a distance and witnessed the beginning of His trials, we understand the more clearly why a startling change gradually overtook him. At first perhaps Judas played with the silver pieces, letting them fall through his fingers, polishing them, placing them in rows, jingling them at his ears, dreaming of the power the money-mad think they can conjure with clicking coins. But *"when he saw that"* Jesus *"was condemned,"* the attraction of that minted silver suddenly vanished. The treachery, which had seemed such an easy, cunning scheme, now became an avalanche of terror.

Do you know that Judas, recoiling from his despicable sin, showed more concern than some of you? He at least realized his monstrous crime and hated it; you see only the sensual appeal of your transgression and love it. You — this is your boast — will do what you want, and no one can stop *you!* The Lord Jesus Christ's name is just an aid to your profanity. For your soul's sake I pray God that He will hurl you down from your self-conceited unbelief, if necessary, into the depth of suffering, so that, helpless, you can learn what even Judas knew, "Sin never pays, while the sinner always pays." If some of you young people who once thought that there could be nothing sweeter than the forbidden fruits begin to experience an after-taste of bitterness, thank God! You will never know Christ until you recognize your own sin!

Judas went a step farther. He returned to the priests, hoping he could secure help in the Temple; yet just as little as people today can find soul-comfort through any religious teacher not blessed by God, so the distracted disciple vainly sought guidance in the Sanctuary. Terrified, he confessed the enormity of his crime, saying, *"I have sinned!"* And then Judas, the hypocrite, the traitor, became the first in the story of the Savior's suffering to declare Jesus not guilty. Hear his cry reecho through the Temple, *"I have betrayed the innocent blood!"* Again, Judas was far in advance of many modern Americans; he confessed his sin, while voices throughout the country in education, literature, philosophy, science, give it new names, excuse it, even justify it, and — this low have they stooped! — even glorify it! Judas told the men who had directed the plot against Christ that Jesus was blameless; let this statement from the lips of our Lord's archenemy urge you to recognize that Jesus has always been innocent of every calumny and attack perverted men have hurled against Him. Unless you understand that our Lord was guiltless and that the death penalty placed on His stainless body and soul was incurred by your transgression, you cannot know true repentance nor find the pathway to heaven.

The priests coldly shrugged their shoulders as they replied, *"What is that to us? See thou to that!"* and showed the devilish unconcern which always marks sin. Many of you recall how friends who coaxed you into wrong-doing were the first to turn against you. Despite priestly indifference, however, Judas's conscience continued to drive him on. He tried to make restitution. As impossible as it was for him to rescue Christ from His enemies, he could at least rid himself of the blood-profit gained through the suffering of the Innocent One, and in despair he hurled the thirty pieces of silver to the Sanctuary floor. — Have you tried to make restitution for your sins? If you have stolen money, have you returned it? If you live in an illicit relationship, are you ready to stop and do what God expects of you? If people have suffered through your greed, have you done anything to compensate them? The nation has a conscience fund in Washington, and through receipt of smaller sums it has grown to sizable proportions; but if all money and property sinfully acquired could be returned to the Government or defrauded individuals, the country's financial problem would be minimized and millions now destitute could live in comfort. It may be too late to make amends, but unless you do everything humanly possible to refund your thefts, you cannot stand before the Almighty!

As the money rolled on the floor, Judas ran from the Temple in headlong flight, the doom of death written on his countenance. Fear such as only the damned can experience pursued him like hellhounds of endless remorse. Completely in Satan's control, he ended eternally damned; for we read, *"He . . . went and hanged himself."* The care-free child that once played in the lanes of Judean Kerioth, the disciple eager to serve Christ, now dangled in a suicide's noose, until either the rope or tree branch broke, and he fell headlong into death and — hell!

Do you say: "What a fool Judas was! People with any degree of intelligence can avoid what he did"? Are you sure? Can you prove the popular theory that education is the best preventive of self-destruction? Why is it that intellectual leaders and university graduates are frequently numbered among those who take their own lives? Unless you are ready to go farther than Judas went, you have absolutely no assurance that your end must be different from his.

II

REAL REPENTANCE IS NECESSARY

Judas's suicide impresses on us that more than remorse is necessary. We must have real repentance — in Christ! None of life's fears is more treacherous and destructive than the gnawing despair of an aroused conscience. Richard III of England, who murdered his two innocent nephews, kept an unsheathed sword at his bedside and constantly fought invisible imaginary foes. Charles IX of France, who signed the death-warrant for tens of thousands of Protestants mowed down in the Saint Bartholomew massacre, asked for music when he awakened at night to soothe his terrorized soul and take his thoughts from the horror of his sin. No matter how intense your remorse may be, if you stop where Judas did, you can cry your eyes dry every day, count each long hour of the night in sleepless anxiety until you collapse in nervous breakdown; without Christ this is all wasted energy, futile suffering!

It is not enough to declare, "I am sorry!" Dogs show a sort of creature sorrow when punished for wrong-doing! It is not sufficient to resolve, "I will stop this evil. I promise to make good what I have done wrong!" Educated Greek and Roman pagans said the same thing; yet they ended without the assurance of forgiveness! It is not enough to know who Jesus is, to proclaim His innocence. Even the Mohammedan Koran gives the Savior greater glory without being able to offer its followers the pledge of pardon. The factor which makes repentance acceptable in God's sight is the faith by which we place our entire hope for pardon on the Lord Jesus. *Only* when repentance is made in His name, but *always* when contrite hearts are lifted first to His cross and then to the open heavens, can we be sure that our sins are removed.

Beholding our Redeemer on the cross, we are to believe, with hearts freed from every doubt, that *"He was wounded for our transgressions, He was bruised for our iniquities, the chastisement of our peace was upon Him, and with His stripes we are healed."* The Beginning and End of our faith based on the plain Bible truth that *"Christ died for our sins,"* the Innocent for the guilty, the Eternal for the mortal, God for man, we not only overcome the fear of consequences, the dread of exposure, the panic of an enraged conscience, the furies of hell itself; but because we believe assuredly that *"the blood of Jesus Christ, His Son, cleanseth us from all sin,"* we know that our iniquities have been taken away forever. Pledged to the Savior we have no reason to cringe before God, fearing that our transgressions may not have been completely forgiven; for the acceptance of divine approval was stamped upon our Lord's redemptive work when after His death-gasp, *"It is finished!"* He was gloriously resurrected from the dead on the third day. Nothing remains undone, nothing necessary for our salvation unfulfilled, not even the most insignificant part still to be accomplished. Judas could have been pardoned and restored had his remorse given way to a true, Christ-centered contrition; and if Jesus would have forgiven even His betrayer had that desperate disciple sought forgiveness in faith, you should believe that, since no sin could possibly be worse than Judas's treachery, the Savior has pardon, love, peace, for you. All you need — however scarlet or bloody your sins may be — after deep penetrating sorrow is sincere trust in the Lord Jesus — nothing more!

When Judas hanged himself and his disfigured body fell headlong to the ground, it was too late for repentance. Thank God, you still have a chance! But if you love your soul, do not postpone your contrite return to the Father! Don't figure on death-bed penitence or plan to live in sin until your last hour comes and then conveniently be converted to God! True, the thief on the cross was saved in the eleventh hour, showing that as long as there is life, it is not too late. A Christian physician in Maine who has systematically observed the dying moments of hundreds of sufferers, writes me to corroborate a happy certainty that often a last-moment word pointing to Christ can be of eternal blessing. Yet it is equally sure, as Christian ministers can testify, that in most cases dying unbelievers are not physically, mentally, spiritually, able to understand the offer of Christ's love. They have toyed with salvation, and it has slipped beyond their grasp!

Several years ago reports from Russia announced that Red atheists would erect a gigantic, widely visible statue of Judas Iscariot to show their defiant rejection of Christ. I have not been able to ascertain how far they succeeded; nor does it matter. Some day the Soviets will learn the whole lesson of which even now they have apparently accepted the first chapters, that no country can long prosper in rebellion against the Almighty. It is of more personal concern that you and I never altogether lose sight of Judas nor forget the lessons which his despair and suicide teach. Look at him once more in that fatal flight from the Temple; for in him we must see our own weaknesses mirrored; but while he ran from Christ, O God of all grace, help us hasten to the Savior with more than remorse — with real, Christ-directed repentance! Make us a truly contrite nation, in which devout citizens, though surrounded by the pomp and parade of the hour, humbly confess their faults and prayerfully seek divine guidance for the United States during the hazardous years ahead! Grant us truly penitent churches, keenly conscious of their reluctance to give everything in bringing the crucified Savior to masses in America! Bless us with repentant homes, so that grim despair may be banished from families united in trustful adoration of Christ! Give us, in our foremost benediction, truly contrite hearts, deep sorrow for our wrong, sincere resolve for the right, through faith in Jesus Christ our own and only Redeemer! We ask it in His name! Amen.

———————

WILL JESUS ANSWER ME?

*"He questioned with Him in many words; but He an-
swered him nothing."* — Saint Luke 23:9
*"Jesus said unto him, Verily I say unto thee, Today
shalt thou be with Me in Paradise."* — Saint Luke 23:43

Father Almighty:

*In the midst of a world crowded with war, hatred, destruction, we
have no refuge but in Thee and the love by which Thy Son gave
Himself into the agonized death of Calvary to make complete atonement for all iniquity. Fill our hearts with gratitude for this mercy
and lead us, by unfaltering faith, ever more deeply into the full
riches of Christ's grace! Bless the invitation of Thy Gospel and
show every sin-weighted soul that the same Savior who in His
dying hours pardoned a penitent criminal has forgiveness and compassion for every one of us despite our black and scarlet sins, if only
we approach Him with the firm assurance that He is our God, our
Savior, our King! Send Thy Spirit to abide in us as our daily
Guide and Comforter! Give us the heavenly wisdom whereby we
can constantly walk humbly and penitently before Thee! And,
O God, triune and triumphant over all enemies, keep our thoughts,
desires, and ambitions ever close to the cross on which the Savior
paid for our transgressions with His life! We ask it in His precious
name. Amen.*

A FEW days ago a copy of Sir John MacDonnell's
book *Historical Trials* came into my hands. As
I read the eminent jurist's account of ten famous legal
cases, from the procedures against Socrates down to the
court actions in the seventeenth century, a comparison with
the Savior's death trial was inevitable. One remarkable
difference separates the prosecution of Jesus from these
other notable hearings. It is not the injustice, the perjury,
the ruthless fracture of all lawful procedure involved in
the sentence that doomed Jesus to the cross; for although
history has never witnessed a miscarriage of justice comparable with the verdict "Guilty of death!" pronounced
upon Christ, there have always been corrupt judges, con-

trolled courts, bought and biased juries. We have them today. The distinctive mark in our Savior's arraignment before His fellow-countrymen and the Roman authorities is this: Not only did Jesus decline to plead in His own behalf, but at each of His hearings the time came when He sealed His lips and refused to speak. Caiaphas, the worldly-minded Sadducee high priest, screamed his blasphemous charges against our Lord; and soon the Savior, serene in the face of death, fell into unbroken silence. When Pontius Pilate, shrewd, unprincipled politician, extended his questioning, the captive Christ deliberately disdained to answer. In the scene we shall study today, after Pilate sent Jesus to Herod, the ruler of Galilee, that sensual weakling hurled question after question at our Lord without receiving a single reply.

This impressive silence was not accidental. Seven and one half centuries before, Isaiah, beholding his suffering Savior, had predicted, *"He was oppressed, and He was afflicted, yet He opened not His mouth: He is brought as a Lamb to the slaughter."* While I speak of fulfilled prophecy, let me take a moment to remind you how our Lord's Passion is foretold with detail hundreds of years before Gethsemane and Calvary. His betrayal by a disciple, the thirty pieces of silver as the traitor's fee, the potter's field bought with that blood-money, the perjury of false witnesses, the crucifixion itself, the vinegar given in His burning thirst, the blasphemy of malicious enemies under the cross, the division of His clothing, Jesus' prayer *"My God, My God, why hast Thou forsaken Me?"* the atoning power of His substitutionary death, His burial, not in an unmarked grave but in a rich man's tomb — these and more are the startling predictions accomplished to the letter on the night of the Savior's capture and on the day of His death. We challenge any unbeliever to

312 WILL JESUS ANSWER ME?

produce completed prophecy, not even a long series like this, but only one instance. Why do some of you skeptics continue to doubt or deny God's Word when you have this convincing evidence of divine foreknowledge?

Yet, while our Savior, in harmony with Isaiah's ancient forecast, refused to answer King Herod, only a few hours later on that same Good Friday, when nailed to the cross, He did speak hope into the soul of a convicted criminal.

Can you not see in this startling contrast: silence for proud rulers, pardon for a crucified thief, that there are two classes of men, some who make Christ turn from them in cold, condemning silence, and others whom He gladly receives? In this day of the question-and-answer craze, when every night the radio features quiz programs, every week many thousands of dollars are spent for intelligence broadcasts, every year winners receive stacks of silver dollars and huge piles of prizes, no issue is of comparable importance with our question for today:

WILL JESUS ANSWER ME?

Will He pardon and welcome me, or will His lips remain locked when I stand before Him? Thank God, you can have a definite understanding on this life-and-death truth. A wide knowledge of geography and history is unnecessary; you need only know what happened on that rough hill of Golgotha and what the cross means to you. No specialized training in chemistry is required; your soul is cleansed, not in research laboratories, but through faith in Christ. Higher mathematics is ruled out; Jesus deals with unnumbered sins and unlimited grace. He demands no literary test; He is concerned with only one Book, and its promises are so clear that even a child can understand them. If your heart holds the right response to this question, "Will Jesus answer me?" Heaven's most magnificent blessings are yours forever. If you give the wrong answer, you are heading for eternal disaster.

May this message, which divine wisdom and love can make a turning-point for many, give you an assured answer to this question of hope or despair, heaven or hell, "Will Jesus hear me when I try to come before Him?" To that blessed end we read this record of the Savior's Lenten suffering in Saint Luke's twenty-third chapter, verse nine: *"He* [Herod] *questioned with Him* [Jesus] *in many words; but He answered him nothing,"* and then in verse forty-three: *"Jesus said unto him* [the thief crucified at the side of His own cross], *Verily I say unto thee, Today shalt thou be with Me in Paradise."*

I

JESUS WILL NOT ANSWER IMPENITENT PRIDE

During the death trial before Pontius Pilate, while one charge after the other was hurled at our Savior, it was mentioned, perhaps in sarcastic scorn, that Jesus had come from Galilee. When Pilate heard this, he resolved to send the captive Christ to Herod, whom the Roman conquerors had permitted to rule over Galilee and who happened to be in Jerusalem at that time for the Passover Festival. What a convenient way, Pilate concluded, to get rid of Jesus! Somehow the mysterious Prisoner disturbed his pagan mind. Convinced that Jesus was innocent, he repeatedly tried to side-step a decision and wash his hands of the whole affair. Finally, however, he had to make a personal, definite choice concerning Jesus, just as every one of you is either for Christ or against Him. There is no straddling, no middle ground, no neutrality here! On Friday morning, then, after three hearings by His own countrymen and the first trial before Pilate, Jesus was once more led through the streets of Jerusalem toward Herod's palace. Don't forget that our Lord had to endure six distinct legal hearings within twelve hours! By contrast, a labor leader who first faced deportation procedures three years ago is still in this country!

Herod, the Galilean king, was *"exceeding glad"* to see Jesus, the Galilean prophet. The Savior's name was on every one's lips. His miracles were the subject of public discussion; and now the moment had come when Herod could gratify his curiosity and perhaps induce Jesus to perform a dazzling wonder. *"He questioned with Him in many words,"* our text summarizes. Herod was like many of the 70,000,000 unchurched people in this country who are indifferent to Christ even in a crisis that should drive men back to their God and Savior. They demand, Christianity must offer modern social miracles by which people can find quick money and light work. Jesus treats them just as He did Herod when throughout that entire questioning *"He answered him nothing."*

It would have been easy for our Lord to produce a spectacular display, answer curious questions, then plead for justice and deliverance. Herod, his favor won, could have had the farcical trial ended with complete vindication for Christ. But Jesus would curry the favor of no man nor ingratiate himself with the rich and important. — Let American churches pause thoughtfully before this scene in which Jesus spurns wealth and influence! The frequent indictment directed against Christianity today charges it with neglecting the working-men and the poor while trying to creep into the good graces of the moneyed classes, paying court to the prominent and powerful. It may be that in some instances certain groups have been guilty. They should learn of Christ now before the most far-reaching social reconstruction in modern history begins after this war, when losses, totaling not billions but hundreds of billions, will create deeper poverty throughout the world! More than ever before in this country churches must follow the Savior in condemning ill-gotten wealth and in rededicating themselves to bring His Gospel to all men, particularly to the lower, underprivileged classes. Today, with the lure of blood-money and excessive profits stronger than ever, we must repeat Christ's warning, *"Verily, I say unto you that a rich man shall hardly enter into the kingdom of heaven!"*

Wealth in itself, of course, can be a bountiful blessing. I have been in large, impressive homes that have had more genuine, humble, and complete trust in Christ than I have sometimes found in middle-class families. Herod, however, was sinfully rich, wicked, and dissolute. Inflamed by carnal passions, he had discarded his wife and taken Herodias, his brother Philip's wife. He thought that he was a law unto himself. The king could do no wrong, he doubtless boasted. Too many crowned heads and national leaders in this generation have followed in Herod's footsteps. Within the last ten years three European kings have practiced immorality before the whole world. One, openly estranged from his wife, was associated with repeated scandals. Another broke his marriage vows and lived in illicit relations with an adventuress. A third married a twice-divorced woman. May God in His grace give the United States men in the Presidency and high national positions whose lives are untouched by public or private scandal! Once the championing of lax marital relations marks our governmental circles, the common people will only too quickly seize upon such examples as justification for their own similar sins.

Sustained immorality regularly goes side by side with unbelief; and Herod was no exception to this rule. His hands were stained with the blood of John the Baptist,

that courageous witness and forerunner of Jesus Christ;
for when the royal adulterer in Galilee married his brother's
wife, Herodias, John had not permitted this flagrant incest
to pass unrebuked. With the courage that I pray the Holy
Spirit will give every true minister of Jesus Christ, this
wilderness preacher, clothed in coarse camel's hair, sternly
denounced the *roué* ruler. Herodias, shrewd, scheming
woman, who dominated her husband, with the fatal results that often follow when an unscrupulous wife con-
trols the family, immediately laid plans to destroy the
meddlesome preacher. At a voluptuous banquet, after the
usual carousal, Herodias's daughter Salome performed an
Oriental dance, disgraceful even in those days, before the
wine-inflamed, passion-filled guests. Keep the following
tragedy in mind, those of you who want the churches to
turn their Sunday-school rooms into dance-halls, you pastors
who tell me that your Sunday-night parish dances are
among the most successful features on your program!
From lewd exhibitions like Salome's performance down to
its modern forms, the dance has hurt the Church, en-
dangered the souls of its young people, robbed unnumbered
devotees of their purity, and ruined thousands of girls.
Not long ago a young man asked me whether he should
accept an offer to become an orchestra leader in a Seattle
ball-room. I answered, "No!" for he would have every
reason to expect that his music would lead to the downfall
of some young women and lure young men into forgetfulness of God. If even the United States Government
officially warns against certain types of dancing, how can
any one who loves the Lord Jesus knowingly support a
project which can undermine decency? Call this old-
fashioned if you will, but facts are stubborn, and there
is much evidence that mothers of unnamed children as
well as lecherous young men were frequently started on

the road to disaster through public dances, with the usual sequence of drinking and seduction. Many of us share the horror of a noted English preacher who said that every time he contemplated the abandonment and sensuality of the immoral dance, he had an uncomfortable feeling about his neck, for he recalled John the Baptist.

You know how Herod, aroused by Salome's wanton display, offered her anything she would name, were it half of his kingdom; how after consultation with her adulterous mother she demanded the head of John the Baptist; and how the wretched king, unwillingly, yet goaded by revengeful Herodias, killed that valiant witness of Jesus Christ. The gory head of the fearless preacher was presented to the lewd dancer, while Herodias smiled in satanic satisfaction. Men, young and old, see in this repulsive story how a loose, shameless woman can lead from enticement to adultery to killing — the fatal sequence revealed daily in metropolitan newspapers. Herod, the son of the royal murderer who slew the innocent babes at Bethlehem, becomes a murderer himself! Like father, like son!

For a while, it seemed, what may have been left of Herod's conscience protested against this bloody butchery. The ghastly specter of Salome, carrying John's blood-drained head on a platter, haunted him, and when he first heard of Jesus, he exclaimed, *"This is John the Baptist; he is risen from the dead."* Gradually, however, these fears wore off. Consciences can be killed so that sin, instead of appearing as the damnable soul-destruction that it is, enshrouds itself in an alluring light. — One day Father Damien, intrepid missionary to the lepers, accidentally poured some boiling hot water on his foot, and when he experienced no pain, knew immediately that he had fallen victim to the fatal disease. If you, as Herod, stop feeling the horror of sin, your soul is leprous.

Herod's whole attitude toward Christ, then, when the captive Savior stood before him, was idle curiosity; and as he plied his quick, repeated questions, Jesus *"answered him nothing."* Why? Not in this instance because the Savior, driven by His consuming desire to die for us, refused to raise His voice in any plea for freedom; not because His face was so unchangeably directed toward the cross that nothing could keep Him from reaching the goal of our redemption. Christ's lips refused to move because that wretched Galilean ruler approached Him in pride, with murder on his hands, doubt in his heart, unbelief in his mouth. Scores of times before Herod could have heard Christ. If he had ever sincerely invited the Lord to explain His Gospel, the Savior would gladly have left everything to give His divine instruction. Herod could have learned the way to life from John the Baptist, a prisoner in his own fortress. Had he gone down to John's cell and shown one sign of repentance and faith, the voice of the forerunner, which had been so uncompromising in its denunciation, would have become tender and appealing in its promise of forgiveness. Now, however, these opportunities for grace spurned, the moment had come for Herod when Jesus turned away from him.

If you now ask whether Jesus will answer you, I know that my God wants me to raise this warning: The Savior of limitless love will remain silent if, like Herod, you approach Him without trust in His atoning love, without deep-rooted contrition over your sins. As long as you continue stubbornly in rebellion against God, in illicit relations, in unbending pride like Herod's, you can ask Christ a thousand curious questions, but He will give no response. As long as your heart is destitute of faith and Christianity is only a try-it-and-see-what-happens experiment, church attendance only a meaningless action motivated by curiosity or the desire for personal gain, you can approach Jesus by day and by night, and always, even on the death-bed, you will find the way closed, barred by unbelief and persistent sin.

While there is time, try to escape that disaster! God's outraged justice quickly overtook Herod. History tells us that he was deposed and died in exile shortly after the crucifixion. Perhaps some of you have lost your work, good name, respect, as a direct punishment for rejecting Christ. Yet if, by God's unsearchable ways, you seem to enjoy earthly prosperity with your defiance, there is no escape from divine punishment in the hereafter. You will be banished from heaven! Those whom Christ will not hear and answer in this life will never be heard and answered in the next. He Himself warns with divine finality, *"Whosoever shall deny Me before men, him will I also deny before My Father which is in heaven!"*

II

JESUS WILL ALWAYS ANSWER PENITENT FAITH

What glorious comfort, however, to know that within a few hours after His silence before Herod our Lord Jesus answered another inquirer, to bestow His overabundant grace. It is now shortly before noon on the day of death. The big, blunt nails have crushed through the Savior's quivering hands and feet. The cross has been raised on Calvary's crest, flanked on each side by crosses bearing two dying criminals. One of these robbers, even in the pain of his approaching end, musters enough strength to vilify Christ, with the same persistence in evil for which some of you suffer heavy punishment, total loss, and yet remain firmly embittered against your God. The second crucified thief begins to see Jesus in a new and wondrous light. He rebukes the other malefactor who had reviled our Lord

and defends Christ with the words, *"We receive the due
reward of our deeds; but this Man hath done nothing
amiss."* His is the first and only voice at Golgotha before
the Savior's death to declare Him not guilty. Even more,
this malefactor sees in Jesus the Lord Himself, King of
a heavenly realm, who, though the crucifixion may take
His earthly life, will soon enter the radiance of the celestial
kingdom. He looks in faith to Christ and, like Herod, he
also asks Jesus to perform a wonder, but a miracle far
mightier than any spectacle for which Herod's curiosity
longed, the supernatural pardoning and cleansing of a
sinner. Acknowledging himself a wretched transgressor,
well deserving the death that soon would claim him, he
implores Jesus, *"Lord, remember me when Thou comest
into Thy kingdom!"*

What astonishing faith! The dying thief sees a
wounded, bleeding Sufferer, reviled both by the religious
and the social leaders and the mocking masses. Yet his
trust beholds in the Crucified the martyred Savior, the
eternal King of kings! He gained more soul-knowledge
during those closing hours of his life confronted with
Jesus in His utter weakness and humility than Bible
critics, worldlings, and wastrels have learned in their entire
existence confronted by our Lord in His glory and power
as His Church spreads from shore to shore. Pray God to
give you that same Christ-directed confidence which never
apologizes for the cross, never obeys the threatening throng
nor listens to the unbelief in the so-called upper classes —
the firm reliance which is not ashamed to confess the dying
Redeemer your own Ransom! Then you, too, will be able
to approach Jesus and pray, "Lord, who hast triumphed
over death, remember me now in Thy kingdom!"

Had Jesus turned His bleeding head from the crucified
thief and permitted His parched lips to remain unmoved,

could we blame Him? There on the cross, in anguish of body and soul that earthly measurements can never gage, our Lord endured the punishment, terror, curse, of all human sins. How can we expect that in the midst of such fierce agony He could consider a single sinner, a man in the lowest depths of human society, a convicted highwayman? Praise be to His eternal mercy! — the same Savior who a few hours before had no reply for an arrogant, stiffnecked monarch now turns to this poor, contrite criminal and shows every generation that no penitent, believing sinner can ever sink too low, commit too many grievous crimes, to be welcomed, pardoned, and cleansed by the Lord Jesus Christ. With the marvel of mercy which has repeatedly brightened the dying hours of Christians since that day, the crucified Lord declares, *"Verily, I say unto thee, Today shalt thou be with Me in Paradise!"*

Study this deathless answer, for these words express the mercy which will save you! *"Verily,"* Jesus begins and by this oath lends His promise double assurance. There can be no hit-or-miss, no guess work, no perhaps or maybe about this pledge, when the Lord of Truth declares, *"I say unto thee!"* We cannot blame those who distrust men's promises when within less than a half year after explicit political and campaign platform promises to keep us out of foreign wars we are being pushed in step by step. But never doubt Jesus' Word!

Consider especially, however, the full and free grace in the Savior's reply! The malefactor's past life had been a career of crime; in the few hours left he could do nothing good, with arms nailed to the cross, nor join a pilgrimage to a sacred place, with feet similarly riveted. He could not even bend his knees or fold his hands to perform any ritual of penance. But to show us from the height of Calvary that we are *saved entirely by grace,* that our *deliverance is all Christ's,* Jesus received the penitent. In his last, lingering moment he was *justified by faith!*

My fellow-redeemed, strain every effort to preserve the pure Gospel in the pulpits of American churches! Testify to it! Work for its continuance! Organize against its opponents! Too many sermons are preached with lavish references to Christ, but not the bleeding, agonized, sin-atoning Sufferer on the cross. We must know more about Jesus than that He died on Calvary; much more even than that He died for us, for soldiers lay down their lives for their country, parents for their children; heroic and self-sacrificing as this is, it cannot influence souls. We must say, and I find that this heart and center of our Christian faith is often missing, "Christ died for us in complete atonement for our sins, so that we may be redeemed by grace without any compensation or payment on our part, saved entirely and eternally by His love." Preaching this free mercy may cut down the revenue of some churches, but it will enrich more souls with heavenly treasures!

Without one condition or demand, then, Jesus promises the repentant malefactor entrance into Paradise, His kingdom on high, where the perfect bliss of the first Eden, lost through sin, will be restored; and as the crowning pledge of mercy the dying thief is to pass through the celestial gates *on that very day* — not after a long period of probation or purifying. Five or six hours at most remained before that Friday ended with nightfall, yet this was ample time for the most radiant of transitions, this change in a twinkling from earth to heaven. — If some of you have believed that when death comes the Savior's mercy is not sufficient to save you completely, read this record again with its clear testimony that the repentant thief, burdened by abhorrent crimes, is directly translated into a blessed eternity without any intermediate stage, without long years of penance and purging. Why detract from this limitless love, *"The blood of Jesus Christ, His Son, cleanseth us from* ALL *sin"?* Because our Lord, who can *"save to the uttermost,"* is God's Son and His self-offering at Calvary the only required and acceptable sacrifice for our sins; because the work of His redemption is forever finished, you, too, can be divinely sure of your immediate entrance into Paradise.

If now, having stood on Calvary, you ask, Will the Savior speak to me when I plead for heaven? you have the answer. See yourself in that penitent thief! Take heart today! Believe that, no matter how far you have wandered from your God, how grievously you have offended His holiness and majesty, when you approach Jesus in faith, plead with Him in contrite trust, acclaim Him your eternal God and Savior, then, as you with all your weakness become less than nothing and Christ with all His mercy becomes more than everything on this earth; the wickedness of the entire race cannot keep Him from answering you and offering pardon, peace, and Paradise.

Ask God's help this minute! Too many of you have been wasting precious years in uncertainty, doubt, and worry, while the joy of salvation, spiritual happiness for your home, could have been yours. We are told that when in the dark, heavily taxed days after the Revolution a rebellion in Massachusetts collapsed, the leader, Captain Daniel Shays, fled into a remote, wooded section of Vermont to avoid capture and death. He stayed in hiding over eleven long, lonely years; his hair turned gray; he grew a beard; his features were altered by sorrow and fear. Yet all the time, without knowing it, he had been fully pardoned by Congress. — Christ has forgiven every one of you, no matter how bitterly you have rebelled against Him. Don't run away from Him and destroy your hopes for heaven's blessing by not hearing and believing that His blood has bought your deliverance and a prepared place in Paradise! Accept His grace! Trust it through life and death!

As we contrast the Savior's silence before self-condemned Herod, with His words of living promise to the penitent thief, God grant that every one of us, though overloaded with sins, heavily weighted with sorrows, may kneel in triumphant faith at Calvary's cross and, beholding our crucified Christ with the eyes of trusting faith, declare, "O Jesus, Thou art mine, and I am Thine! Remember me mercifully in Thy heavenly kingdom!" And as true as that Jesus is the Son of God and the Redeemer of the race, He *will* answer you by sealing salvation forever in your soul! God give you that assurance by Christ's constant grace! Amen.

I PLEDGE ALLEGIANCE TO THE
CRUCIFIED CHRIST

*"There stood by the cross of Jesus His mother and His
mother's sister . . . and Mary Magdalene . . . and the
disciple . . . whom He loved."* — Saint John 19:25, 26

Christ, Our Crucified Redeemer:

*Accept the thankfulness we bring Thee in this broadcast today
for the atoning love which sent Thee to the cross as our Substitute!
Give us the grace to stand at Calvary again, and as we behold the
writhing of Thy death agony let every one of us say, "It was for
me, precious Savior, that Thou didst endure these tortures!" Thou
knowest how frail and faulty we are; therefore give us the spirit
of loyalty and devotion even unto the end! Show us how in the
depth of Thy crucifixion all Thy disciples, save one, fled from grim
Golgotha; how all Thy followers, except a few women, were too
timid to remain with Thee beneath the cross, and strengthen us
for vigilant loyalty! When we waver, forgive us and fortify us
with the Holy Spirit's indwelling, daily and with more devoted
allegiance to pledge our souls and lives anew to Thee! Come to
us, our Christ, and help us consecrate ourselves to Thee! Amen.*

I HAVE a thrilling joy to share with you this afternoon.
First, our Gospel radio system now includes the Hawai-
ian Islands. Second, we are invited to broadcast in British
Guiana. Third, three new American stations were added
last week. Fourth — one of the happiest announcements
I have ever been able to make — the radio committee of
the Lutheran Laymen's League, under whose auspices we
broadcast, has passed the resolution to increase our Mission
of the Air by adding powerful transmitters in Central
and South America. At present we use some fifty Latin
American outlets; and with these new facilities in Argentina, San Salvador, Guatemala, Honduras, Peru, and
Venezuela, we shall broadcast in twenty-two countries outside the United States, Alaska, the Philippine Islands, and
Hawaii. Fifth, arrangements are completed in cooperation

with the Schenectady short-wave station to send our weekly Spanish message for rebroadcasting throughout Latin America. Sixth, by the same means our Portuguese addresses will be received throughout Brazil. Seventh, and in summary, with humble gratitude to God, rejecting every semblance of boasting or reliance on numbers, we report to you that this radio system which seven years ago had two stations will include more than three hundred outlets in North America, South America, Asia — as far as we know, the world's largest regular broadcast. What an astonishing demonstration of God's power! We started entirely on faith. We were told that the modern mind was not interested in Christ, His cross and His blood. But God put all doubts to shame, and today, without any personal guarantors financing this "Bringing Christ to the Nations" endeavor, without the benefit of free hook-up time which certain other religious programs enjoy, we are able to preach the crucified Savior to millions in this country and in two dozen other lands. Thank God with us, you especially who stood by the Lutheran Hour from its start! Vast, immeasurable opportunities still confront us. At this moment a missionary is on the high Pacific with a letter to Generalissimo Chiang Kai Shek outlining a plan by which unoccupied China will hear our messages in the language of its undaunted people. Correspondence in Dutch and French points to the possibility of East Indian and African stations. We must be ready when this war is over — God grant that it will be over soon! — to bring Christ as the divine reconstructing agency for ruined nations, heavenly strength for the trials preceding the new world order. Pray for us as never before! Lend us your help in publicizing these messages and inviting friends, particularly the unchurched, to tune in! Send us your contributions to help maintain and increase this continent-to-continent testimony for Christ!

Some, however, may ask, "Why do you spend these hundreds of thousands of dollars for radio time?" By way of answer I wish you could examine the 182 Spanish letters which came in one mail from a single station in the Dominican Republic, with many heart-stirring expressions of devotion to the Christ whom we preach. You ought to read the correspondence from Mexico, where, despite the technical ban on religious broadcasting, the opposition to our Savior is weakening. You would see how the Holy Spirit works through the radio, how a man in Mexico City who happened to tune in our message from Ecuador was convicted of his sin but convinced of our Savior's greater grace, and with his whole family came to our Mexico City missionary for instruction in the Christian faith. You would recognize, if you could spend a day in our offices, that our efforts are dedicated to only one purpose: the preaching of the atoning Savior from Alaska to Argentina, from the East Indies to the West.

Today, as we continue our Lenten messages, we ask for faithfulness to the cross-riveted Redeemer; and I have prayed God that when this broadcast is over, many of you will be ready to arise, stand before your radios, wherever you may be, and speak this resolution:

I PLEDGE ALLEGIANCE TO THE CRUCIFIED CHRIST!

It will take repentance, faith, and trust in the Savior to express this determination of loyalty, whether you make the promise for the first time or renew your devotion to our Lord. For spiritual encouragement we shall study the Scriptures, which tell of those who stayed with Christ on Calvary to the last, the words of Saint John, chapter nineteen, verses twenty-five and twenty-six: *"There stood by the cross of Jesus His mother and His mother's sister . . . and Mary Magdalene . . . and the disciple . . . whom He loved."*

I

BELIEVERS BENEATH THE CROSS SHOWED THIS LOYALTY

The deepest cruelty at the crucifixion was not the soldiers' brutality but the cowardice and desertion of those who should have befriended Jesus. Today the most vicious criminal doomed to execution may have the sustaining services of a clergyman. Yet, when Jesus, innocent on every charge for which He had been condemned, hung on the cross, He enjoyed practically no comforting companionship.

Where were the multitudes whom He had healed and helped? The least sense of loyalty, the smallest feeling of sympathy should have brought thousands to Calvary to keep the death-watch with Jesus and support Him during His last moments. Yet the Gospel record is tragic in its truth. Not one of those recently benefited by Christ stood beneath the cross! — The same thanklessness marks the modern world. Every blessing of progress, culture, and happiness that is ours, every advantage separating us from the heathen world, comes ultimately from the Savior. Nevertheless millions rise up against Him.

Where were the priests, who should have known from their own Scriptures that Jesus was God's Son? They kept their distance from the cross, or, with a savagery which degenerates show, raised blasphemous voices to revile the dying Savior. Some of them would willingly have supported Christ as long as they thought He could supply loaves and fishes or offer a rallying-point for the overthrow of the Roman rule; but when our Lord deliberately shattered these ambitions and was crucified, their sympathies changed to hatred. Similarly twentieth-century Modernists, rejecting the atonement, are ready to hail Jesus as a social or moral Messiah but not the bleeding, dying Messiah.

They are willing to acclaim Him the mighty Preacher but not the dying Sufferer. They will make room for a human Jesus but not for God's agonized Son. They will lend their support to a reconstructed Christ but never to a redeeming Christ.

Where, during the crucifixion, were the other leaders of society, the scholars, who could have seen through the screaming injustice of the Savior's death sentence and who should have supported the truth for which He was being sacrificed? If any prominent citizens lingered on Calvary, they, too, lost the veneer of their refinement as they cried: *"Let Him save Himself if He be Christ, the Chosen of God!" "Save Thyself and come down from the cross!"* Where, we counter, is the intelligentsia today, if not, for the most part, enthusiastically side by side with those gloating scoffers on Golgotha? When we ask you for the resolution, "I pledge allegiance to the crucified Savior!" you ought to be clear on this: Loyalty to Christ will probably not bring you shoulder to shoulder with Nobel Prize winners, authors of best sellers, society leaders, political tycoons, international bankers. With notable exceptions, you will find yourself in the company of ordinary middle- and lower-class people, and sometimes even here a haunting loneliness may besiege your heart.

One more question arises: Where were the disciples, who during three and a half years with Jesus had seen overwhelming evidence of the Savior's love, who on the previous night had vowed to remain faithful in the face of death? We can understand why those who never knew our Lord kept their distance from Calvary, but it would be altogether impossible to account for His disciples' ingratitude and desertion when with one exception they fled like cowards, were it not that the same disloyalty besets us, who have seen more of Christ's power than even they did.

If Jesus in the Garden before the crucifixion pleaded for His disciples' company, how much more would He have appreciated their presence when He hung on the tree of shame! Today masterpieces of painting and sculpture, the choicest artistry of song and poetry, the skill of reverent crafts executed in precious metals and costly gems, have made the cross an emblem of beauty, splendor, and glory. Yet how completely opposed to this were those two ugly pieces of coarse wood, stained with the Savior's life-blood! We have made the cross a sign of mercy in war and peace, but on that first Good Friday it was a token of humanity's deepest cruelty and hatred. We wear the cross to show our love for the Crucified, but on the day of His death the masses shrank from it. Touch it, they thought, and you are unclean. We place the cross on our churches or enshrine it in sanctuaries as an invitation to find hope, rest, peace, through Him who was once nailed to its post and cross-beam. For Jesus the cross brought tormenting, racking, convulsing pain.

Many in this audience could not even witness the horror of the crucifixion; yet the Savior had to bear it alone. Think of the bodily suffering He endured and remember that He bore its unrelieved agony because He refused to take the opiate, the strong wine mixed with myrrh which could deaden His consciousness and soothe His pain. He confronted death in His full senses, to prevent any one from contesting the sacred truth that He had laid down His life voluntarily. He felt the fiery fever, the burning wounds, the weighted tension of His body, the tormenting thirst, the exposure of the elements, and the other physical misery. How welcome the services of friends and words of consolation would have been! Yet how little help did He receive from His own! When His thirst was to be assuaged, it was a soldier who pressed the sponge against His mouth.

More penetrating and piercing was the torture of His mind. How painful to have mercy and love rudely rejected! Here hung the Christ whose unselfish words and actions, thoughts, and endeavors were directed toward the welfare and happiness of His own countrymen. What was His reward? The most heartless scoffing, blasphemous ridicule, fiendish laughter history has ever seen. *"Save Thyself!" "Come down from the cross!"* — this chant of hatred was dinned into His ears. How reassuring, had a loyal band of believers around the cross shielded Jesus from these cruelties! Yet David's ancient prophecy was fulfilled, *"There is none to help!"* Not one sentence of sympathy is recorded by the gospel-writers! Those who could have aided failed in this supreme crisis!

Soul anguish, however, was the heaviest burden of the cross. We can understand what happened on Calvary only when we realize that Jesus suffered there what no saint or angel could ever endure. His soul writhed under the terror of every man's sin because our transgressions were imputed to Him, our fractures of God's Law laid to His account, our iniquities, with all their guilt and punishment, transferred to Him.

I hope that none of you has become so calloused to God's warning concerning unforgiven sin that you refuse to measure the terrifying consequences of wrong-doing. If a single violation of divine truth and light can open the floodgates of misery; if blind obedience to one man in control of a nation can cause havoc for millions; if in the smaller circles of your lives a single step from the narrow path can start fears and phobias that rob you of your peace, who can even begin to understand the crushing horror which bore down on the innocent Savior when on Calvary God *"laid on Him the iniquity of us all"*? Who can fathom the depths of that desolation when, with His blood flowing from nail-pierced hands and feet, His life ebbing slowly from His martyred body, His soul torn by the pain that cut sharpest, the penalty of my sin, yours, the whole world's, all history's, He gave Himself as the eternal, complete atonement for men's wickedness, cruelty, lechery, greed, falsehood, profanity, unbelief, idolatry?

How welcome the slightest sign of understanding and compassion from Christ's friends and followers would have been! Even helpless tears coursing down the cheeks of Peter, James, Andrew, the other disciples, would have brought some degree of comfort. Yet our text tells us that of the thousands crowding Jerusalem for the Passover, of the multitudes who had heard Christ and seen His miracles, only four remained under the cross until He died our death. Some, particularly the devoted women from Galilee, stayed at a distance, and doubtless others in the motley throng felt a slight compassion for this Victim of priestly hatred. But only four waited close to our Lord, the three Marys and Saint John, the disciple whom Jesus loved.

No one knows how much their loyalty cost them. They had to face constant ridicule, stifle their own misgivings which increased as they saw fond hopes shattered in the crucifixion. The most distressing sorrow, however, must have been their utter helplessness in relieving Christ's anguish. Think of Mary, His mother! She was too thoroughly human, too completely like your Christian mother and mine, not to feel in her sensitive soul the echo of every taunt and the reflex of every pain her Jesus endured. See the other two Marys, their lives and hopes closely related to Christ, who witnessed His God-forsakenness and last terror-filled moments. Picture Saint John, bound to Jesus with special ties of personal devotion, yet powerless to soothe these harrowing blows or shield his Master from heartless mockery. As this scene is reenacted in your mind and you envision these faithful four beneath the cross until the lifeless body is taken away, may the Spirit move you to declare before God and man, "I pledge this allegiance to my crucified Christ!"

II
WE, TOO, SHOULD SHOW THAT LOYALTY

Nothing less than this complete loyalty can ever insure us the full blessings of our Redeemer's self-sacrifice. It is not enough to know that nineteen centuries ago a noble Figure trod the Palestinian pathways and that malicious men crucified this Jesus. We must stay at the cross until we realize He was nailed on that accursed tree for us. No one should be satisfied merely with thinking lofty thoughts about Christ. We must hail Jesus not merely as a glorified Leader but as the crucified Savior; not as one of many redeemers but the only Ransom for sin that God Almighty recognizes. His Gospel must be acclaimed not as a possible truth to be tried and verified but as Heaven's own surety. Faith, if it is to save, must be more than a think-good, speak-good, do-good, be-good life program by which, we hope, God finally *has* to reward us. Spurning all self-justification, each of us must stay at the cross and there, without a single justifying claim, without a glance for any one else besides God's suffering Son, declare, "O Jesus, You, and You alone, are my Savior; the blood that drips from Your wounds, the only cleansing for my sin-stained heart; the agony You endure here, the only assurance of my escape from hell; the death that here makes You cold and still, the only promise of my life!"

With that trust we cannot adopt a take-it-or-leave-it attitude toward Jesus. We cannot be for Him with His friends and against Him with His enemies. If forgiveness, salvation, heaven, are to be ours, then, as true as God is God, we must pledge our full adherence to the crucified Savior.

What a powerful example of this loyalty you American women can find in Mary, the mother of our Lord! With Jesus your position is far more pivotal today than many of you realize. You can do more to build America through allegiance to Jesus than by any political or social program. If you stay with Christ; if you bring up your children *"in the nurture and admonition of the Lord";* if you make your home an abiding place for the blessed Savior, you will contribute more to the welfare of the United States by a life lived in harmony with Christ's precepts than by any present legislative or civic program.

I hope you will not be misled by the nation-wide campaign against motherhood and childbirth recently inaugurated by a national committee for "planned parenthood." Last week a newspaper advertisement covering almost an entire page asked the public for funds to help lower the American birth-rate. "Make America stronger," they cry. How? By using artificial birth-control methods, by stopping the poor from having children! Do these people forget the experiences of France? Are they deaf to the warnings issued by competent sociologists? Are they blind to the fact that one of every three United States homes is childless now and that our population is practically stationary? Have they poisoned their minds against the repeated Biblical command, *"Be fruitful and multiply!"?* I would suppose that these agitators are utterly unconcerned about what the Scriptures say, were it not that at least four clergymen are on this committee. Talk about Herod and Pontius Pilate becoming friends on Good Friday! Look over that roster, and you will find there ministers working together with men who have viciously blasphemed the Lord Jesus Christ! Because the Bible regards children as a blessing and not a burden, parenthood as a privilege and not a social liability; because Jesus Christ Himself, God's Son, was born of an earthly mother, I ask you, American women, to repudiate this unnatural, physically dangerous, morally destructive tendency.

Mothers, stay close to Jesus! Teach your little ones to pray in His name! Sing them to sleep with a lullaby of His love. As He looked down from the cross and provided for Mary, so today He will look down from heaven to help you in your needs. The Savior asked John to take her as his mother; and we often wonder why Jesus did not entrust Mary to some of His own close relatives. May it not be that the kinsfolk who could have taken care of her did not accept Christ and that as the first requirement for every home Jesus wants the spiritual unity by which parents and children, husband and wife, worship with the same hope and assurance? Day by day my contacts with your problems force me to understand with increasing clarity that for a happy, God-pleasing household we need faith-founded families; that the increasing number of religiously mixed marriages as the marital union of Christians and unbelievers are major causes of domestic misery and spiritual collapse. Let our churches do much more to maintain close contact between their young people and ceaselessly show the advantages of establishing homes at the cross!

Some of you women object, "I could never have the courage and strength of Mary, the Savior's mother!" In all friendliness I say you are wrong. The Holy Spirit, through faith, can work the same miracle of loyalty in your life! Besides, there were two other Marys at Calvary, and you can find encouragement in their faith. The one was the wife of Cleophas. We know little about her except that perhaps she was the Savior's aunt; otherwise she seems to have been an average woman with no particular distinctions. Many of you may never enjoy applause and acclaim; no head-lines will commemorate your work. But if you remain loyal to Christ until the end; if, following the injunction *"Whatsoever ye do in word or deed, do all in the name of the Lord Jesus,"* you look after your husband's interests, take care of the children, conscientiously supervise the household, then, as you wash the dishes, dust the rooms, hang up the family laundry, prepare the meals, you can do all this to the glory of Christ. Some day, too, your sons and daughters will rise up to call you blessed. In Boston my own mother is listening to this message, and I know that the joy of faith which is hers under the cross is the same incomparable spiritual happiness which ten thousands of you Christian women experience.

The third Mary is called Magdalene. Much of her past is shrouded in uncertainty; but this much we do know: she had been marvelously healed and cleansed by Jesus. Out of gratitude she gave up everything, left her Galilean home, and devoted her life to the Savior. Her humble service impresses us again with the truth that the highest hope of womanhood lies not in political position or social distinction but in service to Christ. A claim like this sounds medieval, with modern theories and practices seeking to emancipate our women, destroy their finer qualities, and rob them of their greatest usefulness; but I ask you, Has the nation become better since women have received the ballot? Have American homes grown stronger now that wives work, often without necessity? Has our family life been elevated by birth-control programs? Whenever the principles of the Christian faith have been assaulted, womanhood has likewise been attacked.

We need more of the devotion shown by this Mary. If Christian missionaries in Korea were arrested because they urged prayers for peace, the time may come when you will meet resistance in working for the soul calm that Jesus offers. But look to Mary Magdalene beneath the cross; take her for your example and let your service be for Christ, and not for side-issues.

Women of America, Christ can cleanse *you* as He purified Mary of Magdala, and though your tears may flow when you see what your sins cost the Savior, you, too, will share the joy that lifted this Mary's soul to the height of bliss when on Easter she was the first to greet the resurrected Redeemer. If you have been unfaithful, indifferent, unconcerned about Jesus before; if your sins have been dark and repulsive, stand with the three Marys beneath the Savior's cross, and as you say, "I pledge allegiance to the crucified but now risen Christ," a joy that you can never exhaust will come to bless you.

Only one man remained at Calvary with Jesus: John, who had leaned on the Savior's breast and was attached to Christ more closely than any of His fellow-disciples. Those hours with his dying Master became a turning-point in his life. We are often inclined to think of John as meek because of the unparalleled emphasis his gospel and epistles lay on love. He wrote *after* the crucifixion, however; before that time he had been strong-willed, impetuous, and overfilled with resentment toward those who opposed Jesus. John was among those disciples who would have called down fire from heaven to destroy the unbelieving Samaritans. But when on grim Golgotha he heard his Savior pray, *"Father, forgive them, for they know not what they do";* when he saw Christ's unswerving devotion unto death, his faith was strengthened, and he began to learn the lesson of self-sacrifice. His writings, filled with the Gospel of Jesus' heavenly compassion, give twentieth-century manhood the assurance of the Savior's power and blessing.

"More men for the Church!" must be the cry today. As three of the four loyal believers under the cross were women, so in many congregations throughout the United States only one fourth of the attendance is men. In hundreds of missions women are working without the full cooperation that you fathers, brothers, sons, should offer. The cause of Jesus Christ is retarded under the destructive delusion that religion is for women and children but not for you "he-men" — as though this world has ever seen any one more virile than the Savior, braver than His disciples who laid down their lives battling for Christ against a hostile world, more courageous than His missionaries who faced the fury and fiendish torture of heathen empires!

Now, if you insist on rejecting Jesus; if, after you have again heard His appeal, you still turn coldly away from Him, sneer at the Church, oppose your wife's membership, keep your children away from Sunday-school; if you think that you are a "real man" when you curse and swear, laugh at lewd stories, show your contempt for the Bible, shake your fist against the Almighty, all I can say is, May God have mercy on you and somehow shake you out of your self-conceit! Unless you have Christ, you are lost! But if your conscience tells you that you are wrong in spurning His Redemption; that the Church, your wife, your mother, your children, your friends, are right in urging you to accept Jesus; if today, seeing the Savior deserted except by a few, His Spirit has created the desire in your heart to acknowledge Him not only the Redeemer of the world but *your* Ransom and Atonement, then may this appeal find answer in your soul when I tell you that Christ's arms, once stretched wide on the cross, are now extended to you; that nothing more than faith is required if you would approach Him and find the full treasure of His merciful forgiveness! When King Alfonso lay dying in Rome, friends in Spain sent him a cape, a piece of clothing said to possess miraculous power, and asked that the alleged wonder-working mantle be draped over Alfonso. Despite this, the exiled monarch died. If you, without any relics, charms, or superstitions, cling only to the Lord Jesus Christ, you will be so clothed by Him that you will never taste eternal death. You will be able to sing:

> Jesus, Thy blood and righteousness
> My beauty are, my glorious dress;
> Midst flaming worlds, in these arrayed,
> With joy shall I lift up my head.

Men and women of America, old and young, where will you stand on Calvary? If you know the sin-bearing Savior as your Redeemer and understand that you need only come penitently to declare in truth, *"Lord, I believe; help Thou mine unbelief,"* will you not, I ask you in Christ's name, sincerely renounce sin and unbelief, earnestly promise to resist Satan's temptations, the lusts of your flesh, and the world's wicked ways? As agitation increases and our nation is steadily pushed, day after day, week after week, into situations which must soon bring us into war unless the merciful God intervenes; as you read that the present conflict takes the lives of fifty civilians for every one killed in military or naval service, pray for your soul's peace during these dangerous days before us! Give yourself wholly to Christ! Remain loyally with Him to the end, and His promise will be fulfilled, *"Be thou faithful unto death, and I will give thee a crown of life!"*

As a token of this faith and victory, join me wherever you may receive this message, and, your mind's eye directed to the cross, your thoughts riveted on the Savior, resolutely declare, "I pledge allegiance to the crucified Christ! God help me!" Amen.

PALM-BRANCHES — OR HAMMER
AND NAILS?

"Much people . . . took branches of palm-trees and went forth to meet Him and cried, Hosanna." — Saint John 12:12, 13

"And He, bearing His cross, went forth into a place called the place of a skull, which is called in the Hebrew Golgotha, where they crucified Him." — Saint John 19:17, 18

Christ, Meek and Lowly Prince of Peace,
Self-Giving Savior of Our Souls:

Once Thou didst enter Jerusalem amid loud hosannas and waving palm-branches — to be rejected and crucified a few days later. Come to us despite our frailties, our fickleness! Give us Thy Spirit's guidance in building a firm faith, with heartfelt sorrow over our transgressions, unchangeable reliance on the power of Thy blood to cleanse and save to the uttermost! Keep us ever close to Thee, so that we do not acclaim Thee today and betray Thee tomorrow! O Jesus, as we thank Thee for the matchless mercy of Calvary which this Holy Week again commemorates, look down upon our world of widening war, and may it please Thee, who on Palm Sunday didst come in peace, to break the terror of the present conflict and make an end to this bloodshed! Bless the preaching of Thy love as manifested for all men at Calvary and give Thy Church the sustained courage required to proclaim Thee the only Hope for our eternal salvation! Hear us, our Christ of the cross, as throughout the land our hearts now sing: "Hosanna! Blessed is He that cometh in the name of the Lord! Hosanna in the highest!" Amen.

HOW quickly public opinion reverses itself! How easily the mind of the masses is changed! How abruptly a people's mood can turn against a national benefactor! The Bible itself testifies to this fickleness. In ancient Israel David, the psalmist-king and applauded hero, was driven almost overnight from his throne, hunted like a wild animal, stoned by his followers, deserted by practically the entire nation.

Every age has seen the weather-vane of popular favor

swing in opposite directions. In early Greece, after a remarkable sea battle, the victorious admirals were fêted throughout the land, until suddenly, clutched by a wild hysteria, the citizens sentenced the same naval victors to a disgraceful death. During the Middle Ages Jerome Savonarola became the dictator of the Italian city Florence. Impassioned and eloquent, he so completely won the hearts of the people, particularly the rising generation, that they willingly sacrificed their costliest possessions and publicly threw to the flames sinful, luxurious articles valued at many tens of thousands of dollars. A short year after his greatest success Savonarola was burned to death at the stake, while "ferocious screams of triumph rang through the mob."

We see evidences of the same fickleness today. Fourteen years ago a young aviator who conquered the Atlantic in a small airplane became a national hero, acclaimed as no other young man in our history. Because of his modesty, bravery, and determination he was pictured as the ideal for American youth. The entire wing of a large public building in this city is required to house only part of the tributes sent to him from admirers all over the world. Yet because he pleaded that our nation be kept out of Europe's war, he is branded as a Fifth Columnist, and choruses of hate chant their denunciation.

Such turnings of the popular tide, however, hardly deserve mention in comparison with the recoil of the mob spirit under which our Lord Jesus suffered in the change from Palm Sunday to Good Friday. What an unparalleled week of contrast that was! On its first day Jesus blessed as a conquering king and on its sixth day cursed as a blaspheming criminal! When that week began, multitudes removed their outer garments and laid them in the pathway of His procession, but before it was over, greedy hands tore the clothing from His wounded, bleeding body.

He entered Jerusalem while a jubilant throng marched in His honor; He left the city after His own disciples had deserted Him.

On Sunday enthusiastic crowds welcomed Jesus as Israel's King. On Monday Christ entered the Temple as the Lord of that sanctuary, and even the children sang praises to Him. On Tuesday He frustrated the Pharisees, the Sadducees, the scribes, and received the homage of Greek visitors. On Wednesday He rested. On Thursday He was betrayed, arrested, imprisoned; and before Friday closed, He had faced six hearings, only to be sentenced to death in the final analysis by public acclamation. For when the Roman governor asked the mob, *"What shall I do, then, with Jesus?"* and the heartless crowd screamed, *"Crucify Him! Crucify Him!"* they really pronounced the doom of crucifixion on our Lord.

This shift from *"Hosanna! Blessed is the King of Israel that cometh in the name of the Lord"* to *"Away with Him!" "Let Him be crucified!"* concerns us; we either accept Christ with the prayer, "His blood cleanse us and our children!" or reject Him with the damning *"His blood be on us and on our children!"* Ultimately we stand shoulder to shoulder with those who cut down palm-branches and waved them in welcome to Jesus or with those who cut down the tree and in hatred shaped its timbers for His cross. Therefore on this first day of Holy Week I ask you in the name of the Crucified: What are your thoughts toward Jesus? How will you meet Him — with faith or unbelief, with

PALM-BRANCHES — OR HAMMER AND NAILS?

As we seek our answer, may God's Holy Spirit enlighten our minds, warm our hearts, and cleanse our souls to learn the life-or-death lesson contrasted in these two passages:

"Much people . . . took branches of palm-trees and went forth to meet Him and cried, Hosanna" (Saint John, chapter twelve, verses twelve and thirteen) ; *"He, bearing His cross, went forth into a place called the place of a skull, which is called in the Hebrew Golgotha, where they crucified Him"* (Saint John, chapter nineteen, verses seventeen and eighteen).

I

GOD HELP US WELCOME THE PRINCE OF PEACE!

It was a spring Sunday when Jesus began that triumphant procession. Our Lord had been resting at Bethany, apparently at the home of his friends Lazarus, Mary, and Martha. They lived only about two miles from the walls of Jerusalem, yet far enough removed from the turmoil to afford the Savior the recuperation that He, as true man, busy with helping others, sorely needed. How signally blessed that family circle to receive our Lord's repeated instruction and to be strengthened in the hour of their bereavement by His life-giving power! Our households likewise can be enriched by Jesus' presence. Though in His heavenly majesty He no longer requires relaxation, He eagerly awaits an invitation into *your* home; and when Christ crosses your threshold, He brings joy, peace, salvation.

If people had expected Jesus to hold His entry into Jerusalem with imperial pomp, at the head of parading chariots and prancing steeds, they were disappointed. Having no conveyance of His own, our Lord requisitioned an ass and its colt, mounts that served in peace, not in war; and fulfilling Old Testament prophecy, He rode as one who was *"meek and lowly."*

We should not lose sight of Jesus' renouncing military show; for some clergymen are now telling us that to be good Christians we must be ready to send our soldiers across the ocean. Our Lord never raised His hand in war. Amid plenty of oppression, tyranny, dictatorship, under the Roman rule, He, the incomparable Preacher, could have delivered a fiery appeal which would have summoned enthusiasts and fanatics from the far corners of Israel to fight against Caesar's troops. But He left war to the civil authorities; and the world today would be far better if preachers would stop serving as recruiting agents for furthering hostilities. Clergymen of America, on this Palm Sunday behold the humble, peace-loving Christ; and as you remember His instructions to love our enemies, His refusal to defend Himself with the sword, pray God that you, too, may constantly serve one all-absorbing purpose — to bring true, abiding peace into the hearts of your people!

Jesus had hardly started out with His disciples when many pilgrims at Jerusalem for the Passover joined the group. Every few feet, it seemed, the ranks were increased by new supporters, and whatever of formality and splendor the procession may have lacked, the desire to acclaim the miracle-working Teacher from Galilee constantly added larger numbers to the marching column. Soon voices were blended in praise songs; applying the ancient psalms to Christ, the multitudes preceding Him and those following cried: *"Hosanna to the Son of David! Blessed is He that cometh in the name of the Lord; hosanna in the highest!"* So loud and enthusiastic was this welcome that the envious Pharisees asked Christ to stop these hosannas; but the Savior predicted that, if His disciples were silent, the very stones would cry out. How eloquently the stones of Jerusalem do preach a message of warning! Nothing is left of the whole city that existed in the Savior's time but a wailing-wall where Israel even today bemoans its departed glory. The rest has been buried under heaped debris.

Destruction, devastation, desolation — thus the rocks proclaim the tragic fate of a chosen but ungrateful, unbelieving people! Let America, selected by God to enjoy the greatest material blessings any people has ever known, take heed!

The procession moved on, until suddenly, perhaps at Olivet's crest, where Jerusalem burst into view, it stopped, and Christ looked down on the proud metropolis, far more attractive in those days than now. Even Roman writers paid tribute to its splendor. Yet while others might have stopped to survey its grandeur, Jesus halted to measure the sins and sorrows of a doomed city. Tears trickled down His face, not the evidence of mourning for individual bereavement, like the tears at Lazarus' grave, but the sobbing over a nation that would soon destroy itself. Remember those tears shed for Jerusalem! Jesus has also surveyed our cities with their filth, greed, crime, their treachery in high and low places. Former Governor Lloyd C. Stark of Missouri recently declared that organized civic corruption in the United States is more dangerous than any Fifth Column. He asserted: "Grafters and bribers have gained control of our machinery of government in many large cities. They have set up profitable alliances with criminals of the underworld." But forget the sins of politicians and believe that Jesus' tears have been shed for you, too, over the wrong which has blighted your life! He loves every one of you with such personal and intense devotion that He is cut to the quick when those whom He has ransomed with His life reject one merciful invitation after the other.

Our Lord, however, did not stop with weeping and lamenting. He drew close to the city, and about this time, it seems, another throng came from Jerusalem to meet Him. For a few glorious but all too brief hours the Savior was greeted with the greatest enthusiasm. While

modern conquerors parade between heavily armed regiments, Jesus entered the city with cheering crowds flanking
His roadway. Branches had been cut off palm-trees, and
joyfully the people waved this foliage — the symbol of
peace and victory. Longer and longer the procession
stretched; louder and louder the hosannas, stronger and
stronger the waving of the palm-branches! The whole
city was moved. People peered through their latched
windows, ran hurriedly to the street, and one question
sprang from the lips of all, *"Who is this?"*

In answer they called Him *"the prophet of Nazareth
in Galilee."* He *was* a Prophet. No man has ever preached
as He. No Elijah or Elisha, no Isaiah or Jeremiah, ever
revealed God's full counsel with the clarity and conviction
that leaped from His lips. Yet He was more than a
Prophet! They hailed Him King; and indeed He was
of royal lineage. No Alexander, Caesar, Charlemagne,
ever ruled a domain comparable to Christ's realm. But
He was more than a King!

To understand the real Jesus of Palm Sunday, the true
Christ of Holy Week — and no knowledge in your entire
life is as vital as this — you must realize that Christ, our
Prophet and King, is also Christ, our Priest. When He
rode into the city, clad in the ordinary garments of the
common people, He seemed far removed from the imposing splendor of that sacred office. But long after the
Temple had been burned to dust, its holy vessels seized, the
robes, ephods, breastplates with their costly adornment
destroyed, our Lord's priesthood would be acknowledged
throughout the world. He was to have no altar, nothing
but an accursed cross; no sacrifice except — O wondrous
love! — His own holy body, the one sin-offering for the
complete removal of every transgression with which the
myriads of men from the beginning of time until its end

have sent their souls on the road to hell. No blood of rams or bullocks signalized this central sacrifice for all mankind — instead, His own life-blood, the one cleansing power on earth or in heaven itself that can remove our guilt. No elaborate form and ceremonial marked the Savior's self-giving into death, nothing but the ugly echo of hammer-blows, the shriek of unfathomable terror, *"My God, My God, why hast Thou forsaken Me?"* and the other sacred utterances from the cross, particularly the cry of triumphant relief, *"It is finished!"* With that announcement the whole Old Testament system of sacrifice came to its end. The entire old covenant ceremonial, the Levitical sacrifices, the offerings of animals, the circumcision, the Temple, the Sabbath, the religious preeminence of Jerusalem, were abolished. *"Who is this?"* we ask again as we envision Him riding into Jerusalem amid swelling welcome. Oh, may God give you the faith to blend your voice in the chorus which has reechoed from the first Palm Sunday and sing, *" 'Hosanna! Blessed is He that cometh in the name of the Lord,'* my Christ, my Prophet, my King and self-giving High Priest!"

Yet Jesus was even more. To give His sacrifice at Calvary eternal value, to have His blood exert its cleansing throughout the ages, He had to be stronger than mere man. Soldiers are killed on the field of battle; military airplane pilots are hurtled to their death; sailors from torpedoed warships may be devoured by sharks; still, with grateful praise to their heroism we realize that despite their greater love by which they laid down their lives for their fellow-men this has not influenced our souls. All the armies in the world, the tens of millions of men under arms — were they to perish in the defense of their countries — could not save your soul. Angel hosts perform stupendous miracles; they can destroy armies and

mighty cities; but they cannot break the tyranny of sin over
your life.   Only God Himself can accomplish that superhuman, superangelic victory.   And it was God incarnate in
Christ who rode into the royal city amid the waving,
shouting throngs.   I cannot expect you to understand how
this humble Hero of the first Palm Sunday was the almighty
God, whose creative fiats produced the universe and adorned
this globe with its marvels and magnificences, the divine
Sustainer who charts the course of history and *"upholds all
things by the Word of His power."*   Although reason
rebels at this truth, believe it!   If every moment of your
life is built on the acceptance of a hundred facts which
neither you nor any one else will ever be able to explain,
don't let your puny intellect rob you of Christ's most
blessed assurance!   Don't obstruct the Spirit's way into
your heart by a know-it-all attitude and supercilious doubt!
Because Jesus called Himself God, proved Himself God,
permitted Himself to be honored as God; because only our
Lord Himself could fully atone for our sins, pay the appalling total of our moral indebtedness, remove this crushing burden, and completely satisfy the standards of His
own justice by taking our place and suffering as our
Substitute — Christ had to be God!

   This same Jesus, both your God and your Savior, wants
to enter *your* heart.   As He once approached Jerusalem,
so every time you hear the divine assurance, *"Christ died for
our sins,"* in whatever language, by whatever means, in
whatever place, this truth may come to you, the Holy Spirit
seeks to bring the Redeemer to your soul.   This may be the
first time you have heard that the compassionate Christ
wants you regardless of your sins, failures, ingratitudes,
and uprising against God;   or in Heaven's inscrutable wisdom this may be the last time Jesus will seek entrance into
your heart.   But first or last, may this assurance be deeply

impressed on your consciousness: Christ loves you, you in prisons or in palaces, you the ragged or the rich, you the helpless in pain or the powerful in the prime of achieving lives! Jesus wants you as His own!

Many who sang Christ's praises in that happy hour misunderstood Jesus. They were dreaming of an earthly conqueror, and some selfishly looked for a restored kingdom of Israel in which they could assume positions of power. But the greatest glory for which they longed was incomparably less than the blessing with which Christ would enrich us. He comes with peace for our souls, to end the warfare between a sinless God and sinful humanity; to announce the complete, perfect harmony established between Heaven and earth by the blood of His mediating love. He offers every one torn by fear, prodded by a restless conscience, a serene calmness; for by trusting His cross-earned grace, you can reject any inward misgivings as they try to make you doubt the full promises of your salvation. Pointing to the cross and the Crucified, you can say, *"I know whom I have believed and am persuaded that He is able to keep that which I have committed to Him."* You can repulse hell's attacks which would throw many of you into despair, when inner voices whisper: "There is no hope for you! You are too wicked! You have broken God's Law again and again!" For, triumphing over the thought of your own unworthiness, you can hear your Savior say, *"Him that cometh to Me I will in no wise cast out."* The Christ who today wants to enter your heart offers you assurance for a peace-robbed, afflicted life. Only Jesus has been able to solve the mystery of sorrow and to answer the plaintive "why?" that so frequently seeks an explanation for your trials and griefs. As He endured immeasurable anguish only to be exalted, so, if we suffer with Him there, we shall reign with Him. When our lives are wholly dedicated to Christ, they are entrusted to divine wisdom and love, so that every affliction, as hard and inscrutable as it may seem, is only the disguised evidence of His love, by which our faith is refined, our trust strengthened, our love purified. — The Christ of Palm Sunday brings us peace with our neighbors — even our enemies. It is the pledge of the inspired Scriptures, *"If any man be in Christ Jesus, he is a new creature,"* and in that twice-born faith hatreds, selfish ambitions, destructive desires, are restrained. As the Spirit possesses our hearts, we become more Christlike, stronger in the ability to resist temptation, more compassionate toward suffering mankind, more ready to sacrifice ambitions and advantages for the welfare of others. If you want to know what this sin-encrusted world needs today, when the flames of war begin to eat their greedy way over wider areas of the world's surface, I point you to the *"meek and lowly"* Christ, the *"Prince of Peace,"* and say: "Let Him enter the capitals of this world, the hearts of hardened statesmen, the souls of shriveled war-mongers! Let Him, unarmed and unsupported by tanks, airplanes, and massed divisions of panzer troops, march into Berlin, London, Rome, Tokyo, Washington, and other cities! Let Him be genuinely welcomed by national leaders, accepted if He has been previously rejected, embraced with real faith where up till now He has received only lip-service and formal worship! Let people stop talking Christianity to practice it!" and we shall witness the world's greatest demonstration of peace.

If you want these blessings of peace for yourself, welcome Christ today! Stand in spirit along the highways of life, strewn as they are with those wounded by man's cruelty, dying as victims of our hundredfold hatreds! Take your place with all the depressed and sorrowing, the fear-gripped and conscience-stricken, those terrorized by sin; and as

Jesus in this message approaches you as your Savior and your God, raise your voice to sing, *"Hosanna! Blessed is He that cometh in the name of the Lord! Hosanna in the highest!"* Throw everything else away that your hands now clutch, so that they may be free to grasp palm-branches as symbols of the peace that is yours, signs of your victory in Jesus! When Christ passes before you, as He does every time you hear His Gospel, realize that He pauses and appeals to you, asking you to join this procession, and follow Him through death itself into the eternal triumphs of heaven!

II

GOD PRESERVE US FROM CRUCIFYING HIM ANEW!

From Palm Sunday the scene shifts to Good Friday. Instead of entering Jerusalem, Jesus now leaves it. Instead of being borne triumphantly into the city, He now is driven out, bearing a cross until He collapses under its pressure. The hosannas have given way to ridicule. The discarded palm-branches wither in the gutters. Pilate's soldiers carry a heavy hammer and large nails; as our text records, they *"went forth into a place called the place of a skull, which is called in the Hebrew Golgotha, where they crucified Him!"*

Stunned by this change, we ask, "How can we explain this shocking upheaval?" Is the reason for this reverse not to be found in the fatal ease with which the masses may be influenced and their good intentions revoked? Influential, cunning men, priests, Pharisees, social leaders, craftily seeking their own interests and the privileges of their class, stood in the background to plot and manage the crucifixion. Because Temple propaganda knew how to churn the people's emotions, they were able to turn Sunday's cheers into Friday's jeers.

We witness the same process today. Artificially stim-
ulated war hysteria begets the mob spirit, and under the
pressure of skilful propaganda, paid for by interests which
profit through bloodshed, the public can be led to demand
conflict. The people of the United States in overwhelming majority do not want war; but millions are being
persuaded that they should want it. The same psychology
works against you young people. Palm Sunday recalls the
time when you renewed your baptismal vow and pledged
yourself to suffer death rather than deny your Savior.
Today many of you know with particular force that whatever Christ teaches and His Church preaches is the truth;
and with the fervor of your youthful faith you want to
maintain your loyalty to Jesus. Too often, however, you
found yourself in a crowd where Christ was rejected; and
because no one rose to His defense, you hesitated to be
different from the rest. Often you attend classes where
teachers, the twentieth-century counterparts of Caiaphas
and his priestly accomplices, seek to destroy your faith
in Jesus; but because you think you are the only one who
disagrees, your silence gives consent to blasphemies. Let
nothing I say excuse the heartless rabble which, obeying
the satanic direction of the priests, cried for the Savior's
blood; yet it often seems to me that those deserve the
most severe censure who as disciples and pilgrims had followed Christ acclaiming Him five days before, but who
during His six hearings spoke not a word in His behalf.

Can you not see, my fellow-redeemed, that the duty of
protest against every assault on Christ and the responsibility for defending His holy cause dare not be avoided?
Some of you write me to ask whether it is really necessary
to speak out plainly and pointedly against rampant sins
and open assaults on our Christian faith. I answer by
pointing to the highest example, the Savior Himself, during

this last week. On the day after this first Palm Sunday He drove out the money-changers, the profiteers in religion. Can we be true to Christ if we do not disavow all ill-gotten wealth and cry out against the wide-spread notion of making money through religion? On Tuesday of that week Jesus rebuked the scribes, the Pharisees, the Sadducees, in unsoftened terms. The most scathing denunciation He ever uttered was spoken three days before He died. Do you want us to remain silent when our faith is assaulted? Whatever you may think, we will continue, as God gives us the power and the means, to preach the Savior's whole truth to the Americas.

Churches which bear His blessed name should avoid every let-down in Christian principles under the stress of emergencies. It may mean the loss of official favor and public support to send forth the message of the crucified Redeemer. His kingdom is not built by officialdom or popular applause but by loyalty to His sure mercies, the whole Bible, through which the Holy Spirit calls and converts sinners. The true prophets of Israel did not permit sin to pass unchallenged; uncompromisingly they denounced unbelief and the moral weaknesses of their own people. There was another class of religious leaders in ancient Israel. The Bible calls them false prophets, although they often flourished under royal favor and popular support. They saw nothing seriously wicked in Israel. The king and the people of the chosen race could do no wrong. They pointed to the Temple, emphasizing God's goodness to the Hebrew people as assurance for future security. It was their approval of sin and the perpetuation of their selfish ambition that sentenced Jesus to the cross and pronounced the doom of awful destruction on Jerusalem. We have false prophets in the United States today, often in high position and popular favor. God give us the power to protest; for if we remain silent when Jesus is attacked, we have become unfaithful; we have sent Him to Golgotha without one plea on His behalf.

The call of Holy Week, therefore, asks every one of us to come out from our sins and whole-heartedly acclaim Christ our Savior. There can be no half-way loyalty between the palm-branches and the nails; no 50-per-cent acceptance of Christ and 50-per-cent rejection. If this war has shown that it is impossible for any people to remain completely neutral either in thought or in action, all impartiality in the war between Christ and unbelief is utterly precluded!

It is vital, then, that you know Jesus in a personal, assured faith. The events of Holy Week warn us against relying on our emotions. How often this now-hot, now-cold Christianity has led to utter indifference! You do not build your business on emotions. Why, then, entrust your soul merely to impressions, changing whims, and fancies? Do not rely on any one else's faith! There is an intensely personal responsibility about our relation to Christ. On the one hand, do not rest on a cold, intellectual understanding of the Gospel! Is it not significant that the Jerusalem intelligentsia was almost solidly arrayed against our Lord and that His bitterest enemies were those who should have known from the Scriptures that He was the promised Messiah? Do not base your hope for heaven merely on church-membership! That was the mistake of those who defiantly sent Christ to the cross. They found false comfort in the fact that outward religion, the mere performance of rite and ritual, was a sort of charm and protection, while God asks in His Word, *"My son, give Me thine heart!"* Build your hope only on Christ, your royal Redeemer, your very God! Look for pardon and peace only at the cross! As you behold the wounded hands, the lacerated feet, the riven side, find the pledge of healing for earth's sorrow and the guidance to celestial joy only in that *"Lamb of God which taketh away the sin of the world"!* Then wave the palm-branches of peace and victory to acclaim your Savior in deathless loyalty!

Israel's temporal punishment for rejecting Jesus can be measured and tabulated; but who can describe the eternal consequence: separation from God, banishment from heaven into hell? If self-confidently you have always dismissed thoughts of the hereafter from your mind, this week of wondrous love calls to you: "O sinner, look at the crude hammer and the blunt spikes which are to pierce through the hands and feet of your Savior! Your sins are the driving power that will use these instruments of death in riveting Him to the cross! Listen to these hammer-blows reechoing down the corridors of time; for each reverberation warns: 'You struck this blow! You nailed your Christ to the accursed tree!' Behold the blood flowing from each impact and let God's Word preach this truth into your soul, 'He was wounded for your transgressions; He was bruised for your iniquities!'" If nothing in the world, no earnest sermon, no pleading of your parents or pastor, no warning from punishment in your own life, no plea from the horrifying end of other unbelievers, no lashing of your conscience, has ever been able to convince you that you are lost without Christ, stand once more at Calvary; and may the Holy Spirit now, by the miracle of conversion, touch your heart with Christ's grace and bring from your repentant, trustful heart this plea: "Jesus, I cast this hammer and these nails from my hands forever to grasp the palm-branch of peace and victory, because, my suffering Savior, You endured all this soul-agony and pain of body for me. From this moment on, with my sins washed away by Your holy, crimson blood, being justified by faith, pardoned by this matchless mercy, I pledge myself to Thee. O Christ of Calvary's gory cross, hear me and help me so to live that I will not crucify Thee anew by unbelief and ungodly living!"

If the holiday throng at Jerusalem could acclaim Christ before He went to Calvary, how much more should our praises be raised to Him after its blood and agony, its ridicule and rebuke, its darkness and death! In these very moments as the victorious Christ, Golgotha's grief passed forever, comes to us, my fellow-redeemed, let us picture ourselves in spirit first at the roadside of His approach, waving palm-branches in welcome, homage, and thanks! With the host of all the ransomed souls, the myriad times myriad, who from that first Palm Sunday and that first Good Friday have looked forward to the second coming of the Lord Jesus, let us, beholding the clear signs of His imminent return, express our faith in the hymn of Palm Sunday praise: *"Hosanna! . . . Blessed is He that cometh in the name of the Lord! Hosanna in the highest!"* Amen.

EASTER GLADNESS

*"Then were the disciples glad when they saw
the Lord."* — Saint John 20:20

Christ, Our Resurrected Redeemer, Victor over the Grave:

*If all our years were spent in continued praise for Thine Easter
triumph, every moment devoted to heartfelt thanks for Thy bursting
death's bonds, the longest life would be far too short worthily to acknowledge the blessings of this radiant day. Make us understand that
through the Easter faith we in our resurrected bodies and the life
everlasting will be able to glorify Thee eternally! May Thy Spirit
direct us constantly to prepare for the heavenly homeland, assured
that, since Thou hast destroyed sin, the wages of death, the grave
has lost its terror! Since Thou livest and reignest forever, Thou
canst and wilt hear us, help us, save us, and resurrect us, always
to be with Thee! May we never become so engrossed with earthly
affairs that we lose sight of heaven with its celestial radiance, its
sinless beauty, its endless privilege of beholding Thee face to face!
Enrich us with the assurance of these Easter blessings even now and
stir our hearts with the desire to tell others of the everlasting bliss
promised all who acclaim Thee their atoning Christ! Send this assurance of never-ending joy to our souls by the pledge of Thine
own empty tomb! Amen.*

A BLESSED, heart-gladdening Easter to every one of
you! Does not the fulfilment of this wish answer
the greatest need of millions in war-torn 1941? The earth
throbs with the new life of spring, the beauty of the first
emerging flowers, the tinge of early blossoms, the soft
green of reawakening nature. Yet vast areas are strewn
with the hideous wreckage of man's cruelty, ugly evidences
of violence and death. Ours is a world planned by God
with room, food, shelter, opportunity, for myriads more
than the present population; yet, instead of working
shoulder to shoulder, hate-driven armies for the second
time in this generation are destroying lives. We look for

[357]

peace, but the Easter full moon reveals total war, all-out destruction. We hope for light, and blackouts blanket Old World nations.

On this nightmare of ever wider suffering Easter has again dawned to fill our hearts with gladness. Let nothing restrict our joy! In the seventh century Christians were forbidden to sing during church services; however, the Easter exaltation was too real to be passed silently, and many congregations broke forth in hallelujahs. May your resurrection rejoicing likewise reecho irrepressibly! But let it be the true Easter cheer! During the Middle Ages Easter sermons often took a humorous turn. Preachers told ludicrous stories until the congregations rocked with laughter, all in the effort to remove any solemnity that might linger after the Lenten weeks. Our Easter ecstasy must be far deeper.

It is my prayer that this sunrise has brought you more than a holiday, a joyous spring festival when you welcome a reviving nature, more than fashion parades with their new, expensive clothing or a banner business season with sales 18 per cent higher than last year. Forget all this to concentrate your devotion and gladness on the all-absorbing thought that today is the anniversary of your Savior's resurrection!

Millions in the United States and Canada, however, have started this day without joy. Despite the boom of defense projects they are unable to find work, and their financial problems mount steadily. Many are sick, crippled, helpless, or have seen their homes broken during recent weeks. Others realize that their sins have finally caught up with them. The past weeks have brought members of this radio audience deeper grief and personal sorrow than they ever believed possible.

Now, to you who in any way may be disheartened, embittered with life, desperate; and to you for whom Easter should recall double happiness since you have never known real affliction or suffered any heavy pain of body or soul, I bring heaven's highest joy, the promise of God's most glorious peace,   EASTER GLADNESS

With the Spirit's help I want you to experience the same exultant rejoicing which came to Christ's followers after His resurrection, *"Then,"* according to Saint John's gospel (chapter twenty, verse twenty), *"were the disciples glad when they saw the Lord."*

I

WE, TOO, ARE GLAD BECAUSE CHRIST IS RISEN

The evening of the first Easter Sunday found the disciples assembled behind barred doors in a secret hiding-place. Fright was plainly written on their faces, the unmistakable fear that those who had crucified Jesus might vent continued hatred on them. Undisguised disappointment ran through their conversation. They had looked for a crown, only to find a cross. They had hoped Christ would reign as a glorious King; He was crucified as a criminal. Yet during all their lament and disappointment Jesus was *risen*.

Is it not true that also many of you lead dark, secluded lives as though the Savior were still dead? Some unforgiven, unremoved sin disquiets you. You dread its consequences, dismayed because your transgressions will be revealed. You cower before your conscience, while the living Christ has long been ready to pardon you. After peace had been declared ending the War of 1812, hard battles were still fought and much blood unnecessarily shed since it took weeks for the news of the treaty to reach our shores. Don't make a similar mistake in your life! The enemies of your soul were defeated on that first Easter.

In remote sections of the South where Lincoln's emancipation was not known slaves remained in bondage after the Civil War, although they had been legally freed. Your liberty from the tyranny of fear was purchased on the cross and sealed at the open grave. Break the locks that keep you from the joy of life! Come out from your lonely isolation!

Miraculously Christ entered through those closed doors. Bars and barriers meant nothing to Him. He can come to you also, no matter how many obstacles would blockade His way. Mexican governmental authorities prohibit religious broadcasting; yet the Savior's invitation still leaps over their boundaries. A Mexican general happened to hear our message through a foreign station, and he was led to Christ. You may live far beyond the railroad, in inaccessible territory destitute of churches, but Christ will find a way to you or make one, as He does by this Easter message. Listeners on the island of Rooke, across from Borneo, are the only white people for miles around. Yet Christ comes to them by our broadcasts. You may be in jail, but penitentiary walls and locked cell-doors cannot exclude Jesus. A few Sundays ago I mentioned the penitent thief. That message struck the heart of a man in a Minnesota State Prison, who wrote, "I am a thief, too; but how I thank God for your assurance of a merciful Savior!"

Hardly had the risen Lord entered, when, to overcome amazement and remove doubt, He showed the disciples His nail-marked hands and riven side. These are the marks of the true Christ. When the body of Livingstone, mighty evangelist of Africa, arrived in England, skeptics questioned whether the remains actually were those of the intrepid missionary. In this uncertainty some one recalled that Livingstone's arm had been broken by an attacking lion.

Examination of the corpse showed the evidence of that encounter. Scars identified Livingstone; nail-wounds and spear-mark reveal Jesus. If ever men try to show you a Christ without wounds; if they preach a Messiah who was not crucified for your sins, no matter how high their other tributes, turn away from them forever! They have a counterfeit, man-made Jesus!

No longer did uncertainty linger in the disciples' mind. The Lord was risen! They never should have doubted His resurrection, for it was clearly predicted in the Old Testament and foretold by the Savior Himself in the New; but, like us, His followers were sometimes too weak to accept Scripture at face value. Therefore in His overabundant mercy Christ proved the Easter victory by appearing to them.

I say that He "proved" His resurrection because the Easter records are as fully attested by reliable witnesses as any fact of history. In a day when propaganda and distortion often make it impossible to distinguish between truth and error, the story of the open grave should receive ready acceptance as God's own revelation. Many skeptics who are unwilling to endorse the statement of the second article of the Apostles' Creed, "On the third day He rose again from the dead," are constantly being won for absurd isms, which demand far more credulity than the Easter story. Congressman George H. Bender was right when he declared that continued laxity in spiritual education throughout the United States had produced a condition by which almost any kind of fraud can "get by." People believe the most irrational and self-contradictory theories; but when God speaks in His Word, they refuse to listen.

By contrast, hear this testimony to the certainty of Christ's resurrection from Thomas Arnold, famous headmaster at Rugby and modern history professor at Oxford:

"The evidence for our Lord's life and death and resurrection may be, and often has been, shown to be satisfactory; it is good according to the common rules for distinguishing good evidence from bad. Thousands and tens of thousands of persons have gone through it piece by piece, as carefully as every judge summing up on a most important case. I myself have done it many times over, not to persuade others, but to satisfy myself. I have been used for many years to study the histories of other times and to examine and weigh the evidence of those who have written about them, and I know of no one fact in the history of mankind which is proved by better and fuller evidence of every sort, to the understanding of a fair inquirer, than the great sign which God has given us that Christ died and rose again from the dead." Listen to this single sentence by Brooke Foss Westcott, professor at Cambridge, one of the most eminent scholars the Christian Church has known in modern times: "Taking all the evidence together, it is not too much to say that there is not a single historic incident better or more variously supported than the resurrection of Christ." If recognized authorities have accepted the Easter record as unassailable verity, by what right do unbelievers and amateurs, often ignorant of the gospel statements and unacquainted with laws of evidence, seek to discredit their accuracy?

How gloriously the resurrected Christ removed the disciples' fear and sorrow! These men, who had felt themselves completely forsaken, were now transformed by the assurance that their Lord had kept His Word and was truly risen. May this gladness possess your hearts! Can you not see that the Savior's triumph over death and decay proves He is your God? No man could vanquish the grave as Christ did. Where are Mohammed, Buddha, Lao Tse, Confucius, Zoroaster? Where are the other self-appointed prophets of the human race? Have they not disintegrated in their tombs and returned to the dust? Because Jesus is God, *"all power is given unto"* Him, even the rule over death. Safely guarded in Washington is the great seal of the United States. Without its imprint important documents would be valueless. Now, the open, empty grave is heaven's great seal on our Lord's deity. — The first Easter lesson you must learn, then, is this: Christ, crucified, dead, buried, but — praise His holy name! — revived on the third day, is your *Lord* and your *God*.

Don't mar this resurrection radiance by demanding an explanation of this inexplicable mystery! If every day of your life; every inch of ground beneath your feet; every breath of air around and above you; every part of your body, your skin, tissues, blood, bone; every morsel of food; every glass of water, is filled with miracles for which neither you nor any scientific genius can adequately account, why, since you accept these commonplaces, marvels though they be, do you reject the evident truth that the living Jesus is your God?

Easter gladness should likewise take possession of your hearts because this day's events prove beyond question that Christ's sin-atoning, soul-saving, hell-destroying work has been completed for all time. The sweat and agony of Gethsemane, the blood and anguish of Calvary, have fulfilled their purpose. Your sins are entirely atoned, your transgressions removed, the handwriting against you blotted out. Nothing is left that you can or should do for your salvation. You are saved! You need only believe, only claim your redemption!

Let this resurrection day ring with rejoicing! We have in the risen Christ the eternal God, whom you approach in each trial and for repeated sorrows. When you pray to Him, you are not addressing a dead superstition, but a mighty Savior, who can and will answer. If you want additional proof for the Easter verity, take your cares and worries to Jesus; and as His help brings deliverance, you will personally realize that He lives. Last week I received this letter from a discouraged listener: "I have walked the streets for the past four years month after month, week after week, fifteen or twenty miles a day, often without food, trying to get a job. But I am forty-nine years old, and I am told that men over forty are not wanted. I have written about two hundred applications, but to no avail. What am I to do? Become a thief? I am getting desperate." A distracted woman in Oregon writes that she has been dismissed from a WPA project, adding: "I cannot sit by and watch my eighty-year-old mother go without food and medicine. Do you think God has forgotten us altogether? We have nothing but illness and poor food and have lost all our friends because of these conditions." To those who stagger under like hardships or suffer from a thousand other causes, Easter promises: "Because Christ is your God and Savior, because He has the power to destroy death, He certainly can lighten your burdens, provide you with work, clothing, health, happiness. Take heart on this day! Easter has come for all mankind, but especially for you, to make you rejoice, even in your tears. Jesus lives, and therefore in His time and in His blessed way He will lift you from the depths of sorrows."

Only a resurrected Redeemer offers our defeated age the pledge of victory. What would the world be without Easter? To picture that catastrophe, we must imagine the churches torn down; the institutions of mercy — hospitals, orphanages, asylums — by the tens of thousands destroyed; the schools and colleges built by Christians demolished; the foundations on which our culture rests blasted away. Deny the angelic announcement, "He is not here; He is risen," and you will help our age go back to pagan perversions. Not long ago an expedition to New Guinea discovered a valley inhabited by 60,000 natives who had never seen a white man. Cut off from the rest of the world, they had never heard of Jesus Christ. You and I should be like those natives, were it not for the Easter Gospel. I do not mean that we should necessarily follow them in keeping our bodies naked or cutting off a finger whenever death strikes our family. We might still have airplanes; but as we think of women and children lying under the *débris* of bombed cities, we ask ourselves, "Has the conquest of the air not brought much more tragedy than good?" We might still have motion-pictures, but some of us feel that America would be better off without many of them. Deprived of the risen Christ, we might record a hundred other scientific achievements, but ours would be nevertheless a dark, morose, hopeless outlook on life; a code of cruel, grasping principles; a lust-filled heart; a sensual, super-stitious mind; a fear-gripped soul, just as those 60,000 in New Guinea's unexplored valley. Banish the risen Christ from the United States, and you will help revert to the reign of terror that marked France when the revolutionists officially dethroned God or that more recently ruled Russia when Moscow public buildings were plastered with signs denouncing all religion, particularly Christianity, as opiate for the masses. Thank God, we can say with the apostle, *"Now is Christ risen!"*

II

WE ARE GLAD BECAUSE WE, TOO, SHALL SEE JESUS

The disciples' delight was rooted not only in the victory by which Jesus burst the sealed grave, but also in His appearance before their very eyes. The text testifies, *"Then were the disciples glad, when they* SAW *Jesus."* Beholding Him in His resurrected form, they, as witnesses of earth's mightiest miracle, were also blessed by a foregleam of their triumph over death, the glory of their revivified bodies.

Let this also be our Easter joy; we, too, shall see Him. Though our bodies are placed into the ground, where they must decay, if we have truly believed in Christ's triumph over the tomb, they will come forth into a celestial newness. This was leprous Job's confidence when he exulted: *"I know that my Redeemer liveth and that He shall stand at the latter day upon the earth. And though after my skin worms destroy this body, yet in my flesh shall I see God; whom I shall see for myself and mine eyes shall behold."* This was the apostle's anchor of faith when he exclaimed, *"We shall be like Him, for we shall see Him as He is."*

Can you think of a more wondrously welcome message than the promise that in Christ you will have a heavenly Easter, a bodily resurrection? International issues and world problems may change from year to year, but the basic questions regarding death, the fundamental perplexities concerning the hereafter, remain unaltered. The Old Testament query, *"If a man die, shall he live again?"* looms up afresh in every life. Despite the remarkable advances by modern science and culture, the gruesomeness of the grave has not been removed.

How hideous and repelling death can sometimes be! Carefully we try to banish all thoughts that even suggest the disintegration of our bodies. At funerals the mounds of earth are covered with artificial grass. When the solemn words "Ashes to ashes and dust to dust" are spoken, not a piece of the sod but beautiful flowers are thrown into the grave. The entire plan and structure of cemeteries are being revolutionized to make these last resting-places of our beloved, spots of natural beauty and artistic adornment. At some funerals, poems are read, beautiful music

played. Caskets are constructed of costly material, protected with metal or concrete vaults. No previous age
has done as much to reduce the pain of parting. Yet with
all commendable advances we have only lightened some of
its darkness. The heart-clutching sorrow still remains after
every funeral that the body of the loved one laid into the
grave will in the years' relentless succession decay and
be consumed.

Beyond the body's decomposition the question of the
soul's destiny rises up to haunt men. They know that their
lives have abounded with hatred, impurity, cruelty, vice,
covetousness, greed; and they cringe before the thought of
an inescapable retribution, which will right the wrongs of
life. Say what you wish about any other fears, none can
approach death's terror. To escape its clutching skeletal
hand, men will sacrifice anything they own. They will
have their limbs cut off to save the rest of their body.
They will cling to floating wreckage for weeks, crawl across
deserts' withering heat, lie half frozen on floating ice-packs,
if only they can live. Finally the doom of death overtakes them; and what then? How can they be prepared
for severance from the land of the living?

Now, it is common for unbelievers to laugh the whole
issue off, to deny any continued existence once breath ceases
and the heart stops beating. But every rejection of the
hereafter is opposed by a ceaseless questioning and protest
from within. That is why men who have glibly, brazenly
denied the Easter truth, decried the Christian religion, denounced the hope of our resurrection; free-thinkers who
have asserted that man, only a superior animal, dies like the
beast he is have often ended in terror as avenging remorse
tormented their last hours. Voltaire frequently boasted
that he was ready to sell his place in heaven for a Prussian
coin! Yet the nurse who waited on him in his dying days

declared that it would not be worth all the kingdoms of Europe to relive this frightful experience.

Others have vaguely persuaded themselves that there should be another life. They philosophize, theorize, guess; but without certainty they never know peace. At the age of seventy-five the poet Goethe confessed that he had not lived four weeks of his entire caree. completely happy. He was always rolling heavy stones, he admitted, worrying about the hereafter.

Scientists have spent many thousands of dollars and long hours in psychical research designed to answer for all time the questions concerning the next world, but their efforts remain unrewarded. Suicides promised that their spirits would return to reveal death's mysteries, but they have not come back. Against the law o most cities spiritist mediums, who claim to be the connecting links between the seen and the unseen world, feature all ed communications from departed souls; but never has one of their seances proved their assertions. On the contrary, much grief has resulted from disregarding the Scriptural truth that spiritism must be condemned.

Where, then, my fellow-redeemed, amid these failures are we to find positive surety? Where, indeed, if not at the open grave and in the Savior's promise, *"Because I live, ye shall live also."* Whatever else you may have thought concerning the hereafter, behold the living Christ today and let the Easter record engrave these truths on your soul: Death does not end all! There is a life after the grave!

With holy emphasis and sacred repetition Jesus teaches this comforting truth! He tells us that the great purpose of His suffering on the cross was to show: *"God so loved the world that He gave His only-begotten Son, that whosoever believeth on Him should not perish but have everlasting life."* He declares: *"He that believeth on the Son hath everlasting life."* He who says, *"I am the Resurrection and the Life,"* He who during His earthly days commanded the dead to rise, promises, *"I give . . . eternal life."*

Here, then, is Christ's Easter promise to you, the grant of eternal life with Him. First, the Savior pledges that your body, marked by disease, marred by accident, abused by the sins of youth, worn and shriveled by age, weakened through sieges of illness, will be restored without disfigurement, spot, or blemish. What joy for you invalids and cripples, you maimed and shell-shocked victims of war!

The second Easter assurance guarantees us that, when we see Jesus in the realms of resurrected glory, there will be no more sin and therefore none of earth's aches and pains, its sorrow and anguish, its disgrace and dismay, its weeping and moaning; only perfect bliss. Is not this the promise for multitudes today who see only misery on all sides, strife in their homes, unfaithfulness in their families — burden heaped upon burden? Can you not understand why world-weary, continually afflicted souls have found death attractive because it brought them this highest happiness?

The third Easter endowment is the comfort that, when we shall see Jesus, we *"shall know even as also"* we are *"known."* We shall have a resurrected body incomparably superior to our terrestial form, but also a resurrection understanding immeasurably exalted over our present, limited mental powers. In the heavenly homeland the supreme truths of our faith, before which our restricted reason balks, will be understood. In the fuller knowledge God's ways which here in time were past finding out will be revealed as the pathways of His divine love. Questions which seek the reason for our suffering will be answered there. What hope, what promise, for you baffled by trials, to know that your sorrows will be revealed as soul blessing!

The fourth Easter pledge tells us that, when we see Jesus, we shall be reunited with those who have died in the faith. Husband and wife, parents and children, will recognize each other and be bound together not by ties of earthly family life but with unspeakably more blessed heavenly love. What solace for you widows and widowers, orphans and bereft parents, to know that after death your dear ones can await you!

The fifth Easter verity asks you to contemplate, as far as possible, the indescribable perfection of the Paradise to come. The most attractive spots in this world, where majesty and sublimity of nature combine to form the highest pictures of beauty, are but poor shadows of God's peerless city, to which those who are Christ's approach more closely every day. Heaven is so glorious that it far exceeds our powers of understanding; and to help us realize something of its grandeur, the Scriptures employ the symbol of costly metals and precious stones. Recently the newspapers told of the world's largest diamond, a 700-carat Brazilian stone; but this gem is inconsequential, less than a pebble, in comparison with the celestial splendor. Find comfort in *"the glory that shall be revealed in us,"* if life has had little beauty for you, if you have constantly been confronted by the sordid, the ugly, the hideous!

The sixth Easter truth emphasizes that, as the disciples were glad *"when they saw Jesus,"* so in eternity we, too, shall rejoice in the most glorious privilege, the adoration of our crucified and living Savior, the standing face to face with Jesus, the singing of the hallelujahs to our Triune God. Mass choirs, symphonies, orchestras, composed of artists — these highest musical delights at present will be silenced by heaven's incomparable music and melodies, the raptures of the celestial choir. Now some of you hardly dare speak of Jesus. An unbelieving husband, scoffing children, skeptical associates, ridicule you when you open your lips to testify to His grace; but then, what glory to sing to Christ!

Finally, the Easter triumph deals in terms of eternity. Its radiance is everlasting. No one can ever take you from Christ. There is no night or darkness, no farewell in heaven. You are Christ's *always*.

"Oh, that I were there to see Jesus now!" some of you are saying. And it is the mercy of the resurrected Redeemer's grace that you can be with Jesus if only, repenting of your sins, clinging to His grace, you personally accept Him as the Son of God, the Savior of the world, and, today especially, the Victor over the grave. Nothing else besides your own faith and trust in Christ is required.

May your grateful hearts direct you to follow the risen Savior's command *"Go, tell!"* and spread the Easter message to others! Last year I explained that the United States is the only large country in which the customary greeting for this day contains no reference to Jesus. While our people say, "Happy Easter!" millions throughout most of the Old World, in scores of languages, salute one another with "Christ is risen!" and answer, "He is risen indeed!" I repeat my appeal, for this glad message is so beyond measure in its mercy that our entire lives should be devoted to its spread. During the last weeks I have received several anonymous letters. Written in the abusive, uncouth language used by moral cowards who are afraid to sign their names, these communications take me to task for preaching the Scriptural Christ and His blood atonement. You, too, will meet hard-hearted opposition if you put Jesus into your Easter greetings. But can we who have been saved eternally do less than proclaim His victorious conquest of death to friend and foe alike? God bless you, as in the larger or smaller circle of your influence you tell others, *"Christ is risen!"* "He is risen indeed!" Amen.

COURAGE IN CHRIST

"The Lord shall deliver me from every evil work and will preserve me unto His heavenly kingdom: to whom be glory forever and ever. . . . The Lord Jesus Christ be with thy spirit. Grace be with you. Amen." — 2 Timothy 4:18 and 22

God, Creator, Redeemer, Sanctifier:

Accept the praise of our thankful hearts for Thy protecting watchfulness over our lives and for the love by which all things, even the hardest blows of adversity, work together for good, because we are Thine, purchased forever by the Savior's redeeming blood! Especially, O Triune God of power, mercy, and strength, do we beseech Thee: keep us constantly grateful for the victory over sin and death won by Jesus in His crucifixion and glorious resurrection. Preserve the saving Gospel to our country, our homes, our churches! Let it be a light for every darkened pathway before us, a heavenly comfort in the hour of personal or national suffering! As we plead with Thee for honorable peace among the nations, we know not what the approaching weeks may bring; yet teach us always to find courage in Christ, inner peace for our distressed souls at the cross and His empty grave! Bless this broadcast and this congregation of the air! May Thy Holy Spirit employ the message, hymns, and prayer to call sinners from their evil ways, bring back those who have wandered from Thy truth, comfort the afflicted, and grant us all the joy of life; through Christ, our only Savior, both now and forever! Amen.

TODAY we broadcast the last message in our present series. We had fervently hoped to continue this Mission of the Air unbroken through the whole year; for during the critical period before us the masses in our country will need Christ's Gospel above all else. The cost of maintaining our network intact for the entire summer would be at least $100,000 additional, and our heavenly Father has not yet shown us how we can secure this immense sum.

We thank God nevertheless that much of our radio testimony will continue. In scores of large cities these

Bringing-Christ-to-the-Nations messages, transcribed to reduce expense, will be heard Sunday after Sunday. Our foreign program in twenty-four countries outside the United States will uninterruptedly send the Savior's truth from continent to continent. We ask your prayers and support in a greater degree than previously, so that, our broadcasting richly blessed through the summer, we may return in the fall over an even greater hook-up and more closely approach our ultimate objective, a year-round, world-wide radio system which will proclaim the eternal Gospel in dozens of languages to the very ends of the earth.

This may therefore be the last time I speak to you. Before the ninth Lutheran Hour begins about 750,000 people in the United States and Canada will have died. What assurance have we, in the uncertainty of modern existence, that next October you and I will still be numbered among the living? Who can forecast the tragic changes which may occur in a brief half year? Do you think that six months ago people in Belgrade believed their city would be swept by a devastation which would leave 10,000 corpses covered by the smoldering ruins of their own homes? Did King Peter anticipate on the Sunday before last that he would reign less than two weeks before fleeing into exile? If an army of a million men surrenders unconditionally after only twelve days of warfare; if a thousand lives are crushed out during a single night's bombing; if in a few seconds aerial torpedoes can irreparably shatter the toil of long years, even centuries, how terrifying the destruction which can intervene before we are privileged to resume our testimony to Christ!

Don't make the mistake of denying that disaster can come or imagine the United States secure from all perils! We are closer to war than at any other time since the conflagration started in September, 1939. A review of the

past months reveals a gradual, day-after-day edging closer
to actual fighting. Even if divine mercy prevails and we
are spared the horrors of active participation, our beloved,
God-blessed country may face trying days, with financial,
industrial, social, moral, political, religious difficulties the
like of which this nation has never witnessed. Add to this
uncertainty the pressing weight of personal problems, inner
sorrows, invisible griefs, insistent conscience claims, and
you will agree that multitudes inside our borders face
question-marked weeks, a fear-freighted future.

Yet — praise be to God! — you can meet with immovable calm the worst the veiled months may produce.
Whatever the approaching crisis brings, however crushing
your individual trials, I offer you in this season's last broadcast an unfailing source of strength. For all darkened
hours, each sudden reverse, every collapse of cherished
plans; for war and bloodshed, pain and agony, desertion
and loneliness, sin and sorrow; for the crowded moment
of life and the lonely hour of death, there is

Courage in Christ —

help for earth's cruelties, hope for heaven's happiness. This
double promise is found in the glorious confidence at the
close of Saint Paul's Second Letter to Timothy (chapter
four, verses eighteen and twenty-two): *"The Lord shall
deliver me from every evil work and will preserve me unto
His heavenly kingdom: to whom be glory forever and
ever. . . . The Lord Jesus Christ be with thy spirit. Grace
be with you. Amen."*

I

WE TAKE COURAGE BECAUSE CHRIST WILL "DELIVER US FROM ALL EVIL"

These were the last words of Scripture Saint Paul
wrote. During the reign of blood-crazed Nero the apostle
was rearrested and again brought to Rome. Deserted by

most of his friends, he defended himself alone against malicious accusations, including perhaps the charge that he, a Christian leader, had conspired to burn Rome. The hearing concluded, he was sent back to prison to await judgment. There in bonds this Second Letter to Timothy was composed. Paul knew that he would not be acquitted, for he asserted: *"I am now ready to be offered, and the time of my departure is at hand. I have fought a good fight, I have finished my course, I have kept the faith. Henceforth there is laid up for me a crown of righteousness, which the Lord, the righteous Judge, shall give me at that day."* Peering into the darkened future, dictating the final lines of his farewell epistle, the preeminent apostle (author of the Letter to the Romans, with its unparalleled explanation of justification by faith, the Letter to the Galatians, with its marvelous emphasis on Gospel freedom, and other sacred writings which have stirred the souls of millions since his day) declared resolutely, *"The Lord shall deliver me from every evil work."*

May God give us the same courage, for we in the United States also face a trying future! What I say now will find little applause, but the Church dare not cater to the popularity that blindly sets divine truth aside. Every minister of Jesus Christ is to be a watchman who, studying the trends of his times, warns and comforts his people. Therefore, when disturbed Christians, repeating the ancient Bible question, ask, *"Watchman, what of the night?"* we must be guided by complete honesty and absolute indifference to public acclaim. Under this conviction I tell you that in the deliberate opinion of many sober-minded investigators, within the Church as without, the United States faces the possibility of more numerous, more subtle, more imminent disasters than in our entire previous history. The most dangerous perils arise not from without but from within. Small countries may be overrun by military machines, but rich, powerful peoples succumb to internal treachery, the consequences of their own sins, the disregard of God's Word. As Christians we must whole-heartedly do our share in building and strengthening the nation's defenses; but we dare not overlook the truth that the contempt of divine will in American life can become a hundred times more destructive than any foreign invasion.

As Saint Paul, looking out on an age of rebellion against God, knew that evil would confront him, so present-day followers of Christ must have discerning eyes to recognize the uprisings against the Almighty continually flaunted before them. We should think, for example, of the anti-religious, atheistic tendency in American culture. For years unbelievers have boasted that the overthrow of our democratic life would spring from academic circles. They have systematically endeavored to tear the love for God from the hearts of our young people. Denying man's divine origin and his divine destiny in Jesus, they have deliberately reduced the human race to the animal level. University professors who tell their students that the Ten Commandments are as out of date as the 4,000-year-old Code of Hammurabi; that the Bible is full of mistakes, contradictions, even immoralities; that Jesus, if He ever existed, was a misguided, mistaken idealist — these men constitute a far greater menace to our country than Hitler. The United States can repel any foreign foe, but if youthful hearts are mobilized against Christ, the Bible, the Church, we can only plead: God help America!

Another national weakness is found in many godless homes. Easy, quick, cheap divorce; wilfully childless marriages; condoned unfaithfulness in wedlock; children without reverence for God and respect for parents, suffering from spiritual malnutrition but overdosed with sordid dramas, underworld stories, gangster romances — all this foreshadows disastrous consequences.

A third national sin is our notorious crime record. The Federal Bureau of Investigation in Washington reveals that one of every twenty-eight Americans is a criminal. Almost five million criminals are in this country, at present a greater army, doubtless, than any invading forces which will ever assail us. About one and one half million serious crimes — murder, manslaughter, rape, robbery, burglary, assault — are annually committed in the United States. We lead the world in lawmaking as in lawbreaking; and we ought to be intelligent enough to understand the retribution that a holy God may demand.

We are similarly depressed by the corruption of justice, according to the Old Testament, a definite cause for national collapse. Eminent jurists have admitted that collusion is widely practiced, particularly before domestic courts. In some cities it is impossible to convict those who manufacture or distribute immoral books and pictures. Judges have repeatedly been the puppets of politicians. Their decisions could be bought and sold.

An additional liability is class conflict. The violent battle between the employee and the working-man; the atheistic, Communist leadership in some sectors of organized labor and the selfishness of certain capitalists; the growing disdain of hard work, thrift, economy; the clash of color, with cruel discrimination against the Negro — these are conditions that God will not tolerate indefinitely.

We must further condemn the greed and oppression by which the poor are continually becoming poorer. The number of those without the proper food, clothing, and shelter is alarming, while some on the top rung of the financial ladder have steadily exploited the masses.

Deeply significant is the current world philosophy that nations can get along without God. We must help bar this delusion from our country. It should be a basic principle that nothing in American law or administration contradicts the divide code of governmental morality; but legislatures legalize gambling and champion the disruption of the home. Civic affairs, according to the admission of authorities, are often controlled by corrupt leaders allied with the underworld.

Another moral danger is the selfish promotion of war either for personal gain or for national conquest. The Bible emphatically denounces such bloodshed, as the psalmist asks God, "*Scatter Thou the people that delight in war!*" Yet there are those who would cast this country into conflict (regardless of the disasters which can follow even a complete victory) and seek the same private profits (through the blood of our American youth) that in the last hostilities created an army of war millionaires, but left masses destitute.

More dangerous, however, is the spiritual tragedy in many churches, which by maintaining loyalty to Christ and the Scriptures should prove a defense against national peril but have lost their allegiance to the Savior. Not merely from hundreds but thousands of American pulpits sermons are preached each Sunday in which the Trinity, Christ's deity and atonement, the inerrancy of the Scriptures, and every foundation truth of our faith are deliberately assaulted.

This religious treachery, in turn, contributes to widespread irreligion and unbelief. More than half of our people belong to no church whatever, and among those officially listed on congregational rosters a lamentably large percentage gives God only occasional lip-service.

As we thus survey the future with Saint Paul in our text, we, too, must be aware of the threat to our national and individual welfare exerted by those menacing forces. Unless a wave of religious reawakening and repentance sweeps across the country (of which we can see no signs at present); unless churches undertake an intense, all-out preaching of the crucified and risen Christ, we must be prepared to face the most difficult days that have ever dawned on America. No people can continually prosper in disregard of the Almighty. No country is rich enough to purchase exemption from the consequences of its sins. God is too holy to permit evil to flourish unrebuked. With prospects of heavy, continued taxes; confronted by the serious financial problems of a postwar and practically bankrupt world; face to face with the astounding growth of anti-American radicalism, we should not be surprised if startling upheavals shake this country and impose new restrictions on the Church's work.

The Holy Spirit help us to use the power of our faith in bringing America closer to the Almighty! The Christian walking humbly before God is a greater asset to the country than all the gold stored in subterranean treasuries at Fort Knox. Followers of Jesus on their knees in fervent prayer for their homeland can defeat hostile hordes. A spiritually prepared people, armed in a soul-defense program, can succeed where armaments fail.

Yet, come what may, we should find courage in Christ. We can join the Apostle's triumph over doubt, *"The Lord shall deliver me from every evil work!"* This assurance is grounded in God's eternal mercy as revealed in the Savior's crucifixion and resurrection. Christ loved every one of us with a heavenly devotion. He suffered the punishment of our sins, shed His blood to wash our iniquities away, died on the cross to pay the penalties of our transgressions with His death, so that we, pure and holy in God's sight, might be reawakened by the power of His Easter victory into the glories of eternal life. Now assuredly the heavenly Father, who, sacrificing His Son for our sins, proved His divine compassion, will not leave those who approach Him in faith without hope and help in this world. He cannot look on indifferently when we are tossed about by the hurricanes of hatred nor sit by unconcernedly while we are ground under the heel of hatred. Strikingly the apostle argues, *"God, who spared not His own Son but delivered Him up for us all, how shall He not with Him also freely give us all things?"* If our Father has offered us the treasures of eternity, He will not refuse the comparative trifles of this world. If He enriches our souls with the Bread of Life and the Living Water, He will not permit our bodies to starve. Granting the greater, He will not withhold the lesser.

Millions of Christians know, as Saint Paul did, that God can and does answer their prayer, *"Deliver us from evil!"* Last Sunday we told you of a woman in Oregon, discharged from the WPA, completely destitute, with a dependent eighty-year-old mother. Her trust in Christ soared over despair, and during the past week her prayers were remarkably answered. Some one who had borrowed money from her twenty-one years ago unexpectedly came to make a small payment. Friends, entirely unsolicited, offered their help. Daily the Lord shows similar grace to multitudes as He fulfils His promise, *"Call upon Me in the day of trouble; I will deliver thee!"* Every hour Christ's love binds up the soul-wounds of thousands who, bowed down under repeated adversity, accept His invitation, *"Come unto Me, all ye that labor and are heavy laden, and I will give you rest!"* Every moment the Holy Spirit, called *"the Comforter"* because He can give our souls peace, changes darkness into light, sorrow into joy. While Christians hope, pray, and work for better times and blessings on their country, they know that, even if these problem years bring their worst, if their own lives, quite apart from such world-moving issues, are afflicted with sorrows that cut to the quick, they can always find courage in Christ.

Will you not agree, then, that you need Jesus above all else? If up till this moment you have remained untouched by His grace, distant from His blood-bought love, may the Holy Spirit accompany the appeal of this farewell broadcast to create within you a desire to acclaim Christ yours and find in Him forgiveness and the pledge of His protection! The Savior, who died and rose again, offers all you require for the best possible life! There is no substitute for Jesus; neither wealth, position, learning, nor power can grant the trust and the joy which will be yours even in affliction through humble allegiance to the resurrected Redeemer! While the Spirit urges you, write us, so that we can help you solve your problems and send you a Christian pastor with Heaven's own pledge for God's help in any present trouble or for any future trial! Accept Jesus as your Savior now, and you will be blessed eternally!

Some of you, however, may protest that despite his confident assertion, "*the Lord shall deliver me from every evil work!*" Saint Paul was not rescued; that he was taken from his Roman prison to die a martyr's death. But this objection misunderstands entirely the extent of divine power and the wider reach of heavenly love. God could have liberated the apostle from his bonds. Remember what happened at Philippi, when in the depths of night a miracle opened the prison-doors to free the apostle! At dozens of other places Saint Paul had been in danger of destruction, yet each time the Almighty intervened to save him. Now the Lord has another deliverance, the greatest which even

He can give, the end of earthly sorrow and the beginning of unending happiness.

In Christ we can find the same guidance for our lives. Hundreds of Scripture-passages assure us of His providing, sustaining, protecting love. Were it not for the fact that our God *"neither slumbers nor sleeps";* that He has given *"His angels charge concerning"* us; that He has promised, *"There shall no evil come nigh thy dwelling,"* you and I would not be here today. In unnumbered instances disaster and death might have overtaken us. Often, however, situations arise when for our own good, the purifying of our desires, the strengthening of faith, the fortifying of trust, God permits reverses to check our plans, sorrows of many sorts to surround us. Despite prayers for relief the thorn in our flesh may not be immediately removed. But at His own time, in His heavenly way, always higher than ours, He will surely deliver us, if necessary by a miracle. Though He answers in His own manner, He never gives us less than we need; His help never comes at the wrong hour or place. Finally, however, the time arrives when He wants us to come home; and through the most magnificent of deliverances, the complete escape from all evil, we enter heaven's joy. What courage in Christ, therefore, to know that, when life's battles turn against us, the final victory still is ours; to realize that, even if our friends or family desert us, Jesus will abide with His own forever; to have the confidence that, though God permits us to lose our money, work, home, good name, health, and finally even life itself, ultimately we gain so much more that *"the sufferings of this present time are not worthy to be compared with the glory that shall be revealed in us"!* For the unspeakable joy of this eternal deliverance I beseech you once more in the name of the risen Redeemer: Acclaim Him your Savior from every sin and the Deliverer from every sorrow!

II

WE TAKE COURAGE BECAUSE CHRIST WILL PRESERVE US FOR HEAVEN

The bars of no Roman prison could prevent Saint Paul from looking assuredly into the open heaven and beholding, far beyond the executioner's block, the throne of his eternal Lord. Therefore in the last recorded triumph of his trust the stalwart witness to Christ unflinchingly cries out, *"The Lord . . . will preserve me unto His heavenly kingdom."* No "if," "perhaps," "maybe," lingered in the apostle's mind. He was *assured* of his salvation. Loyal, even as death's shadow approached, he trusted his Savior's promise, *"He that endureth unto the end shall be saved."*

The faith which can give us courage must likewise be an immovable conviction of Christ's sustaining, preserving power. I do not want to complete this season's broadcast and leave any of you uncertain concerning your salvation. We do not deal with guesses and wishful thinking in our Christian assurance of a blessed hereafter. We have advanced beyond the laboratory stage or the experimental level. Therefore you can do much more than hope, wish, or pray for your salvation. You can face a world arrayed against you and with Christ at your side exult confidently in the apostle's confident challenge: *"Who shall separate us from the love of Christ? Shall tribulation or distress or persecution or famine or nakedness or peril or sword? . . . Nay, in all these things we are more than conquerors through Him that loved us. For I am persuaded that neither death nor life nor angels nor principalities nor powers nor things present nor things to come nor height nor depth nor any other creature shall be able to separate us from the love of God which is in Christ Jesus, our Lord."*

Here, then, you stand before the glorious climax of

divine mercy. When the Savior is yours, you can say not only, "Jesus loved me. He gave Himself for me. He died on the cross for me. He rose again on that first Easter for me. He intercedes with His heavenly Father for me. He promised me help in every need"; but with Saint Paul's confidence you should triumph, *"He will preserve me unto His heavenly kingdom."* Is there a more radiant reassurance than this? Can even God in His limitless might grant a more marvelous blessing than the sacred conviction that Christ will *"preserve"* us *"unto His heavenly kingdom"?* Don't let anything keep you from this glorious hope! If you feel unworthy because your faith is small, wavering, inconsistent, ask Jesus to intensify it, and the blessed Savior who said, *"My strength is made perfect in weakness,"* will fortify your trust! Don't think that you can assure yourself of a place in heaven by your self-sacrifice, self-denial, self-imposed penances, by your personal virtues, achievements, and accomplishments! Everything involved in our salvation is 100-per-cent pure mercy. Saint Paul says here, not, "I will preserve myself unto the heavenly kingdom," but, *"He"* — the Lord Jesus — *"will preserve me."* Our title to the prepared place is bestowed only by grace; it comes entirely from Christ's undeserved love.

This does not mean, however, that you make your redemption automatic and boast, "Once saved, always saved!" What folly to risk your blessed eternity on the delusion that, if you have once believed on Christ, you can spend the rest of your life in sin, rebellion against God, denial of His mercy, and somehow before death be brought back to the Lord! What false comfort backsliders and nominal Christians find in this misinterpretation of Scripture! Many who once followed Jesus have deserted Him and died with unbelief, blasphemy, despair, on their lips.

Therefore the Bible warns against falling from the faith, and it mentions some who believed only for a short time and then were lost. We should rather follow the Scriptures and maintain close contact with our Savior in the sacred Word by which the Holy Spirit grants us constant grace and the strength to abide in Jesus. Read the Bible, study it, hear it explained in a true church, apply it to your own life, to your family — and the Christ, who can *"preserve"* you *"unto His heavenly kingdom,"* will come constantly closer to give you more complete victory over sin! Combine with this love of God's Word, *"which is able to build you up,"* your fervent, personal, penetrating prayer to God in Jesus' name! Come before Him when temptations seek to entice you, doubts dissuade you, afflictions drive you to despair, and as He promised, *"Verily, verily, I say unto you, Whatsoever ye shall ask the Father in My name, He will give it you,"* you will have Heaven's own help in securing this benediction, *"Be thou faithful unto death, and I will give thee a crown of life!"*

To emphasize this truth, let me repeat what I have tried to tell you in each one of the more than two hundred sermons I have preached over a radio network: For this courage by which you can rejoice even in adversity you need a firm personal trust in the Savior. More books are written about religion today than at any other period in human affairs; but too much of this printed material is vague, hazy unbelief, which specializes in individual theories and man-made claims but completely rejects the true Christ. Last Sunday, on the day of the resurrection, a weekly magazine featured what was called "A Message for Easter Day" by a famous scientist and Nobel Prize winner. The article mentioned Albert Einstein, Thomas Mann, Sigrid Undset, Jules Romains, Franz Werfel, Maurice Maeterlinck, Thomas Edison, and other notables, some of whom deny the existence of a personal God or who have written immoral books; yet that entire Easter discussion did not once even refer to our resurrected Lord and Savior. A creed of this kind will never save any one. It will not rescue even the American democracy which it proposes to help preserve.

So that none of you can say: "I was never warned; no one ever told me the truth," I now solemnly assert: There is no other way to a courageous life and a blessed death than through Jesus Christ, who declares, *"I am the Way, the Truth, and the Life. No man cometh unto the Father but by Me."* There is no other volume of everlasting verity besides our Bible; no saving Gospel other than the message of Jesus' cross, His blood, His atoning death; no possibility of your getting right with God, if you are not justified by faith in that Savior.

In this last broadcast I give you a summary of our Christian hope (which, printed on a small card, I shall be happy to send you as a constant reminder of the holy Gospel), words distilled from Scripture by that mighty hero of the Reformation, Martin Luther: "I believe that Jesus Christ, true God, begotten of the Father from eternity, and also true man, born of the Virgin Mary, is my Lord, who has redeemed me, a lost and condemned creature, purchased and won me from all sins, from death, and from the power of the devil, not with gold or silver, but with His holy, precious blood and with His innocent suffering and death, that I may be His own and live under Him in His kingdom and serve Him in everlasting righteousness, innocence, and blessedness, even as He is risen from the dead, lives and reigns to all eternity. This is most certainly true." Cling to that Christ, and you can find courage to face both time and eternity!

I cannot close this period in our Mission of the Air

without thanking God publicly for the privilege of being able to serve you in Jesus' name nor without expressing sincere gratitude to the members of this far-flung radio congregation for their generous support, particularly their fervent intercession in my behalf. It is not easy to leave you even for a few months in times like these, but I want you, particularly those who have not yet joined the Church, to feel that we shall be happy to assist you in any way the Lord permits. Our parting appeal asks you not to postpone giving yourself wholly to Jesus. Your heavenly Father wants you *now!* Why delay when *"all things are now ready"?* God grant that you will resolve immediately to accept Jesus as your Savior!

For you, my tried and true Christian friends, I have the assurance that, though most of us will never meet personally here on earth, in Christ every one of us can say, *"The Lord . . . will preserve me unto His heavenly kingdom, to whom be glory forever and ever!"* Glory for His mercy! Glory for His preserving guidance! Glory for His heaven! Confident that I shall stand in that celestial radiance with you who are Christ's, I look forward through Jesus, my only Savior, to the joy of knowing personally many millions who have joined us in this worship.

If this eighth annual series of broadcasts is to conclude, as it began, with God's Word, what passage could be more appropriate as I plead with you to keep your courageous trust in Christ than these last words in Saint Paul's last letter, the final wish of our text, the petition with which I commend you to our Savior's love until, God willing, we meet again in spirit, the parting prayer of this broadcast for every one of you: *"The Lord Jesus Christ be with thy spirit! Grace be with you! Amen."*